Free as in Freedom (2.0): Richard Stallman and the Free Software Revolution

Sam Williams
Second edition revisions by Richard M. Stallman

i

This is *Free as in Freedom 2.0: Richard Stallman and the Free Software Revolution*, a revision of *Free as in Freedom: Richard Stallman's Crusade for Free Software*.

Published by the Free Software Foundation
51 Franklin St., Fifth Floor
Boston, MA 02110-1335
USA
ISBN: 9780983159216

The cover photograph of Richard Stallman is by Peter Hinely. The PDP-10 photograph in Chapter 7 is by Rodney Brooks. The photograph of St. IGNUcius in Chapter 8 is by Stian Eikeland.

Contents

Foreword
by Richard M. Stallman

I have aimed to make this edition combine the advantages of my knowledge and Williams' interviews and outside viewpoint. The reader can judge to what extent I have achieved this.

I read the published text of the English edition for the first time in 2009 when I was asked to assist in making a French translation of *Free as in Freedom*. It called for more than small changes.

Many facts needed correction, but deeper changes were also needed. Williams, a non-programmer, blurred fundamental technical and legal distinctions, such as that between modifying an existing program's code, on the one hand, and implementing some of its ideas in a new program, on the other. Thus, the first edition said that both Gosmacs and GNU Emacs were developed by modifying the original PDP-10 Emacs, which in fact neither one was. Likewise, it mistakenly described Linux as a "version of Minix." SCO later made the same false claim in its infamous lawsuit against IBM, and both Torvalds and Tanenbaum rebutted it.

The first edition overdramatized many events by projecting spurious emotions into them. For instance, it said that I "all but shunned" Linux in 1992, and then made a "a dramatic about-face" by deciding in 1993 to sponsor Debian GNU/Linux. Both my interest in 1993 and my lack of interest in 1992 were pragmatic means to pursue the same end: to complete the GNU system. The launch of the GNU Hurd kernel in 1990 was also a pragmatic move directed at that same end.

For all these reasons, many statements in the original edition were mistaken or incoherent. It was necessary to correct them, but not straightforward to do so with integrity short of a total rewrite, which was undesirable for other reasons. Using explicit notes for the corrections was suggested, but in most chapters the amount of change made explicit notes prohibitive. Some errors were too pervasive or too ingrained to be corrected by notes. Inline or footnotes for the rest would have overwhelmed the text in some places and made the text hard to read; footnotes would have been skipped by readers tired of looking down for them. I have therefore made corrections directly in the text.

However, I have not tried to check all the facts and quotations that are outside my knowledge; most of those I have simply carried forward on Williams' authority.

Williams' version contained many quotations that are critical of me. I have preserved all these, adding rebuttals when appropriate. I have not deleted any quotation, except in chapter 11 where I have deleted some that were about open source and did not pertain to my life or work. Likewise I have preserved (and sometimes commented on) most of Williams' own interpretations that criticized me, when they did not represent misunderstanding of facts or technology, but I have freely corrected inaccurate assertions about my work and my thoughts and feelings. I have preserved his personal impressions when presented as such, and "I" in the text of this edition always refers to Williams except in notes labeled "RMS:".

In this edition, the complete system that combines GNU and Linux is always "GNU/Linux," and "Linux" by itself always refers to Torvalds' kernel, except in quotations where the other usage is marked with "[*sic*]". See http://www.gnu.org/gnu/gnu-linux-faq.html for more explanation of why it is erroneous and unfair to call the whole system "Linux."

I would like to thank John Sullivan for his many useful criticisms and suggestions.

Preface by Sam Williams

This summer marks the 10th anniversary of the email exchange that set in motion the writing of *Free as in Freedom: Richard Stallman's Crusade for Free Software* and, by extension, the work prefaced here, *Richard Stallman and the Free Software Revolution.*

Needless to say, a lot has changed over the intervening decade.

Originally conceived in an era of American triumphalism, the book's main storyline – about one man's Jeremiah-like efforts to enlighten fellow software developers as to the ethical, if not economic, shortsightedness of a commercial system bent on turning the free range intellectual culture that gave birth to computer science into a rude agglomeration of proprietary gated communities – seems almost nostalgic, a return to the days when the techno-capitalist system seemed to be working just fine, barring the criticism of a few outlying skeptics.

Now that doubting the system has become almost a common virtue, it helps to look at what narrative threads, if any, remained consistent over the last ten years.

While I don't follow the software industry as closely as I once did, one thing that leaps out now, even more than it did then, is the ease with which ordinary consumers have proven willing to cede vast swaths of private information and personal user liberty in exchange for riding atop the coolest technology "platform" or the latest networking trend.

A few years ago, I might have dubbed this the "iPod Effect," a shorthand salute to Apple co-founder Steve Jobs' unrivaled success in getting both the music industry and digital music listeners to put aside years of doubt and mutual animosity to rally around a single, sexy device – the Apple iPod – and its restrictive licensing regime, iTunes. Were I pitching the story to a magazine or newspaper nowadays, I d probably have to call it the "iPad Effect" or maybe the "Kindle Effect" both in an attempt to keep up with the evolving brand names and to acknowledge parallel, tectonic shifts in the realm of daily journalism and electronic book publishing.

Lest I appear to be gratuitously plugging the above-mentioned brand names, RMS suggests that I offer equal time to a pair of web sites that can spell out their many disadvantages, especially in the realm of software liberty. I have agreed to this suggestion in the spirit of equal time. The web sites he recommends are `DefectiveByDesign.org` and `BadVista.org`.

Regardless of title, the notion of corporate brand as sole guarantor of software quality in a swiftly changing world remains a hard one to dislodge, even at a time when most corporate brands are trading at or near historic lows.

Ten years ago, it wasn't hard to find yourself at a technology conference listening in on a conversation (or subjected to direct tutelage) in which some old-timer, Richard Stallman included, offered a compelling vision of an alternate possibility. It was the job of these old-timers, I ultimately realized, to make sure we newbies in the journalism game recognized that the tools we prided ourselves in finally knowing how to use – Microsoft Word, PowerPoint, Internet Explorer, just to name a few popular offerings from a single oft-cited vendor – were but a pale shadow of towering edifice the original architects of the personal computer set out to build.

Nowadays, it's almost as if the opposite situation is at hand. The edifice is now a sprawling ecosystem, a jungle teeming with ideas but offering only a few stable niches for sustainable growth. While one can still find plenty of hackers willing to grumble about, say, Vista's ongoing structural flaws, Apple's dictatorial oversight of the iPhone App Store or Google's shifting definition of the word "evil" – each year brings with it a fresh crop of "digital native" consumers willing to trust corporate guidance in this Hobbesian realm. Maybe that's because many of the problems that once made using your desktop computer such a teeth-grinding experience have largely been paved over with the help of free software.

Whatever. As consumer software reliability has improved, the race to stay one step ahead of consumer taste has put application developers in an even tighter embrace with moneyed interests. I'm not saying that the hacker ethos no longer exists or that it has even weakened in any noticeable way. I'm just saying that I doubt the programmer who generated the Facebook algorithm that rewrites the "info" pages so that each keyword points to a sponsored page, with an 80-percent semantic error rate to boot, spends much time in his new Porsche grousing about what the program really could have achieved if only the "suits" hadn't gotten in the way.

True, millions of people now run mostly free software on their computers with many running free software exclusively. From an ordinary consumer perspective, however, terms like "software" and "computer" have become increasingly distant. Many 2010-era cell phones could give a 2000-era laptop a run for its money in the functionality department. And yet, when it comes time to make a cell phone purchase, how many users lend any thought to the computer or software operating system making that functionality possible? The vast majority of modern phone users base their purchasing decisions almost entirely on the number of applications offered, the robustness of the network and, most important of all, the monthly service plan.

Getting a consumer in this situation to view his or her software purchase through the lens of personal liberty, as opposed to personal convenience, is becoming, if not more difficult, certainly a more complex endeavor.

Given this form of pessimistic introduction, why should anyone want go on and read this book?

I can offer two major reasons.

The first reason is a personal one. As noted in the Epilogue of *Free as in Freedom*, Richard and I parted on less than cordial terms shortly before the publication of that book. The fault, in large part, was mine. Having worked with Richard to make sure that my biographical sketch didn't run afoul of free software principles – an effort that, I'm proud to say, made *Free as in Freedom* one of the first works to employ the GNU Free Documentation License (GFDL) as a copyright mechanism – I abruptly ended the cooperative relationship when it came time to edit the work and incorporate Richard's lengthy list of error corrections and requests for clarification.

Though able to duck behind my own principles of authorial independence and journalistic objectivity, I have since come to lament not begging the book's publisher – O'Reilly and Associates – for additional time. Because O'Reilly had already granted my one major stipulation – the GFDL – and had already put up with a heavy stream of last-minute changes on my part, however, I was hesitant to push my luck.

In the years immediately following the publication of *Free as in Freedom*, I was able to justify my decision by noting that the GFDL, just like the GNU General Public License in the software realm, makes it possible for any reader to modify the book and resell it as a competitive work. As Ernest Hemingway once put it, "the first draft of anything is shit." If Stallman or others within the hacker community saw *Free as in Freedom* as a first draft at best, well, at least I had spared them the time and labor of generating their own first draft.

Now that Richard has indeed delivered what amounts to a significant rewrite, I can only but remain true to my younger self and endorse the effort. Indeed, I salute it. My only remaining hope is that, seeing as how Richard's work doesn't show any sign of slowing, additional documentation gets added to the mix.

Before moving on to the next reason, I should note that one of the pleasant by-products of this book is a re-opening of email communication channels between Richard and myself. The resulting communication has reacquainted me with the razor-sharp Stallman writing style.

An illustrative and perhaps amusing anecdote for anyone out there who has wrangled with Richard in text: In the course of discussing the passage in which I observe and document the process of Richard losing his cool amid the rush hour traffic of Kihei, Maui, a passage that served as the basis for Chapter 7 ("A Brief Journey through Hacker Hell") in the original book, I acknowledged a common complaint among the book's reviewers – namely, that the episode seemed out of place, a fragment of magazine-style profile interrupting a book-length biography. I told Richard that he could discard the episode for that reason alone but noted that my decision to include it was based on two justifications. First, it offered a glimpse of the Stallman temper, something I'd been warned about but had yet to experience in a firsthand manner. Second, I felt the overall scene possessed a certain metaphorical value. Hence the chapter title.

Stallman, to my surprise, agreed on both counts. His concern lay more in the two off-key words. At one point I quote him accusing the lead driver of our two-vehicle caravan with "deliberately" leading us down a dead-end street, an accusation that, if true, suggested a level of malice outside the bounds of the actual situation. Without the benefit of a recorded transcript – I only had a notebook at the time, I allowed that it was likely I'd mishandled Stallman's actual wording and had made it more hurtful than originally intended.

On a separate issue, meanwhile, Stallman questioned his quoted use of the word "fucking." Again, I didn't have the moment on tape, but I wrote back that I distinctly recalled an impressive display of profanity, a reminder of Richard's New York roots, and was willing to stand by that memory.

An email response from Richard, received the next day, restated the critique in a way that forced me to go back and re-read the first message. As it turned out, Stallman wasn't so much objecting to the "fuck" as the "-ing" portion of the quote.

"Part of the reason I doubt [the words] is that they involve using fucking as an adverb," Stallman wrote. "I have never spoken that way. So I am sure the words are somewhat altered."

Touché.

The second reason a person should feel compelled to read this book cycles back to the opening theme of this preface – how different a future we face in 2010 compared to the one we were still squinting our eyes to see back in 2000. I ll be honest: Like many Americans (and non-Americans), my worldview was altered by the events of September 11, 2001, so much so that it wasn't much longer after the publication of *Free as in Freedom* that my attention drifted sharply away from the free software movement and Stallman's efforts to keep it on course. While I have managed to follow the broad trends and major issues, the day-to-day drama surrounding software standards, software copyrights and software patents has become something I largely skip over – the Internet news equivalent of the Water Board notes in the local daily newspaper, in other words.

[RMS: The September 2001 attacks, not mentioned later in the book, deserve brief comment here. Far from "changing everything," as many proclaim, the attacks have, in fact, changed very little in the U.S.: There are still scoundrels in power who hate our freedoms. The only major difference is that they can now cite "terrorists" as an excuse for laws to take them away. See the political notes on `stallman.org` for more about this.]

This is a lamentable development in large part because, ten years in, I finally see the maturing 21st century in what I believe to be a clear light. Again, if this were a pitch letter to some editor, I'd call it "The Process Century."

By that I mean I we stand at a rare point in history where, all cynicism aside, the power to change the world really does delegate down to the ordinary citizen's level. The catch, of course, is that the same power that belongs to you also belongs to everyone else. Where in past eras one might have secured change simply by winning the sympathies of a few well-placed insiders, today's reformer must bring into alignment an entire vector field of competitive ideas and interests. In short, being an effective reformer nowadays requires more than just titanic stamina and a willingness to cry out in the wilderness for a decade or more, it requires knowing how to articulate durable, scalable ideas, how to beat the system at its own game.

On all counts, I would argue that Richard M. Stallman, while maybe not the archetype, is at the very least an ur-type of the successful reformer just described.

While some might lament a future in which every problem seems to take a few decades of committee meetings and sub-committee hearings just to reach the correction stage, I, for one, see the alternative – a future so responsive to individual or small group action that some self-appointed actor finally decides to put that responsiveness to the test – as too chilling to contemplate.

In short, if you are the type of person who, like me, hopes to see the 21st century follow a less bloody course than the 20th century, the Water Board – in its many frustrating guises – is where that battle is currently being fought. As hinted by the Virgil-inspired epigraph introducing the book's first chapter, I've always held out hope that this book might in some way become a sort of epic poem for the Internet Age. Built around a heroic but flawed central figure, its authorial stamp should be allowed to blur with age.

On that note, I would like to end this preface the same way I always end this preface – with a request for changes and contributions from any reader wishing to improve the text. Appendix B – GNU Free Documentation License offers a guide on your rights as a reader to submit changes, make corrections, or even create your own spin-off version of the book. If you prefer to simply run the changes through

Richard or myself, you can find the pertinent contact information on the Free Software Foundation web site.

In the meantime, good luck and enjoy the book!

Sam Williams
Staten Island, USA

.

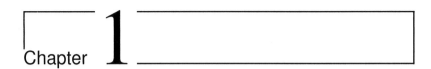

Chapter 1

For Want of a Printer

> I fear the Greeks. Even when they bring gifts.
> – Virgil, *The Aeneid*

The new printer was jammed, again.

Richard M. Stallman, a staff software programmer at the Massachusetts Institute of Technology's Artificial Intelligence Laboratory (AI Lab), discovered the malfunction the hard way. An hour after sending off a 50-page file to the office laser printer, Stallman, 27, broke off a productive work session to retrieve his documents. Upon arrival, he found only four pages in the printer's tray. To make matters even more frustrating, the four pages belonged to another user, meaning that Stallman's print job and the unfinished portion of somebody else's print job were still trapped somewhere within the electrical plumbing of the lab's computer network.

Waiting for machines is an occupational hazard when you're a software programmer, so Stallman took his frustration with a grain of salt. Still, the difference between waiting for a machine and waiting on a machine is a sizable one. It wasn't the first time he'd been forced to stand over the printer, watching pages print out one by one. As a person who spent the bulk of his days and nights improving the efficiency of machines and the software programs that controlled them, Stallman

1

felt a natural urge to open up the machine, look at the guts, and seek out the root of the problem.

Unfortunately, Stallman's skills as a computer programmer did not extend to the mechanical-engineering realm. As freshly printed documents poured out of the machine, Stallman had a chance to reflect on other ways to circumvent the printing jam problem.

How long ago had it been that the staff members at the AI Lab had welcomed the new printer with open arms? Stallman wondered. The machine had been a donation from the Xerox Corporation. A cutting edge prototype, it was a modified version of a fast Xerox photocopier. Only instead of making copies, it relied on software data piped in over a computer network to turn that data into professional-looking documents. Created by engineers at the world-famous Xerox Palo Alto Research Facility, it was, quite simply, an early taste of the desktop-printing revolution that would seize the rest of the computing industry by the end of the decade.

Driven by an instinctual urge to play with the best new equipment, programmers at the AI Lab promptly integrated the new machine into the lab's sophisticated computing infrastructure. The results had been immediately pleasing. Unlike the lab's old printer, the new Xerox machine was fast. Pages came flying out at a rate of one per second, turning a 20-minute print job into a 2-minute print job. The new machine was also more precise. Circles came out looking like circles, not ovals. Straight lines came out looking like straight lines, not low-amplitude sine waves.

It was, for all intents and purposes, a gift too good to refuse.

Once the machine was in use, its flaws began to surface. Chief among the drawbacks was the machine's susceptibility to paper jams. Engineering-minded programmers quickly understood the reason behind the flaw. As a photocopier, the machine generally required the direct oversight of a human operator. Figuring that these human operators would always be on hand to fix a paper jam, if it occurred, Xerox engineers had devoted their time and energies to eliminating other pesky problems. In engineering terms, user diligence was built into the system.

In modifying the machine for printer use, Xerox engineers had changed the user-machine relationship in a subtle but profound way. Instead of making the machine subservient to an individual human operator, they made it subservient to an entire networked population of human operators. Instead of standing directly over the machine, a human user on one end of the network sent his print command through an extended bucket brigade of machines, expecting the desired content to arrive at the targeted destination and in proper form. It wasn't until he finally went to check up on the final output that he realized how little of it had really been printed.

Stallman was hardly the only AI Lab denizen to notice the problem, but he also thought of a remedy. Years before, for the lab's previous printer, Stallman had solved a similar problem by modifying the software program that regulated the printer, on a small PDP-11 machine, as well as the Incompatible Timesharing System that ran on the main PDP-10 computer. Stallman couldn't eliminate paper jams, but he could insert software code that made the PDP-11 check the printer periodically, and report jams back to the PDP-10. Stallman also inserted code on the PDP-10 to notify every user with a waiting print job that the printer was jammed. The notice was simple, something along the lines of "The printer is jammed, please fix it," and because it went out to the people with the most pressing need to fix the problem, chances were that one of them would fix it forthwith.

As fixes go, Stallman's was oblique but elegant. It didn't fix the mechanical side of the problem, but it did the next best thing by closing the information loop between user and machine. Thanks to a few additional lines of software code, AI Lab employees could eliminate the 10 or 15 minutes wasted each week in running back and forth to check on the printer. In programming terms, Stallman's fix took advantage of the amplified intelligence of the overall network.

"If you got that message, you couldn't assume somebody else would fix it," says Stallman, recalling the logic. "You had to go to the printer. A minute or two after the printer got in trouble, the two or three people who got messages arrive to fix the machine. Of those two or three people, one of them, at least, would usually know how to fix the problem."

Such clever fixes were a trademark of the AI Lab and its indigenous population of programmers. Indeed, the best programmers at the AI Lab disdained the term programmer, preferring the more slangy occupational title of hacker instead. The job title covered a host of activities – everything from creative mirth making to the improve-

ment of existing software and computer systems. Implicit within the
title, however, was the old-fashioned notion of Yankee ingenuity. For
a hacker, writing a software program that worked was only the beginning. A hacker would try to display his cleverness (and impress other
hackers) by tackling an additional challenge: to make the program
particularly fast, small, powerful, elegant, or somehow impressive in a
clever way.[1]

Companies like Xerox made it a policy to donate their products
(and software) to places where hackers typically congregated. If hackers used these products, they might go to work for the company later
on. In the 60s and early 70s, they also sometimes developed programs
that were useful for the manufacturer to distribute to other customers.

When Stallman noticed the jamming tendency in the Xerox laser
printer, he thought of applying the old fix or "hack" to this printer.
In the course of looking up the Xerox laser-printer software, however,
Stallman made a troubling discovery. The printer didn't have any
software, at least nothing Stallman or a fellow programmer could read.
Until then, most companies had made it a form of courtesy to publish
source-code files–readable text files that documented the individual
software commands that told a machine what to do. Xerox, in this
instance, had provided software files only in compiled, or binary, form.
If programmers looked at the files, all they would see was an endless
stream of ones and zeroes – gibberish.

There are programs, called "disassemblers," to convert the ones
and zeroes into low-level machine instructions, but figuring out what
those instructions actually "do" is a long and hard task, known as
"reverse engineering." To reverse engineer this program could have
taken more time than five years' worth of jammed printouts. Stallman
wasn't desperate enough for that, so he put the problem aside.

Xerox's unfriendly policy contrasted blatantly with the usual practices of the hacker community. For instance, to develop the program
for the PDP-11 that ran the old printer, and the program for another PDP-11 that handled display terminals, the AI Lab needed a
cross-assembler program to build PDP-11 programs on the PDP-10
main computer. The lab's hackers could have written one, but Stallman, a Harvard student, found such a program at Harvard's computer
lab. That program was written to run on the same kind of computer,
the PDP-10, albeit with a different operating system. Stallman never

knew who had written the program, since the source code did not say. But he brought a copy back to the AI Lab. He then altered the source code to make it run on the AI Lab's Incompatible Timesharing System (ITS). With no muss and little fuss, the AI Lab got the program it needed for its software infrastructure. Stallman even added a few features not found in the original version, making the program more powerful. "We wound up using it for several years," Stallman says.

From the perspective of a 1970s-era programmer, the transaction was the software equivalent of a neighbor stopping by to borrow a power tool or a cup of sugar from a neighbor. The only difference was that in borrowing a copy of the software for the AI Lab, Stallman had done nothing to deprive anyone else of the use of the program. If anything, other hackers gained in the process, because Stallman had introduced additional features that other hackers were welcome to borrow back. For instance, Stallman recalls a programmer at the private engineering firm, Bolt, Beranek & Newman, borrowing the program. He made it run on Twenex and added a few additional features, which Stallman eventually reintegrated into the AI Lab's own source-code archive. The two programmers decided to maintain a common version together, which had the code to run either on ITS or on Twenex at the user's choice.

"A program would develop the way a city develops," says Stallman, recalling the software infrastructure of the AI Lab. "Parts would get replaced and rebuilt. New things would get added on. But you could always look at a certain part and say, 'Hmm, by the style, I see this part was written back in the early 60s and this part was written in the mid-1970s.'"

Through this simple system of intellectual accretion, hackers at the AI Lab and other places built up robust creations. Not every programmer participating in this culture described himself as a hacker, but most shared the sentiments of Richard M. Stallman. If a program or software fix was good enough to solve your problems, it was good enough to solve somebody else's problems. Why not share it out of a simple desire for good karma?

This system of cooperation was being undermined by commercial secrecy and greed, leading to peculiar combinations of secrecy and cooperation. For instance, computer scientists at UC Berkeley had built up a powerful operating system called BSD, based on the Unix system they had obtained from AT&T. Berkeley made BSD available for the cost of copying a tape, but would only give these tapes to schools that could present a $50,000 source license obtained from AT&T. The Berkeley hackers continued to share as much as AT&T let them, but they had not perceived a conflict between the two practices.

Likewise, Stallman was annoyed that Xerox had not provided the source-code files, but not yet angry. He never thought of asking Xerox for a copy. "They had already given us the laser printer," Stallman says. "I could not say they owed us something more. Besides, I took for granted that the absence of source code reflected an intentional decision, and that asking them to change it would be futile."

Good news eventually arrived: word had it that a scientist at the computer-science department at Carnegie Mellon University had a copy of the laser printer source code.

The association with Carnegie Mellon did not augur well. In 1979, Brian Reid, a doctoral student there, had shocked the community by refusing to share his text-formatting program, dubbed Scribe. This text formatter was the first to have mark-up commands oriented towards the desired semantics (such as "emphasize this word" or "this paragraph is a quotation") rather than low-level formatting details ("put this word in italics" or "narrow the margins for this paragraph"). Instead Reid sold Scribe to a Pittsburgh-area software company called Unilogic. His graduate-student career ending, Reid says he simply was looking for a way to unload the program on a set of developers that would take pains to keep it from slipping into the public domain. (Why one would consider such an outcome particularly undesirable is not clear.) To sweeten the deal, Reid also agreed to insert a set of time-dependent functions – "time bombs" in software-programmer parlance – that deactivated freely copied versions of the program after a 90-day expiration date. To avoid deactivation, users paid the software company, which then issued a code that defused the internal time-bomb anti-feature.

For Stallman, this was a betrayal of the programmer ethos, pure and simple. Instead of honoring the notion of share-and-share alike, Reid had inserted a way for companies to compel programmers to pay for information access. But he didn't think deeply about the question, since he didn't use Scribe much.

Unilogic gave the AI Lab a gratis copy to use, but did not remove or mention the time bomb. It worked, for a while; then one day a user reported that Scribe had stopped working. System hacker Howard Cannon spent hours debugging the binary until he found the time-bomb and patched it out. Cannon was incensed, and wasn't shy about telling the other hackers how mad he was that Unilogic had wasted his time with an intentional bug.

Stallman had a Lab-related reason, a few months later, to visit the Carnegie Mellon campus. During that visit, he made a point of looking for the person reported to have the printer software source code. By good fortune, the man was in his office.

In true engineer-to-engineer fashion, the conversation was cordial but blunt. After briefly introducing himself as a visitor from MIT, Stallman requested a copy of the laser-printer source code that he wanted to modify. To his chagrin, the researcher refused.

"He told me that he had promised not to give me a copy," Stallman says.

Memory is a funny thing. Twenty years after the fact, Stallman's mental history tape is blank in places. Not only does he not remember the motivating reason for the trip or even the time of year during which he took it, he also has no recollection of who was on the other end of the conversation. According to Reid, the person most likely to have fielded Stallman's request is Robert Sproull, a former Xerox PARC researcher and current director of Sun Laboratories, a research division of the computer-technology conglomerate Sun Microsystems. During the 1970s, Sproull had been the primary developer of the laser-printer software in question while at Xerox PARC. Around 1980, Sproull took a faculty research position at Carnegie Mellon where he continued his laser-printer work amid other projects.

When asked directly about the request, however, Sproull draws a blank. "I can't make a factual comment," writes Sproull via email. "I have absolutely no recollection of the incident."

"The code that Stallman was asking for was leading-edge, state-of-the-art code that Sproull had written in the year or so before going to Carnegie Mellon," recalls Reid. If so, that might indicate a misunderstanding that occurred, since Stallman wanted the source for the program that MIT had used for quite some time, not some newer version. But the question of which version never arose in the brief conversation.

In talking to audiences, Stallman has made repeated reference to the incident, noting that the man's unwillingness to hand over the source code stemmed from a nondisclosure agreement, a contractual agreement between him and the Xerox Corporation giving the signatory access to the software source code in exchange for a promise of secrecy. Now a standard item of business in the software industry, the nondisclosure agreement, or NDA, was a novel development at the time, a reflection of both the commercial value of the laser printer to Xerox and the information needed to run it. "Xerox was at the time trying to make a commercial product out of the laser printer," recalls Reid. "They would have been insane to give away the source code."

For Stallman, however, the NDA was something else entirely. It was a refusal on the part of some CMU researcher to participate in a society that, until then, had encouraged software programmers to regard programs as communal resources. Like a peasant whose centuries-old irrigation ditch had grown suddenly dry, Stallman had followed the ditch to its source only to find a brand-spanking-new hydroelectric dam bearing the Xerox logo.

For Stallman, the realization that Xerox had compelled a fellow programmer to participate in this newfangled system of compelled secrecy took a while to sink in. In the first moment, he could only see the refusal in a personal context. "I was so angry I couldn't think of a way to express it. So I just turned away and walked out without another word," Stallman recalls. "I might have slammed the door. Who knows? All I remember is wanting to get out of there. I went to his office expecting him to cooperate, so I had not thought about how I would respond if he refused. When he did, I was stunned speechless as well as disappointed and angry."

Twenty years after the fact, the anger still lingers, and Stallman presents the event as one that made him confront an ethical issue, though not the only such event on his path. Within the next few months, a series of events would befall both Stallman and the AI Lab hacker community that would make 30 seconds worth of tension in a remote Carnegie Mellon office seem trivial by comparison. Nevertheless, when it comes time to sort out the events that would transform Stallman from a lone hacker, instinctively suspicious of centralized authority, to a crusading activist applying traditional notions of liberty, equality, and fraternity to the world of software development, Stallman singles out the Carnegie Mellon encounter for special attention.

"It was my first encounter with a nondisclosure agreement, and it immediately taught me that nondisclosure agreements have victims," says Stallman, firmly. "In this case I was the victim. [My lab and I] were victims."

Stallman later explained, "If he had refused me his cooperation for personal reasons, it would not have raised any larger issue. I might have considered him a jerk, but no more. The fact that his refusal was impersonal, that he had promised in advance to be uncooperative, not just to me but to anyone whatsoever, made this a larger issue."

Although previous events had raised Stallman's ire, he says it wasn't until his Carnegie Mellon encounter that he realized the events were beginning to intrude on a culture he had long considered sacrosanct. He said, "I already had an idea that software should be shared, but I wasn't sure how to think about that. My thoughts weren't clear and organized to the point where I could express them in a concise fashion to the rest of the world. After this experience, I started to recognize what the issue was, and how big it was."

As an elite programmer at one of the world's elite institutions, Stallman had been perfectly willing to ignore the compromises and bargains of his fellow programmers just so long as they didn't interfere with his own work. Until the arrival of the Xerox laser printer, Stallman had been content to look down on the machines and programs other computer users grimly tolerated.

Now that the laser printer had insinuated itself within the AI Lab's network, however, something had changed. The machine worked fine, barring the paper jams, but the ability to modify software according to personal taste or community need had been taken away. From the viewpoint of the software industry, the printer software represented a change in business tactics. Software had become such a valuable asset that companies no longer accepted the need to publicize source code, especially when publication meant giving potential competitors a chance to duplicate something cheaply. From Stallman's viewpoint, the printer was a Trojan Horse. After a decade of failure, software that users could not change and redistribute – future hackers would use the term "proprietary" software – had gained a foothold inside the

AI Lab through the sneakiest of methods. It had come disguised as a gift.

That Xerox had offered some programmers access to additional gifts in exchange for secrecy was also galling, but Stallman takes pains to note that, if presented with such a quid pro quo bargain at a younger age, he just might have taken the Xerox Corporation up on its offer. The anger of the Carnegie Mellon encounter, however, had a firming effect on Stallman's own moral lassitude. Not only did it give him the necessary anger to view such future offers with suspicion, it also forced him to turn the situation around: what if a fellow hacker dropped into Stallman's office someday and it suddenly became Stallman's job to refuse the hacker's request for source code?

"When somebody invited me to betray all my colleagues in that way, I remembered how angry I was when somebody else had done that to me and my whole lab," Stallman says. "So I said, 'Thank you very much for offering me this nice software package, but I can't accept it on the conditions that you're asking for, so I'm going to do without it.'"

It was a lesson Stallman would carry with him through the tumultuous years of the 1980s, a decade during which many of his MIT colleagues would depart the AI Lab and sign nondisclosure agreements of their own. They may have told themselves that this was a necessary evil so they could work on the best projects. For Stallman, however, the NDA called the the moral legitimacy of the project into question. What good is a technically exciting project if it is meant to be withheld from the community?

As Stallman would quickly learn, refusing such offers involved more than personal sacrifice. It involved segregating himself from fellow hackers who, though sharing a similar distaste for secrecy, tended to express that distaste in a more morally flexible fashion. Refusing another's request for source code, Stallman decided, was not only a betrayal of the scientific mission that had nurtured software development since the end of World War II, it was a violation of the Golden Rule, the baseline moral dictate to do unto others as you would have them do unto you.

Hence the importance of the laser printer and the encounter that resulted from it. Without it, Stallman says, his life might have followed a more ordinary path, one balancing the material comforts of a commercial programmer with the ultimate frustration of a life spent writing invisible software code. There would have been no sense of clarity, no urgency to address a problem others weren't addressing. Most importantly, there would have been no righteous anger, an emotion that, as we soon shall see, has propelled Stallman's career as surely as any political ideology or ethical belief.

"From that day forward, I decided this was something I could never participate in," says Stallman, alluding to the practice of trading personal liberty for the sake of convenience – Stallman's description of the NDA bargain – as well as the overall culture that encouraged such ethically suspect deal-making in the first place. "I decided never to make other people victims as I had been a victim."

Endnotes

[1] For more on the term "hacker," see Appendix A – Hack, Hackers, and Hacking.

.

Chapter **2**

2001: A Hacker's Odyssey

The New York University computer-science department sits inside
Warren Weaver Hall, a fortress-like building located two blocks east of
Washington Square Park. Industrial-strength air-conditioning vents
create a surrounding moat of hot air, discouraging loiterers and solici-
tors alike. Visitors who breach the moat encounter another formidable
barrier, a security check-in counter immediately inside the building's
single entryway.

Beyond the security checkpoint, the atmosphere relaxes somewhat.
Still, numerous signs scattered throughout the first floor preach the
dangers of unsecured doors and propped-open fire exits. Taken as
a whole, the signs offer a reminder: even in the relatively tranquil
confines of pre-September 11, 2001, New York, one can never be too
careful or too suspicious.

The signs offer an interesting thematic counterpoint to the growing
number of visitors gathering in the hall's interior atrium. A few look
like NYU students. Most look like shaggy-haired concert-goers milling
outside a music hall in anticipation of the main act. For one brief
morning, the masses have taken over Warren Weaver Hall, leaving the
nearby security attendant with nothing better to do but watch Ricki
Lake on TV and shrug her shoulders toward the nearby auditorium
whenever visitors ask about "the speech."

Once inside the auditorium, a visitor finds the person who has forced this temporary shutdown of building security procedures. The person is Richard M. Stallman, founder of the GNU Project, original president of the Free Software Foundation, winner of the 1990 MacArthur Fellowship, winner of the Association of Computing Machinery's Grace Murray Hopper Award (also in 1990), corecipient of the Takeda Foundation's 2001 Takeda Award for Social/Economic Betterment, and former AI Lab hacker. As announced over a host of hacker-related web sites, including the GNU Project's own `http://www.gnu.org` site, Stallman is in Manhattan, his former hometown, to deliver a much anticipated speech in rebuttal to the Microsoft Corporation's recent campaign against the GNU General Public License.

The subject of Stallman's speech is the history and future of the free software movement. The location is significant. Less than a month before, Microsoft senior vice president Craig Mundie appeared at the nearby NYU Stern School of Business, delivering a speech blasting the GNU General Public License, or GNU GPL, a legal device originally conceived by Stallman 16 years before. Built to counteract the growing wave of software secrecy overtaking the computer industry – a wave first noticed by Stallman during his 1980 troubles with the Xerox laser printer – the GPL has evolved into a central tool of the free software community. In simplest terms, the GPL establishes a form of communal ownership – what today's legal scholars now call the "digital commons" – through the legal weight of copyright. The GPL makes this irrevocable; once an author gives code to the community in this way, that code can't be made proprietary by anyone else. Derivative versions must carry the same copyright license, if they use a substantial amount of the original source code. For this reason, critics of the GPL have taken to calling it a "viral" license, suggesting inaccurately that it spreads itself to every software program it touches.[1]

In an information economy increasingly dependent on software and increasingly beholden to software standards, the GPL has become the proverbial "big stick." Even companies that once derided it as "software socialism" have come around to recognize the benefits. Linux, the kernel developed by Finnish college student Linus Torvalds in 1991, is licensed under the GPL, as are most parts of the GNU system: GNU Emacs, the GNU Debugger, the GNU C Compiler, etc. Together, these tools form the components of the free software GNU/Linux operating system, developed, nurtured, and owned by the worldwide hacker community. Instead of viewing this community as a threat, high-tech companies like IBM, Hewlett Packard, and Sun Microsystems have come to rely upon it, selling software applications and services built to ride atop the ever-growing free software infrastructure.[2]

They've also come to rely upon it as a strategic weapon in the hacker community's perennial war against Microsoft, the Redmond, Washington-based company that has dominated the PC-software marketplace since the late 1980s. As owner of the popular Windows operating system, Microsoft stands to lose the most in an industry-wide shift to the GPL license. Each program in the Windows colossus is covered by copyrights and contracts (End User License Agreements, or EULAs) asserting the proprietary status of the executable, as well as the underlying source code that users can't get anyway. Incorporating code protected by the "viral" GPL into one of these programs is forbidden; to comply with the GPL's requirements, Microsoft would be legally required to make that whole program free software. Rival companies could then copy, modify, and sell improved versions of it, taking away the basis of Microsoft's lock over the users.

Hence the company's growing concern over the GPL's rate of adoption. Hence the recent Mundie speech blasting the GPL and the "open source" approach to software development and sales. (Microsoft does not even acknowledge the term "free software," preferring to use its attacks to direct attention towards the apolitical "open source" camp described in chapter 11, and away from the free software movement.) And hence Stallman's decision to deliver a public rebuttal to that speech on the same campus here today.

20 years is a long time in the software industry. Consider this: in 1980, when Richard Stallman was cursing the AI Lab's Xerox laser printer, Microsoft, which dominates the worldwide software industry, was still a privately held startup. IBM, the company then regarded as the most powerful force in the computer hardware industry, had yet to introduce its first personal computer, thereby igniting the current low-cost PC market. Many of the technologies we now take for granted – the World Wide Web, satellite television, 32-bit video-game consoles – didn't even exist. The same goes for many of the companies that now fill the upper echelons of the corporate establishment, companies

like AOL, Sun Microsystems, Amazon.com, Compaq, and Dell. The list goes on and on.

Among those who value progress above freedom, the fact that the high-technology marketplace has come so far in such little time is cited both for and against the GNU GPL. Some argue in favor of the GPL, pointing to the short lifespan of most computer hardware platforms. Facing the risk of buying an obsolete product, consumers tend to flock to companies with the best long-term survival. As a result, the software marketplace has become a winner-take-all arena.[3] The proprietary software environment, they say, leads to monopoly abuse and stagnation. Strong companies suck all the oxygen out of the marketplace for rival competitors and innovative startups.

Others argue just the opposite. Selling software is just as risky, if not more risky, than buying software, they say. Without the legal guarantees provided by proprietary software licenses, not to mention the economic prospects of a privately owned "killer app" (i.e., a breakthrough technology that launches an entirely new market),[4] companies lose the incentive to participate. Once again, the market stagnates and innovation declines. As Mundie himself noted in his May 3rd address on the same campus, the GPL's "viral" nature "poses a threat" to any company that relies on the uniqueness of its software as a competitive asset. Added Mundie:

> It also fundamentally undermines the independent commercial software sector because it effectively makes it impossible to distribute software on a basis where recipients pay for the product rather than just the cost of distribution.[5]

The mutual success of GNU/Linux and Windows over the last 10 years suggests that both sides on this question are sometimes right. However, free software activists such as Stallman think this is a side issue. The real question, they say, isn't whether free or proprietary software will succeed more, it's which one is more ethical.

Nevertheless, the battle for momentum is an important one in the software industry. Even powerful vendors such as Microsoft rely on the support of third-party software developers whose tools, programs, and computer games make an underlying software platform such as

Windows more attractive to the mainstream consumer. Citing the rapid evolution of the technology marketplace over the last 20 years, not to mention his own company's impressive track record during that period, Mundie advised listeners to not get too carried away by the free software movement's recent momentum:

> Two decades of experience have shown that an economic model that protects intellectual property and a business model that recoups research and development costs can create impressive economic benefits and distribute them very broadly.[6]

Such admonitions serve as the backdrop for Stallman's speech today. Less than a month after their utterance, Stallman stands with his back to one of the chalk boards at the front of the room, edgy to begin.

If the last two decades have brought dramatic changes to the software marketplace, they have brought even more dramatic changes to Stallman himself. Gone is the skinny, clean-shaven hacker who once spent his entire days communing with his beloved PDP-10. In his place stands a heavy-set middle-aged man with long hair and rabbinical beard, a man who now spends the bulk of his time writing and answering email, haranguing fellow programmers, and giving speeches like the one today. Dressed in an aqua-colored T-shirt and brown polyester pants, Stallman looks like a desert hermit who just stepped out of a Salvation Army dressing room.

The crowd is filled with visitors who share Stallman's fashion and grooming tastes. Many come bearing laptop computers and cellular modems, all the better to record and transmit Stallman's words to a waiting Internet audience. The gender ratio is roughly 15 males to 1 female, and 1 of the 7 or 8 females in the room comes in bearing a stuffed penguin, the official Linux mascot, while another carries a stuffed teddy bear.

Agitated, Stallman leaves his post at the front of the room and takes a seat in a front-row chair, tapping commands into an already-opened laptop. For the next 10 minutes Stallman is oblivious to the growing number of students, professors, and fans circulating in front of him at the foot of the auditorium stage.

Before the speech can begin, the baroque rituals of academic formality must be observed. Stallman's appearance merits not one but two introductions. Mike Uretsky, codirector of the Stern School's Center for Advanced Technology, provides the first.

"The role of a university is to foster debate and to have interesting discussions," Uretsky says. "This particular presentation, this seminar falls right into that mold. I find the discussion of open source particularly interesting."

Before Uretsky can get another sentence out, Stallman is on his feet waving him down like a stranded motorist.

"I do free software," Stallman says to rising laughter. "Open source is a different movement."

The laughter gives way to applause. The room is stocked with Stallman partisans, people who know of his reputation for verbal exactitude, not to mention his much publicized 1998 falling out with the open source software proponents. Most have come to anticipate such outbursts the same way radio fans once waited for Jack Benny's trademark, "Now cut that out!" phrase during each radio program.

Uretsky hastily finishes his introduction and cedes the stage to Edmond Schonberg, a professor in the NYU computer-science department. As a computer programmer and GNU Project contributor, Schonberg knows which linguistic land mines to avoid. He deftly summarizes Stallman's career from the perspective of a modern-day programmer.

"Richard is the perfect example of somebody who, by acting locally, started thinking globally [about] problems concerning the unavailability of source code," says Schonberg. "He has developed a coherent philosophy that has forced all of us to reexamine our ideas of how software is produced, of what intellectual property means, and of what the software community actually represents."[7]

Schonberg welcomes Stallman to more applause. Stallman takes a moment to shut off his laptop, rises out of his chair, and takes the stage.

At first, Stallman's address seems more Catskills comedy routine than political speech. "I'd like to thank Microsoft for providing me the opportunity to be on this platform," Stallman wisecracks. "For the past few weeks, I have felt like an author whose book was fortuitously banned somewhere."

For the uninitiated, Stallman dives into a quick free software warm-up analogy. He likens a software program to a cooking recipe. Both provide useful step-by-step instructions on how to complete a desired task and can be easily modified if a user has special desires or circumstances. "You don't have to follow a recipe exactly," Stallman notes. "You can leave out some ingredients. Add some mushrooms, 'cause you like mushrooms. Put in less salt because your doctor said you should cut down on salt – whatever."

Most importantly, Stallman says, software programs and recipes are both easy to share. In giving a recipe to a dinner guest, a cook loses little more than time and the cost of the paper the recipe was written on. Software programs require even less, usually a few mouse-clicks and a modicum of electricity. In both instances, however, the person giving the information gains two things: increased friendship and the ability to borrow interesting recipes in return.

"Imagine what it would be like if recipes were packaged inside black boxes," Stallman says, shifting gears. "You couldn't see what ingredients they're using, let alone change them, and imagine if you made a copy for a friend. They would call you a pirate and try to put you in prison for years. That world would create tremendous outrage from all the people who are used to sharing recipes. But that is exactly what the world of proprietary software is like. A world in which common decency towards other people is prohibited or prevented."

With this introductory analogy out of the way, Stallman launches into a retelling of the Xerox laser-printer episode. Like the recipe analogy, the laser-printer story is a useful rhetorical device. With its parable-like structure, it dramatizes just how quickly things can change in the software world. Drawing listeners back to an era before Amazon.com one-click shopping, Microsoft Windows, and Oracle databases, it asks the listener to examine the notion of software ownership free of its current corporate logos.

Stallman delivers the story with all the polish and practice of a local district attorney conducting a closing argument. When he gets to the part about the Carnegie Mellon professor refusing to lend him a copy of the printer source code, Stallman pauses.

"He had betrayed us," Stallman says. "But he didn't just do it to us. Chances are he did it to you."

On the word "you," Stallman points his index finger accusingly at an unsuspecting member of the audience. The targeted audience member's eyebrows flinch slightly, but Stallman's own eyes have moved on. Slowly and deliberately, Stallman picks out a second listener to nervous titters from the crowd. "And I think, mostly likely, he did it to you, too," he says, pointing at an audience member three rows behind the first.

By the time Stallman has a third audience member picked out, the titters have given away to general laughter. The gesture seems a bit staged, because it is. Still, when it comes time to wrap up the Xerox laser-printer story, Stallman does so with a showman's flourish. "He probably did it to most of the people here in this room – except a few, maybe, who weren't born yet in 1980," Stallman says, drawing more laughs. "[That's] because he had promised to refuse to cooperate with just about the entire population of the planet Earth."

Stallman lets the comment sink in for a half-beat. "He had signed a nondisclosure agreement," Stallman adds.

Richard Matthew Stallman's rise from frustrated academic to political leader over the last 20 years speaks to many things. It speaks to Stallman's stubborn nature and prodigious will. It speaks to the clearly articulated vision and values of the free software movement Stallman helped build. It speaks to the high-quality software programs Stallman has built, programs that have cemented Stallman's reputation as a programming legend. It speaks to the growing momentum of the GPL, a legal innovation that many Stallman observers see as his most momentous accomplishment.

Most importantly, it speaks to the changing nature of political power in a world increasingly beholden to computer technology and the software programs that power that technology.

Maybe that's why, even at a time when most high-technology stars are on the wane, Stallman's star has grown. Since launching the GNU Project in 1984,[8] Stallman has been at turns ignored, satirized, vilified, and attacked–both from within and without the free software movement. Through it all, the GNU Project has managed to meet its milestones, albeit with a few notorious delays, and stay relevant in a software marketplace several orders of magnitude more complex than the one it entered 18 years ago. So too has the free software ideology, an ideology meticulously groomed by Stallman himself.

To understand the reasons behind this currency, it helps to examine Richard Stallman both in his own words and in the words of the people who have collaborated and battled with him along the way. The Richard Stallman character sketch is not a complicated one. If any person exemplifies the old adage "what you see is what you get," it's Stallman.

"I think if you want to understand Richard Stallman the human being, you really need to see all of the parts as a consistent whole," advises Eben Moglen, legal counsel to the Free Software Foundation and professor of law at Columbia University Law School. "All those personal eccentricities that lots of people see as obstacles to getting to know Stallman really 'are' Stallman: Richard's strong sense of personal frustration, his enormous sense of principled ethical commitment, his inability to compromise, especially on issues he considers fundamental. These are all the very reasons Richard did what he did when he did."

Explaining how a journey that started with a laser printer would eventually lead to a sparring match with the world's richest corporation is no easy task. It requires a thoughtful examination of the forces that have made software ownership so important in today's society. It also requires a thoughtful examination of a man who, like many political leaders before him, understands the malleability of human memory. It requires an ability to interpret the myths and politically laden code words that have built up around Stallman over time. Finally, it requires an understanding of Stallman's genius as a programmer and his failures and successes in translating that genius to other pursuits.

When it comes to offering his own summary of the journey, Stallman acknowledges the fusion of personality and principle observed by Moglen. "Stubbornness is my strong suit," he says. "Most people who attempt to do anything of any great difficulty eventually get discouraged and give up. I never gave up."

He also credits blind chance. Had it not been for that run-in over the Xerox laser printer, had it not been for the personal and political conflicts that closed out his career as an MIT employee, had it not been for a half dozen other timely factors, Stallman finds it very easy to picture his life following a different career path. That being said, Stallman gives thanks to the forces and circumstances that put him in the position to make a difference.

"I had just the right skills," says Stallman, summing up his decision for launching the GNU Project to the audience. "Nobody was there but me, so I felt like, 'I'm elected. I have to work on this. If not me, who?'"

Endnotes

[1] Actually, the GPL's powers are not quite that potent: just putting your code in the same computer with a GPL-covered program does not put your code under the GPL.

"To compare something to a virus is very harsh," says Stallman. "A spider plant is a more accurate comparison; it goes to another place if you actively take a cutting."

For more information on the GNU General Public License, visit http://www.gnu.org/copyleft/gpl.html.

[2] Although these applications run on GNU/Linux, it does not follow that they are themselves free software. On the contrary, most of them applications are proprietary software, and respect your freedom no more than Windows does. They may contribute to the success of GNU/Linux, but they don't contribute to the goal of freedom for which it exists.

[3] See Shubha Ghosh, "Revealing the Microsoft Windows Source Code," *Gigalaw.com* (January, 2000), http://www.gigalaw.com/.

[4] Killer apps don't have to be proprietary. Still, I think the reader gets the point: the software marketplace is like the lottery. The bigger the potential payoff, the more people want to participate. For a good summary of the killer-app phenomenon, see Philip Ben-David, "Whatever Happened to the 'Killer App'?", *e-Commerce News* (December 7, 2000), http://www.ecommercetimes.com/story/5893.html.

[5] See Craig Mundie, "The Commercial Software Model," senior vice president, Microsoft Corp., excerpted from an online transcript of Mundie's May 3, 2001, speech to the New York University Stern School of Business, http://www.microsoft.com/presspass/exec/craig/05-03sharedsource.asp.

[6] *Ibid.*

[7] If this were to be said today, Stallman would object to the term "intellectual property" as carrying bias and confusion. See http://www.gnu.org/philosophy/not-ipr.html.

[8] The acronym GNU stands for "GNU's not Unix." In another portion of the May 29, 2001, NYU speech, Stallman summed up the acronym's origin:

> We hackers always look for a funny or naughty name for a program, because naming a program is half the fun of writing the program. We also had a tradition of recursive acronyms, to say that the program that you're writing is similar to some existing program... I looked for a recursive acronym for Something Is Not UNIX. And I tried all 26 letters and discovered that none of them was a word. I decided to make it a contraction. That way I could have a three-letter acronym,

for Something's Not UNIX. And I tried letters, and I came across the word "GNU." That was it.

Although a fan of puns, Stallman recommends that software users pronounce the "g" at the beginning of the acronym (i.e., "gah-new"). Not only does this avoid confusion with the word "gnu," the name of the African antelope, Connochaetes gnou, it also avoids confusion with the adjective "new." "We've been working on it for 17 years now, so it is not exactly new any more," Stallman says.

Source: author notes and online transcript of "Free Software: Freedom and Cooperation," Richard Stallman's May 29, 2001, speech at New York University, http://www.gnu.org/events/rms-nyu-2001-transcript.txt.

.

Chapter 3

A Portrait of the Hacker as a Young Man

Richard Stallman's mother, Alice Lippman, still remembers the moment she realized her son had a special gift.

"I think it was when he was eight," Lippman recalls.

The year was 1961, and Lippman, a recently divorced single mother, was whiling away a weekend afternoon within the family's tiny one-bedroom apartment on Manhattan's Upper West Side. Leafing through a copy of Scientific American, Lippman came upon her favorite section, the Martin Gardner-authored column titled "Mathematical Games." A substitute art teacher at the time, Lippman enjoyed Gardner's column for the brain-teasers it provided. With her son already ensconced in a book on the nearby sofa, Lippman decided to take a crack at solving the week's feature puzzle.

"I wasn't the best person when it came to solving the puzzles," she admits. "But as an artist, I found they really helped me work through conceptual barriers."

Lippman says her attempt to solve the puzzle met an immediate brick wall. About to throw the magazine down in disgust, Lippman was surprised by a gentle tug on her shirt sleeve.

"It was Richard," she recalls, "He wanted to know if I needed any help."

Looking back and forth, between the puzzle and her son, Lippman says she initially regarded the offer with skepticism. "I asked Richard if he'd read the magazine," she says. "He told me that, yes, he had and what's more he'd already solved the puzzle. The next thing I know, he starts explaining to me how to solve it."

Hearing the logic of her son's approach, Lippman's skepticism quickly gave way to incredulity. "I mean, I always knew he was a bright boy," she says, "but this was the first time I'd seen anything that suggested how advanced he really was."

Thirty years after the fact, Lippman punctuates the memory with a laugh. "To tell you the truth, I don't think I ever figured out how to solve that puzzle," she says. "All I remember is being amazed he knew the answer."

Seated at the dining-room table of her second Manhattan apartment – the same spacious three-bedroom complex she and her son moved to following her 1967 marriage to Maurice Lippman, now deceased – Alice Lippman exudes a Jewish mother's mixture of pride and bemusement when recalling her son's early years. The nearby dining-room credenza offers an eight-by-ten photo of Stallman glowering in full beard and doctoral robes. The image dwarfs accompanying photos of Lippman's nieces and nephews, but before a visitor can make too much of it, Lippman makes sure to balance its prominent placement with an ironic wisecrack.

"Richard insisted I have it after he received his honorary doctorate at the University of Glasgow," says Lippman. "He said to me, 'Guess what, mom? It's the first graduation I ever attended.'" [1]

Such comments reflect the sense of humor that comes with raising a child prodigy. Make no mistake, for every story Lippman hears and reads about her son's stubbornness and unusual behavior, she can deliver at least a dozen in return.

"He used to be so conservative," she says, throwing up her hands in mock exasperation. "We used to have the worst arguments right here at this table. I was part of the first group of public city school teachers that struck to form a union, and Richard was very angry with me. He saw unions as corrupt. He was also very opposed to social security. He thought people could make much more money investing it on their own. Who knew that within 10 years he would become so idealistic? All I remember is his stepsister coming to me and saying, 'What is he going to be when he grows up? A fascist?'"[2]

As a single parent for nearly a decade – she and Richard's father, Daniel Stallman, were married in 1948, divorced in 1958, and split custody of their son afterwards – Lippman can attest to her son's aversion to authority. She can also attest to her son's lust for knowledge. It was during the times when the two forces intertwined, Lippman says, that she and her son experienced their biggest battles.

"It was like he never wanted to eat," says Lippman, recalling the behavior pattern that set in around age eight and didn't let up until her son's high-school graduation in 1970. "I'd call him for dinner, and he'd never hear me. I'd have to call him 9 or 10 times just to get his attention. He was totally immersed."

Stallman, for his part, remembers things in a similar fashion, albeit with a political twist.

"I enjoyed reading," he says. "If I wanted to read, and my mother told me to go to the kitchen and eat or go to sleep, I wasn't going to listen. I saw no reason why I couldn't read. No reason why she should be able to tell me what to do, period. Essentially, what I had read about, ideas such as democracy and individual freedom, I applied to myself. I didn't see any reason to exclude children from these principles."

The belief in individual freedom over arbitrary authority extended to school as well. Two years ahead of his classmates by age 11, Stallman endured all the usual frustrations of a gifted public-school student. It wasn't long after the puzzle incident that his mother attended the first in what would become a long string of parent-teacher conferences.

"He absolutely refused to write papers," says Lippman, recalling an early controversy. "I think the last paper he wrote before his senior year in high school was an essay on the history of the number system in the west for a fourth-grade teacher." To be required to choose a specific topic when there was nothing he actually wanted to write about was almost impossible for Stallman, and painful enough to make him go to great lengths to avoid such situations.

Gifted in anything that required analytical thinking, Stallman gravitated toward math and science at the expense of his other studies.

What some teachers saw as single-mindedness, however, Lippman saw
as impatience. Math and science offered simply too much opportunity
to learn, especially in comparison to subjects and pursuits for which
her son seemed less naturally inclined. Around age 10 or 11, when the
boys in Stallman's class began playing a regular game of touch football,
she remembers her son coming home in a rage. "He wanted to play
so badly, but he just didn't have the coordination skills," Lippman
recalls. "It made him so angry."

The anger eventually drove her son to focus on math and science
all the more. Even in the realm of science, however, her son's impatience could be problematic. Poring through calculus textbooks by
age seven, Stallman saw little need to dumb down his discourse for
adults. Sometime, during his middle-school years, Lippman hired a
student from nearby Columbia University to play big brother to her
son. The student left the family's apartment after the first session and
never came back. "I think what Richard was talking about went over
his head," Lippman speculates.

Another favorite maternal memory dates back to the early 1960s,
shortly after the puzzle incident. Around age seven, two years after
the divorce and relocation from Queens, Richard took up the hobby of
launching model rockets in nearby Riverside Drive Park. What started
as aimless fun soon took on an earnest edge as her son began recording
the data from each launch. Like the interest in mathematical games,
the pursuit drew little attention until one day, just before a major
NASA launch, Lippman checked in on her son to see if he wanted to
watch.

"He was fuming," Lippman says. "All he could say to me was, 'But
I'm not published yet.' Apparently he had something that he really
wanted to show NASA." Stallman doesn't remember the incident, but
thinks it more likely that he was anguished because he didn't have
anything to show.

Such anecdotes offer early evidence of the intensity that would become Stallman's chief trademark throughout life. When other kids
came to the table, Stallman stayed in his room and read. When other
kids played Johnny Unitas, Stallman played spaceman. "I was weird,"
Stallman says, summing up his early years succinctly in a 1999 interview. "After a certain age, the only friends I had were teachers."[3]
Stallman was not ashamed of his weird characteristics, distinguishing

them from the social ineptness that he did regard as a failing. However, both contributed together to his social exclusion.

Although it meant courting more run-ins at school, Lippman decided to indulge her son's passion. By age 12, Richard was attending science camps during the summer and private school during the school year. When a teacher recommended her son enroll in the Columbia Science Honors Program, a post-Sputnik program designed for gifted middle- and high-school students in New York City, Stallman added to his extracurriculars and was soon commuting uptown to the Columbia University campus on Saturdays.

Dan Chess, a fellow classmate in the Columbia Science Honors Program, recalls Richard Stallman seeming a bit weird even among the students who shared a similar lust for math and science. "We were all geeks and nerds, but he was unusually poorly adjusted," recalls Chess, now a mathematics professor at Hunter College. "He was also smart as shit. I've known a lot of smart people, but I think he was the smartest person I've ever known."

Seth Breidbart, a fellow Columbia Science Honors Program alumnus, offers bolstering testimony. A computer programmer who has kept in touch with Stallman thanks to a shared passion for science fiction and science-fiction conventions, he recalls the 15-year-old, buzz-cut-wearing Stallman as "scary," especially to a fellow 15-year-old.

"It's hard to describe," Breidbart says. "It wasn't like he was unapproachable. He was just very intense. [He was] very knowledgeable but also very hardheaded in some ways."

Such descriptions give rise to speculation: are judgment-laden adjectives like "intense" and "hardheaded" simply a way to describe traits that today might be categorized under juvenile behavioral disorder? A December, 2001, *Wired* magazine article titled "The Geek Syndrome" paints the portrait of several scientifically gifted children diagnosed with high-functioning autism or Asperger Syndrome. In many ways, the parental recollections recorded in the *Wired* article are eerily similar to the ones offered by Lippman. Stallman also speculates about this. In the interview for a 2000 profile for the *Toronto Star*, Stallman said he wondered if he were "borderline autistic." The article inaccurately cited the speculation as a certainty.[4]

Such speculation benefits from the fast and loose nature of most so-called "behavioral disorders" nowadays, of course. As Steve Silberman, author of "The Geek Syndrome," notes, American psychiatrists have only recently come to accept Asperger Syndrome as a valid umbrella term covering a wide set of behavioral traits. The traits range from poor motor skills and poor socialization to high intelligence and an almost obsessive affinity for numbers, computers, and ordered systems.[5]

"It's possible I could have had something like that," Stallman says. "On the other hand, one of the aspects of that syndrome is difficulty following rhythms. I can dance. In fact, I love following the most complicated rhythms. It's not clear cut enough to know." Another possibility is that Stallman had a "shadow syndrome" which goes some way in the direction of Asperger's syndrome but without going beyond the limits of normality.[6]

Chess, for one, rejects such attempts at back-diagnosis. "I never thought of him [as] having that sort of thing," he says. "He was just very unsocialized, but then, we all were."

Lippman, on the other hand, entertains the possibility. She recalls a few stories from her son's infancy, however, that provide fodder for speculation. A prominent symptom of autism is an oversensitivity to noises and colors, and Lippman recalls two anecdotes that stand out in this regard. "When Richard was an infant, we'd take him to the beach," she says. "He would start screaming two or three blocks before we reached the surf. It wasn't until the third time that we figured out what was going on: the sound of the surf was hurting his ears." She also recalls a similar screaming reaction in relation to color: "My mother had bright red hair, and every time she'd stoop down to pick him up, he'd let out a wail."

In recent years, Lippman says she has taken to reading books about autism and believes that such episodes were more than coincidental. "I do feel that Richard had some of the qualities of an autistic child," she says. "I regret that so little was known about autism back then."

Over time, however, Lippman says her son learned to adjust. By age seven, she says, her son had become fond of standing at the front window of subway trains, mapping out and memorizing the labyrinthian system of railroad tracks underneath the city. It was a hobby that relied on an ability to accommodate the loud noises that accompanied each train ride. "Only the initial noise seemed to bother him," says Lippman. "It was as if he got shocked by the sound but his nerves learned how to make the adjustment."

For the most part, Lippman recalls her son exhibiting the excitement, energy, and social skills of any normal boy. It wasn't until after a series of traumatic events battered the Stallman household, she says, that her son became introverted and emotionally distant.

The first traumatic event was the divorce of Alice and Daniel Stallman, Richard's father. Although Lippman says both she and her ex-husband tried to prepare their son for the blow, she says the blow was devastating nonetheless. "He sort of didn't pay attention when we first told him what was happening," Lippman recalls. "But the reality smacked him in the face when he and I moved into a new apartment. The first thing he said was, 'Where's Dad's furniture?'"

For the next decade, Stallman would spend his weekdays at his mother's apartment in Manhattan and his weekends at his father's home in Queens. The shuttling back and forth gave him a chance to study a pair of contrasting parenting styles that, to this day, leaves Stallman firmly opposed to the idea of raising children himself. Speaking about his father, a World War II vet who died in early 2001, Stallman balances respect with anger. On one hand, there is the man whose moral commitment led him to learn French just so he could be more helpful to Allies when they'd finally fight the Nazis in France. On the other hand, there was the parent who always knew how to craft a put-down for cruel effect.[7]

"My father had a horrible temper," Stallman says. "He never screamed, but he always found a way to criticize you in a cold, designed-to-crush way."

As for life in his mother's apartment, Stallman is less equivocal. "That was war," he says. "I used to say in my misery, 'I want to go home,' meaning to the nonexistent place that I'll never have."

For the first few years after the divorce, Stallman found the tranquility that eluded him in the home of his paternal grandparents. One died when he was 8, and the other when he was 10. For Stallman, the loss was devastating. "I used to go and visit and feel I was in a loving, gentle environment," Stallman recalls. "It was the only place I ever found one, until I went away to college."

Lippman lists the death of Richard's paternal grandparents as the second traumatic event. "It really upset him," she says. He was very close to both his grandparents. Before they died, he was very outgoing, almost a leader-of-the-pack type with the other kids. After they died, he became much more emotionally withdrawn.

From Stallman's perspective, the emotional withdrawal was merely an attempt to deal with the agony of adolescence. Labeling his teenage years a "pure horror," Stallman says he often felt like a deaf person amid a crowd of chattering music listeners.

"I often had the feeling that I couldn't understand what other people were saying," says Stallman, recalling his sense of exclusion. "I could understand the words, but something was going on underneath the conversations that I didn't understand. I couldn't understand why people were interested in the things other people said."

For all the agony it produced, adolescence would have an encouraging effect on Stallman's sense of individuality. At a time when most of his classmates were growing their hair out, Stallman preferred to keep his short. At a time when the whole teenage world was listening to rock and roll, Stallman preferred classical music. A devoted fan of science fiction, *Mad* magazine, and late-night TV, Stallman came to have a distinctly off-the-wall personality that met with the incomprehension of parents and peers alike.

"Oh, the puns," says Lippman, still exasperated by the memory of her son's teenage personality. "There wasn't a thing you could say at the dinner table that he couldn't throw back at you as a pun."

Outside the home, Stallman saved the jokes for the adults who tended to indulge his gifted nature. One of the first was a summer-camp counselor who lent Stallman a manual for the IBM 7094 computer during his 8th or 9th year. To a preteenager fascinated with numbers and science, the gift was a godsend.[8] Soon, Stallman was writing out programs on paper in the instructions of the 7094. There was no computer around to run them on, and he had no real applications to use one for, but he yearned to write a program – any program whatsoever. He asked the counselor for arbitrary suggestions of something to code.

With the first personal computer still a decade away, Stallman would be forced to wait a few years before getting access to his first computer. His chance finally came during his senior year of high school. The IBM New York Scientific Center, a now-defunct research facility in downtown Manhattan, offered Stallman the chance to try to write his first real program. His fancy was to write a pre-processor for the programming language PL/I, designed to add the tensor algebra summation convention as a feature to the language. "I first wrote it in PL/I, then started over in assembler language when the compiled PL/I program was too big to fit in the computer," he recalls.

For the summer after high-school graduation, the New York Scientific Center hired him. Tasked with writing a numerical analysis program in Fortran, he finished that in a few weeks, acquiring such a distaste for the Fortran language that he vowed never to write anything in it again. Then he spent the rest of the summer writing a text-editor in APL.

Simultaneously, Stallman had held a laboratory-assistant position in the biology department at Rockefeller University. Although he was already moving toward a career in math or physics, Stallman's analytical mind impressed the lab director enough that a few years after Stallman departed for college, Lippman received an unexpected phone call. "It was the professor at Rockefeller," Lippman says. "He wanted to know how Richard was doing. He was surprised to learn that he was working in computers. He'd always thought Richard had a great future ahead of him as a biologist."

Stallman's analytical skills impressed faculty members at Columbia as well, even when Stallman himself became a target of their ire. "Typically once or twice an hour [Stallman] would catch some mistake in the lecture," says Breidbart. "And he was not shy about letting the professors know it immediately. It got him a lot of respect but not much popularity."

Hearing Breidbart's anecdote retold elicits a wry smile from Stallman. "I may have been a bit of a jerk sometimes," he admits. "But I found kindred spirits among teachers, because they, too, liked to learn. Kids, for the most part, didn't. At least not in the same way."

Hanging out with the advanced kids on Saturday nevertheless encouraged Stallman to think more about the merits of increased socialization. With college fast approaching, Stallman, like many in his Columbia Science Honors Program, had narrowed his list of desired schools down to two choices: Harvard and MIT. Hearing of her son's desire to move on to the Ivy League, Lippman became concerned. As a 15-year-old high-school junior, Stallman was still having run-ins with teachers and administrators. Only the year before, he had pulled straight A's in American History, Chemistry, French, and Algebra, but a glaring F in English reflected the ongoing boycott of writing assignments. Such miscues might draw a knowing chuckle at MIT, but at Harvard, they were a red flag.

During her son's junior year, Lippman says she scheduled an appointment with a therapist. The therapist expressed instant concern over Stallman's unwillingness to write papers and his run-ins with teachers. Her son certainly had the intellectual wherewithal to succeed at Harvard, but did he have the patience to sit through college classes that required a term paper? The therapist suggested a trial run. If Stallman could make it through a full year in New York City public schools, including an English class that required term papers, he could probably make it at Harvard. Following the completion of his junior year, Stallman promptly enrolled in public summer school downtown and began making up the mandatory humanities classes he had shunned earlier in his high-school career.

By fall, Stallman was back within the mainstream population of New York City high-school students, at Louis D. Brandeis High School on on West 84th Street. It wasn't easy sitting through classes that seemed remedial in comparison with his Saturday studies at Columbia, but Lippman recalls proudly her son's ability to toe the line.

"He was forced to kowtow to a certain degree, but he did it," Lippman says. "I only got called in once, which was a bit of a miracle. It was the calculus teacher complaining that Richard was interrupting his lesson. I asked how he was interrupting. He said Richard was always accusing the teacher of using a false proof. I said, 'Well, is he right?' The teacher said, 'Yeah, but I can't tell that to the class. They wouldn't understand.'"

By the end of his first semester at Brandeis High, things were falling into place. A 96 in English wiped away much of the stigma of the 60 earned 2 years before. For good measure, Stallman backed it up with top marks in American History, Advanced Placement Calculus, and Microbiology. The crowning touch was a perfect 100 in Physics. Though still a social outcast, Stallman finished his 10 months at Brandeis as the fourth-ranked student in a class of 789.

Outside the classroom, Stallman pursued his studies with even more diligence, rushing off to fulfill his laboratory-assistant duties at Rockefeller University during the week and dodging the Vietnam protesters on his way to Saturday school at Columbia. It was there, while the rest of the Science Honors Program students sat around discussing their college choices, that Stallman finally took a moment to participate in the preclass bull session.

Recalls Breidbart, "Most of the students were going to Harvard and MIT, of course, but you had a few going to other Ivy League schools. As the conversation circled the room, it became apparent that Richard hadn't said anything yet. I don't know who it was, but somebody got up the courage to ask him what he planned to do."

Thirty years later, Breidbart remembers the moment clearly. As soon as Stallman broke the news that he, too, would be attending Harvard University in the fall, an awkward silence filled the room. Almost as if on cue, the corners of Stallman's mouth slowly turned upward into a self-satisfied smile.

Says Breidbart, "It was his silent way of saying, 'That's right. You haven't got rid of me yet.'"

Endnotes

[1] One of the major background sources for this chapter was the interview "Richard Stallman: High School Misfit, Symbol of Free Software, MacArthur-Certified Genius" by Michael Gross, author of the 1999 book *Talking About My Generation*, a collection of interviews with notable personalities from the so-called "Baby Boom" generation. Although Stallman did not make it into the book, Gross published the interview as an online supplement to the book's web site. The URL for the interview has changed several times since I first came across it. According to various readers who have gone searching for it, you can now find the interview at http://www.mgross.com/MoreThgsChng/interviews/stallman1.html.

[2] RMS: I don't remember telling her this. All I can say is I strongly disagree with those views now. When I was in my teens, I lacked compassion for the difficulties most people encounter in life; my problems were different. I did not appreciate how the wealthy will reduce most people to poverty unless we organize at all levels to stop them. I did not understand how hard it is for most people to resist social pressure to do foolish things, such as spend all their money instead of saving, since I hardly even noticed the pressure myself. In addition, unions in the 60s, when they were very powerful, were sometimes arrogant or corrupt. But they are much weaker today, and the result is that economic growth, when it occurs, benefits mainly the rich.

[3] *Ibid.*

[4] See Judy Steed, *Toronto Star*, *BUSINESS*, (October 9, 2000): C03.

> His vision of free software and social cooperation stands in stark contrast to the isolated nature of his private life. A Glenn Gould-

like eccentric, the Canadian pianist was similarly brilliant, articulate, and lonely. Stallman considers himself afflicted, to some degree, by autism: a condition that, he says, makes it difficult for him to interact with people.

[5]See Steve Silberman, "The Geek Syndrome," *Wired* (December, 2001), `http://www.wired.com/wired/archive/9.12/aspergers_pr.html`.

[6]See John Ratey and Catherine Johnson, "Shadow Syndromes."

[7]Regrettably, I did not get a chance to interview Daniel Stallman for this book. During the early research for this book, Stallman informed me that his father suffered from Alzheimer's. When I resumed research in late 2001, I learned, sadly, that Daniel Stallman had died earlier in the year.

[8]Stallman, an atheist, would probably quibble with this description. Suffice it to say, it was something Stallman welcomed. See Gross (1999): "As soon as I heard about computers, I wanted to see one and play with one."

Chapter 4

Impeach God

Although their relationship was fraught with tension, Richard Stallman would inherit one noteworthy trait from his mother: a passion for progressive politics.

It was an inherited trait that would take several decades to emerge, however. For the first few years of his life, Stallman lived in what he now admits was a "political vacuum."[1] Like most Americans during the Eisenhower age, the Stallman family spent the Fifties trying to recapture the normalcy lost during the wartime years of the 1940s.

"Richard's father and I were Democrats but happy enough to leave it at that," says Lippman, recalling the family's years in Queens. "We didn't get involved much in local or national politics."

That all began to change, however, in the late 1950s when Alice divorced Daniel Stallman. The move back to Manhattan represented more than a change of address; it represented a new, independent identity and a jarring loss of tranquility.

"I think my first taste of political activism came when I went to the Queens public library and discovered there was only a single book on divorce in the whole library," recalls Lippman. "It was very controlled by the Catholic church, at least in Elmhurst, where we lived. I think that was the first inkling I had of the forces that quietly control our lives."

Returning to her childhood neighborhood, Manhattan's Upper West Side, Lippman was shocked by the changes that had taken place since her departure to Hunter College a decade and a half before. The skyrocketing demand for post-war housing had turned the neighborhood into a political battleground. On one side stood the pro-development city-hall politicians and businessmen hoping to rebuild many of the neighborhood's blocks to accommodate the growing number of white-collar workers moving into the city. On the other side stood the poor Irish and Puerto Rican tenants who had found an affordable haven in the neighborhood.

At first, Lippman didn't know which side to choose. As a new resident, she felt the need for new housing. As a single mother with minimal income, however, she shared the poorer tenants' concern over the growing number of development projects catering mainly to wealthy residents. Indignant, Lippman began looking for ways to combat the political machine that was attempting to turn her neighborhood into a clone of the Upper East Side.

Lippman says her first visit to the local Democratic party headquarters came in 1958. Looking for a day-care center to take care of her son while she worked, she had been appalled by the conditions encountered at one of the city-owned centers that catered to low-income residents. "All I remember is the stench of rotten milk, the dark hallways, the paucity of supplies. I had been a teacher in private nursery schools. The contrast was so great. We took one look at that room and left. That stirred me up."

The visit to the party headquarters proved disappointing, however. Describing it as "the proverbial smoke-filled room," Lippman says she became aware for the first time that corruption within the party might actually be the reason behind the city's thinly disguised hostility toward poor residents. Instead of going back to the headquarters, Lippman decided to join up with one of the many clubs aimed at reforming the Democratic party and ousting the last vestiges of the Tammany Hall machine. Dubbed the Woodrow Wilson/FDR Reform Democratic Club, Lippman and her club began showing up at planning and city-council meetings, demanding a greater say.

"Our primary goal was to fight Tammany Hall, Carmine DeSapio and his henchman,"[2] says Lippman. "I was the representative to the city council and was very much involved in creating a viable urban-renewal plan that went beyond simply adding more luxury housing to the neighborhood."

Such involvement would blossom into greater political activity during the 1960s. By 1965, Lippman had become an "outspoken" supporter for political candidates like William Fitts Ryan, a Democrat elected to Congress with the help of reform clubs and one of the first U.S. representatives to speak out against the Vietnam War.

It wasn't long before Lippman, too, was an outspoken opponent of U.S. involvement in Indochina. "I was against the Vietnam War from the time Kennedy sent troops," she says. "I had read the stories by reporters and journalists sent to cover the early stages of the conflict. I really believed their forecast that it would become a quagmire."

Such opposition permeated the Stallman-Lippman household. In 1967, Lippman remarried. Her new husband, Maurice Lippman, a major in the Air National Guard, resigned his commission to demonstrate his opposition to the war. Lippman's stepson, Andrew Lippman, was at MIT and temporarily eligible for a student deferment. Still, the threat of induction should that deferment disappear, as it eventually did, made the risk of U.S. escalation all the more immediate. Finally, there was Richard who, though younger, faced the prospect of being drafted as the war lasted into the 1970s.

"Vietnam was a major issue in our household," says Lippman. "We talked about it constantly: what would we do if the war continued, what steps Richard or his stepbrother would take if they got drafted. We were all opposed to the war and the draft. We really thought it was immoral."

For Stallman, the Vietnam War elicited a complex mixture of emotions: confusion, horror, and, ultimately, a profound sense of political impotence. As a kid who could barely cope in the mild authoritarian universe of private school, Stallman experienced a shiver whenever the thought of Army boot camp presented itself. He did not think he could get through it and emerge sane.

"I was devastated by the fear, but I couldn't imagine what to do and didn't have the guts to go demonstrate," recalls Stallman, whose March 16th birthday earned him a low number in the dreaded draft lottery. This did not affect him immediately, since he had a college deferment, one of the last before the U.S. stopped granting them; but it would affect him in a few years. "I couldn't envision moving to Canada or Sweden. The idea of getting up by myself and moving somewhere. How could I do that? I didn't know how to live by myself. I wasn't the kind of person who felt confident in approaching things like that."

Stallman says he was impressed by the family members who did speak out. Recalling a sticker, printed and distributed by his father, likening the My Lai massacre to similar Nazi atrocities in World War II, he says he was "excited" by his father's gesture of outrage. "I admired him for doing it," Stallman says. "But I didn't imagine that I could do anything. I was afraid that the juggernaut of the draft was going to destroy me."

However, Stallman says he was turned off by the tone and direction of much of that movement. Like other members of the Science Honors Program, he saw the weekend demonstrations at Columbia as little more than a distracting spectacle.[3] Ultimately, Stallman says, the irrational forces driving the anti-war movement became indistinguishable from the irrational forces driving the rest of youth culture. Instead of worshiping the Beatles, girls in Stallman's age group were suddenly worshiping firebrands like Abbie Hoffman and Jerry Rubin. To a kid already struggling to comprehend his teenage peers, slogans like "make love not war" had a taunting quality. Stallman did not want to make war, at least not in Southeast Asia, but nobody was inviting him to make love either.

"I didn't like the counter culture much," Stallman recalls. "I didn't like the music. I didn't like the drugs. I was scared of the drugs. I especially didn't like the anti-intellectualism, and I didn't like the prejudice against technology. After all, I loved a computer. And I didn't like the mindless anti-Americanism that I often encountered. There were people whose thinking was so simplistic that if they disapproved of the conduct of the U.S. in the Vietnam War, they had to support the North Vietnamese. They couldn't imagine a more complicated position, I guess."

Such comments underline a trait that would become the key to Stallman's own political maturation. For Stallman, political confidence was directly proportionate to personal confidence. By 1970, Stallman had become confident in few things outside the realm of math and science. Nevertheless, confidence in math gave him enough of a foundation to examine the extremes of the anti-war movement in purely logical terms. Doing so, Stallman found the logic wanting.

Although opposed to the war in Vietnam, Stallman saw no reason to disavow war as a means for defending liberty or correcting injustice.

In the 1980s, a more confident Stallman decided to make up for his past inactivity by participating in mass rallies for abortion rights in Washington DC. "I became dissatisfied with my earlier self for failing in my duty to protest the Vietnam War," he explains.

In 1970, Stallman left behind the nightly dinnertime conversations about politics and the Vietnam War as he departed for Harvard. Looking back, Stallman describes the transition from his mother's Manhattan apartment to life in a Cambridge dorm as an "escape." At Harvard, he could go to his room and have peace whenever he wanted it. Peers who watched Stallman make the transition, however, saw little to suggest a liberating experience.

"He seemed pretty miserable for the first while at Harvard," recalls Dan Chess, a classmate in the Science Honors Program who also matriculated at Harvard. "You could tell that human interaction was really difficult for him, and there was no way of avoiding it at Harvard. Harvard was an intensely social kind of place."

To ease the transition, Stallman fell back on his strengths: math and science. Like most members of the Science Honors Program, Stallman breezed through the qualifying exam for Math 55, the legendary "boot camp" class for freshman mathematics "concentrators" at Harvard. Within the class, members of the Science Honors Program formed a durable unit. "We were the math mafia," says Chess with a laugh. "Harvard was nothing, at least compared with the SHP."

To earn the right to boast, however, Stallman, Chess, and the other SHP alumni had to get through Math 55. Promising four years worth of math in two semesters, the course favored only the truly devout. "It was an amazing class," says David Harbater, a former "math mafia" member and now a professor of mathematics at the University of Pennsylvania. "It's probably safe to say there has never been a class for beginning college students that was that intense and that advanced. The phrase I say to people just to get it across is that, among other things, by the second semester we were discussing the differential geometry of Banach manifolds. That's usually when their eyes bug out, because most people don't start talking about Banach manifolds until their second year of graduate school."

Starting with 75 students, the class quickly melted down to 20 by the end of the second semester. Of that 20, says Harbater, "only 10 really knew what they were doing." Of that 10, 8 would go on to become future mathematics professors, 1 would go on to teach physics.

"The other one," emphasizes Harbater, "was Richard Stallman."

Seth Breidbart, a fellow Math 55 classmate, remembers Stallman distinguishing himself from his peers even then.

"He was a stickler in some very strange ways," says Breidbart. There is a standard technique in math which everybody does wrong. It's an abuse of notation where you have to define a function for something and what you do is you define a function and then you prove that it's well defined. Except the first time he did and presented it, he defined a relation and proved that it's a function. It's the exact same proof, but he used the correct terminology, which no one else did. That's just the way he was."

It was in Math 55 that Richard Stallman began to cultivate a reputation for brilliance. Breidbart agrees, but Chess, whose competitive streak refused to yield, says the realization that Stallman might be the best mathematician in the class didn't set in until the next year. "It was during a class on Real Analysis," says Chess, now a math professor at Hunter College. "I actually remember in a proof about complex valued measures that Richard came up with an idea that was basically a metaphor from the calculus of variations. It was the first time I ever saw somebody solve a problem in a brilliantly original way."

For Chess, it was a troubling moment. Like a bird flying into a clear glass window, it would take a while to realize that some levels of insight were simply off limits.

"That's the thing about mathematics," says Chess. "You don't have to be a first-rank mathematician to recognize first-rate mathematical talent. I could tell I was up there, but I could also tell I wasn't at the first rank. If Richard had chosen to be a mathematician, he would have been a first-rank mathematician."[4]

For Stallman, success in the classroom was balanced by the same lack of success in the social arena. Even as other members of the math mafia gathered to take on the Math 55 problem sets, Stallman preferred to work alone. The same went for living arrangements. On the housing application for Harvard, Stallman clearly spelled out his preferences. "I said I preferred an invisible, inaudible, intangible roommate," he says. In a rare stroke of bureaucratic foresight, Harvard's housing office accepted the request, giving Stallman a one-room single for his freshman year.

Breidbart, the only math-mafia member to share a dorm with Stallman that freshman year, says Stallman slowly but surely learned how to interact with other students. He recalls how other dorm mates, impressed by Stallman's logical acumen, began welcoming his input whenever an intellectual debate broke out in the dining club or dorm commons.

"We had the usual bull sessions about solving the world's problems or what would be the result of something," recalls Breidbart. "Say somebody discovers an immortality serum. What do you do? What are the political results? If you give it to everybody, the world gets overcrowded and everybody dies. If you limit it, if you say everyone who's alive now can have it but their children can't, then you end up with an underclass of people without it. Richard was just better able than most to see the unforeseen circumstances of any decision."

Stallman remembers the discussions vividly. "I was always in favor of immortality," he says. "How else would we be able to see what the world is like 200 years from now?" Curious, he began asking various acquaintances whether they would want immortality if offered it. "I was shocked that most people regarded immortality as a bad thing." Many said that death was good because there was no use living a decrepit life, and that aging was good because it got people prepared for death, without recognizing the circularity of the combination.

Although perceived as a first-rank mathematician and first-rate informal debater, Stallman shied away from clear-cut competitive events that might have sealed his brilliant reputation. Near the end of freshman year at Harvard, Breidbart recalls how Stallman conspicuously ducked the Putnam exam, a prestigious test open to math students throughout the U.S. and Canada. In addition to giving students a chance to measure their knowledge in relation to their peers, the Putnam served as a chief recruiting tool for academic math departments. According to campus legend, the top scorer automatically qualified for a graduate fellowship at any school of his choice, including Harvard.

Like Math 55, the Putnam was a brutal test of merit. A six-hour exam in two parts, it seemed explicitly designed to separate the wheat from the chaff. Breidbart, a veteran of both the Science Honors

Program and Math 55, describes it as easily the most difficult test he ever took. "Just to give you an idea of how difficult it was," says Breidbart, "the top score was a 120, and my score the first year was in the 30s. That score was still good enough to place me 101st in the country."

Surprised that Stallman, the best student in the class, had skipped the test, Breidbart says he and a fellow classmate cornered him in the dining common and demanded an explanation. "He said he was afraid of not doing well," Breidbart recalls.

Breidbart and the friend quickly wrote down a few problems from memory and gave them to Stallman. "He solved all of them," Breidbart says, "leading me to conclude that by not doing well, he either meant coming in second or getting something wrong."

Stallman remembers the episode a bit differently. "I remember that they did bring me the questions and it's possible that I solved one of them, but I'm pretty sure I didn't solve them all," he says. Nevertheless, Stallman agrees with Breidbart's recollection that fear was the primary reason for not taking the test. Despite a demonstrated willingness to point out the intellectual weaknesses of his peers and professors in the classroom, Stallman hated and feared the notion of head-to-head competition – so why not just avoid it?

"It's the same reason I never liked chess," says Stallman. "Whenever I'd play, I would become so consumed by the fear of making a single mistake and losing that I would start making stupid mistakes very early in the game. The fear became a self-fulfilling prophecy." He avoided the problem by not playing chess.

Whether such fears ultimately prompted Stallman to shy away from a mathematical career is a moot issue. By the end of his freshman year at Harvard, Stallman had other interests pulling him away from the field. Computer programming, a latent fascination throughout Stallman's high-school years, was becoming a full-fledged passion. Where other math students sought occasional refuge in art and history classes, Stallman sought it in the computer-science laboratory.

For Stallman, the first taste of real computer programming at the IBM New York Scientific Center had triggered a desire to learn more. "Toward the end of my first year at Harvard school, I started to have enough courage to go visit computer labs and see what they had. I'd ask them if they had extra copies of any manuals that I could read."

Taking the manuals home, Stallman would examine the machine specifications to learn about the range of different computer designs.

One day, near the end of his freshman year, Stallman heard about a special laboratory near MIT. The laboratory was located on the ninth floor of a building in Tech Square, the mostly-commercial office park MIT had built across the street from the campus. According to the rumors, the lab itself was dedicated to the cutting-edge science of artificial intelligence and boasted the cutting-edge machines and software to match.

Intrigued, Stallman decided to pay a visit.

The trip was short, about 2 miles on foot, 10 minutes by train, but as Stallman would soon find out, MIT and Harvard can feel like opposite poles of the same planet. With its maze-like tangle of interconnected office buildings, the Institute's campus offered an aesthetic yin to Harvard's spacious colonial-village yang. Of the two, the maze of MIT was much more Stallman's style. The same could be said for the student body, a geeky collection of ex-high school misfits known more for its predilection for pranks than its politically powerful alumni.

The yin-yang relationship extended to the AI Lab as well. Unlike Harvard computer labs, there was no grad-student gatekeeper, no clipboard waiting list for terminal access, no atmosphere of "look but don't touch." Instead, Stallman found only a collection of open terminals and robotic arms, presumably the artifacts of some AI experiment. When he encountered a lab employee, he asked if the lab had any spare manuals it could loan to an inquisitive student. "They had some, but a lot of things weren't documented," Stallman recalls. "They were hackers, after all," he adds wryly, referring to hackers' tendency to move on to a new project without documenting the last one.

Stallman left with something even better than a manual: A job. His first project was to write a PDP-11 simulator that would run on a PDP-10. He came back to the AI Lab the next week, grabbing an available terminal, and began writing the code.

Looking back, Stallman sees nothing unusual in the AI Lab's willingness to accept an unproven outsider at first glance. "That's the way it was back then," he says. "That's the way it still is now. I'll hire somebody when I meet him if I see he's good. Why wait? Stuffy people who insist on putting bureaucracy into everything really miss the point. If a person is good, he shouldn't have to go through a long, detailed hiring process; he should be sitting at a computer writing code."

To get a taste of "bureaucratic and stuffy," Stallman need only visit the computer labs at Harvard. There, access to the terminals was doled out according to academic rank. As an undergrad, Stallman sometimes had to wait for hours. The waiting wasn't difficult, but it was frustrating. Waiting for a public terminal, knowing all the while that a half dozen equally usable machines were sitting idle inside professors' locked offices, seemed the height of irrational waste. Although Stallman continued to pay the occasional visit to the Harvard computer labs, he preferred the more egalitarian policies of the AI Lab. "It was a breath of fresh air," he says. "At the AI Lab, people seemed more concerned about work than status."

Stallman quickly learned that the AI Lab's first-come, first-served policy owed much to the efforts of a vigilant few. Many were holdovers from the days of Project MAC, the Department of Defense-funded research program that had given birth to the first time-share operating systems. A few were already legends in the computing world. There was Richard Greenblatt, the lab's in-house Lisp expert and author of MacHack, the computer chess program that had once humbled AI critic Hubert Dreyfus. There was Gerald Sussman, original author of the robotic block-stacking program HACKER. And there was Bill Gosper, the in-house math whiz already in the midst of an 18-month hacking bender triggered by the philosophical implications of the computer game LIFE.[5]

Members of the tight-knit group called themselves "hackers." Over time, they extended the "hacker" description to Stallman as well. In the process of doing so, they inculcated Stallman in the ethical traditions of the "hacker ethic." In their fascination with exploring the limits of what they could make a computer do, hackers might sit at a terminal for 36 hours straight if fascinated with a challenge. Most importantly, they demanded access to the computer (when no one else was using it) and the most useful information about it. Hackers spoke openly about changing the world through software, and Stallman learned the instinctual hacker disdain for any obstacle that prevented a hacker from fulfilling this noble cause. Chief among these obstacles were poor software, academic bureaucracy, and selfish behavior.

Stallman also learned the lore, stories of how hackers, when presented with an obstacle, had circumvented it in creative ways. This included various ways that hackers had opened professors' offices to "liberate" sequestered terminals. Unlike their pampered Harvard counterparts, MIT faculty members knew better than to treat the AI Lab's limited stock of terminals as private property. If a faculty member made the mistake of locking away a terminal for the night, hackers were quick to make the terminal accessible again – and to remonstrate with the professor for having mistreated the community. Some hackers did this by picking locks ("lock hacking"), some by removing ceiling tiles and climbing over the wall. On the 9th floor, with its false floor for the computers' cables, some spelunked under it. "I was actually shown a cart with a heavy cylinder of metal on it that had been used to break down the door of one professor's office,"[6] Stallman says.

The hackers' insistence served a useful purpose by preventing the professors from egotistically obstructing the lab's work. The hackers did not disregard people's particular needs, but insisted that these be met in ways that didn't obstruct everyone else. For instance, professors occasionally said they had something in their offices which had to be protected from theft. The hackers responded, "No one will object if you lock your office, although that's not very friendly, as long as you don't lock away the lab's terminal in it."

Although the academic people greatly outnumbered the hackers in the AI Lab, the hacker ethic prevailed. The hackers were the lab staff and students who had designed and built parts of the computers, and written nearly all the software that users used. They kept everything working, too. Their work was essential, and they refused to be downtrodden. They worked on personal pet projects as well as features users had asked for, but sometimes the pet projects revolved around improving the machines and software even further. Like teenage hotrodders, most hackers viewed tinkering with machines as its own form of entertainment.

Nowhere was this tinkering impulse better reflected than in the operating system that powered the lab's central PDP-10 computer. Dubbed ITS, short for the Incompatible Time Sharing system, the operating system incorporated the hacking ethic into its very design. Hackers had built it as a protest to Project MAC's original operating system, the Compatible Time Sharing System, CTSS, and named it accordingly. At the time, hackers felt the CTSS design too restrictive, limiting programmers' power to modify and improve the program's own internal architecture if needed. According to one legend passed down by hackers, the decision to build ITS had political overtones as well. Unlike CTSS, which had been designed for the IBM 7094, ITS was built specifically for the PDP-6. In letting hackers write the system themselves, AI Lab administrators guaranteed that only hackers would feel comfortable using the PDP-6. In the feudal world of academic research, the gambit worked. Although the PDP-6 was co-owned in conjunction with other departments, AI researchers soon had it to themselves. Using ITS and the PDP-6 as a foundation, the Lab had been able to declare independence from Project MAC shortly before Stallman's arrival.[7]

By 1971, ITS had moved to the newer but compatible PDP-10, leaving the PDP-6 for special stand-alone uses. The AI PDP-10 had a very large memory for 1971, equivalent to a little over a megabyte; in the late 70s it was doubled. Project MAC had bought two other PDP-10s; all were located on the 9th floor, and they all ran ITS. The hardware-inclined hackers designed and built a major hardware addition for these PDP-10s, implementing paged virtual memory, a feature lacking in the standard PDP-10.[8]

As an apprentice hacker, Stallman quickly became enamored with ITS. Although forbidding to some non-hackers, ITS boasted features most commercial operating systems wouldn't offer for years (or even to this day), features such as multitasking, applying the debugger immediately to any running program, and full-screen editing capability.

"ITS had a very elegant internal mechanism for one program to examine another," says Stallman, recalling the program. "You could examine all sorts of status about another program in a very clean, well-specified way." This was convenient not only for debugging, but also for programs to start, stop or control other programs.

Another favorite feature would allow the one program to freeze another program's job cleanly, between instructions. In other operating systems, comparable operations might stop the program in the middle of a system call, with internal status that the user could not see and that had no well-defined meaning. In ITS, this feature made sure that monitoring the step-by-step operation of a program was reliable and consistent.

"If you said, 'Stop the job,' it would always be stopped in user mode. It would be stopped between two user-mode instructions, and everything about the job would be consistent for that point," Stallman says. "If you said, 'Resume the job,' it would continue properly. Not only that, but if you were to change the (explicitly visible) status of the job and continue it, and later change it back, everything would be consistent. There was no hidden status anywhere."

Starting in September 1971, hacking at the AI Lab had become a regular part of Stallman's weekly school schedule. From Sunday through Friday, Stallman was at Harvard. As soon as Friday afternoon arrived, however, he was on the subway, heading down to MIT for the weekend. Stallman usually made sure to arrive well before the ritual food run. Joining five or six other hackers in their nightly quest for Chinese food, he would jump inside a beat-up car and head across the Harvard Bridge into nearby Boston. For the next hour or so, he and his hacker colleagues would discuss everything from ITS to the internal logic of the Chinese language and pictograph system. Following dinner, the group would return to MIT and hack code until dawn, or perhaps go to Chinatown again at 3 a.m.

Stallman might stay up all morning hacking, or might sleep Saturday morning on a couch. On waking he would hack some more, have another Chinese dinner, then go back to Harvard. Sometimes he would stay through Sunday as well. These Chinese dinners were not only delicious; they also provided sustenance lacking in the Harvard dining halls, where on the average only one meal a day included anything he could stomach. (Breakfast did not enter the count, since he didn't like most breakfast foods and was normally asleep at that hour.)

For the geeky outcast who rarely associated with his high-school peers, it was a heady experience to be hanging out with people who shared the same predilection for computers, science fiction, and Chinese food. "I remember many sunrises seen from a car coming back from Chinatown," Stallman would recall nostalgically, 15 years after the fact in a speech at the Swedish Royal Technical Institute. "It was actually a very beautiful thing to see a sunrise, 'cause that's such a calm time of day. It's a wonderful time of day to get ready to go to bed. It's so nice to walk home with the light just brightening and the birds starting to chirp; you can get a real feeling of gentle satisfaction, of tranquility about the work that you have done that night."[9]

The more Stallman hung out with the hackers, the more he adopted the hacker world view. Already committed to the notion of personal liberty, Stallman began to infuse his actions with a sense of communal duty. When others violated the communal code, Stallman was quick to speak out. Within a year of his first visit, Stallman was the one opening locked offices to recover the sequestered terminals that belonged to the lab community as a whole. In true hacker fashion, Stallman also sought to make his own personal contribution to the art. One of the most artful door-opening tricks, commonly attributed to Greenblatt, involved bending a stiff wire into several right angles and attaching a strip of tape to one end. Sliding the wire under the door, a hacker could twist and rotate the wire so that the tape touched the inside doorknob. Provided the tape stuck, a hacker could turn the doorknob by pulling the handle formed from the outside end of the wire.

When Stallman tried the trick, he found it hard to execute. Getting the tape to stick wasn't always easy, and twisting the wire in a way that turned the doorknob was similarly difficult. Stallman thought about another method: sliding away ceiling tiles to climb over the wall. This always worked, if there was a desk to jump down onto, but it generally covered the hacker in itchy fiberglass. Was there a way to correct that flaw? Stallman considered an alternative approach. What if, instead of slipping a wire under the door, a hacker slid away two ceiling panels and reached over the wall with a wire?

Stallman took it upon himself to try it out. Instead of using a wire, Stallman draped out a long U-shaped loop of magnetic tape with a short U of adhesive tape attached sticky-side-up at the base. Reaching across over the door jamb, he dangled the tape until it looped under the inside doorknob. Lifting the tape until the adhesive stuck, he then pulled on one end of the tape, thus turning the doorknob. Sure enough, the door opened. Stallman had added a new twist to the art of getting into a locked room.

"Sometimes you had to kick the door after you turned the door knob," says Stallman, recalling a slight imperfection of the new method. "It took a little bit of balance to pull it off while standing on a chair on a desk."

Such activities reflected a growing willingness on Stallman's part to speak and act out in defense of political beliefs. The AI Lab's spirit of direct action had proved inspirational enough for Stallman to break out of the timid impotence of his teenage years. Opening up an office to free a terminal wasn't the same as taking part in a protest march, but it was effective in a way that most protests weren't: it solved the problem at hand.

By the time of his last years at Harvard, Stallman was beginning to apply the whimsical and irreverent lessons of the AI Lab back at school.

"Did he tell you about the snake?" his mother asks at one point during an interview. "He and his dorm mates put a snake up for student election. Apparently it got a considerable number of votes."

The snake was a candidate for election within Currier House, Stallman's dorm, not the campus-wide student council. Stallman does remember the snake attracting a fair number of votes, thanks in large part to the fact that both the snake and its owner both shared the same last name. "People may have voted for it because they thought they were voting for the owner," Stallman says. "Campaign posters said that the snake was 'slithering for' the office. We also said it was an 'at large' candidate, since it had climbed into the wall through the ventilating unit a few weeks before and nobody knew where it was."

Stallman and friends also "nominated" the house master's 3-year-old son. "His platform was mandatory retirement at age seven," Stallman recalls. Such pranks paled in comparison to the fake-candidate pranks on the MIT campus, however. One of the most successful fake-candidate pranks was a cat named Woodstock, which actually managed to outdraw most of the human candidates in a campus-wide election. "They never announced how many votes Woodstock got, and they treated those votes as spoiled ballots," Stallman recalls. "But the large number of spoiled ballots in that election suggested that Woodstock had actually won. A couple of years later, Woodstock was suspiciously run over by a car. Nobody knows if the driver was working for the MIT administration." Stallman says he had nothing to do with Woodstock's candidacy, "but I admired it." [10]

At the AI Lab, Stallman's political activities had a sharper-edged tone. During the 1970s, hackers faced the constant challenge of faculty members and administrators pulling an end-run around ITS and its hacker-friendly design. ITS allowed anyone to sit down at a console and do anything at all, even order the system to shut down in five minutes. If someone ordered a shutdown with no good reason, some other user canceled it. In the mid-1970s some faculty members (usually those who had formed their attitudes elsewhere) began calling for a file security system to limit access to their data. Other operating systems had such features, so those faculty members had become accustomed to living under security, and to the feeling that it was protecting them from something dangerous. But the AI Lab, through the insistence of Stallman and other hackers, remained a security-free zone.

Stallman presented both ethical and practical arguments against adding security. On the ethical side, Stallman appealed to the AI Lab community's traditions of intellectual openness and trust. On the practical side, he pointed to the internal structure of ITS, which was built to foster hacking and cooperation rather than to keep every user under control. Any attempt to reverse that design would require a major overhaul. To make it even more difficult, he used up the last empty field in each file's descriptor for a feature to record which user had most recently changed the file. This feature left no place to store file security information, but it was so useful that nobody could seriously propose to remove it.

"The hackers who wrote the Incompatible Timesharing System decided that file protection was usually used by a self-styled system manager to get power over everyone else," Stallman would later explain. "They didn't want anyone to be able to get power over them that way, so they didn't implement that kind of a feature. The result was, that whenever something in the system was broken, you could always fix it" (since access control did not stand in your way).[11]

Through such vigilance, hackers managed to keep the AI Lab's machines security-free. In one group at the nearby MIT Laboratory for Computer Sciences, however, security-minded faculty members won the day. The DM group installed its first password system in 1977. Once again, Stallman took it upon himself to correct what he saw as ethical laxity. Gaining access to the software code that controlled the password system, Stallman wrote a program to decrypt the encrypted passwords that the system recorded. Then he started an email campaign, asking users to choose the null string as their passwords. If the user had chosen "starfish," for example, the email message looked something like this:

> I see you chose the password "starfish". I suggest that you switch to the password "carriage return", which is what I use. It's easier to type, and also opposes the idea of passwords and security.

The users who chose "carriage return" – that is, users who simply pressed the Enter or Return button, entering a blank string instead of a unique password – left their accounts accessible to the world at large, just as all accounts had been, not long before. That was the point: by refusing to lock the shiny new locks on their accounts, they ridiculed the idea of having locks. They knew that the weak security implemented on that machine would not exclude any real intruders, and that this did not matter, because there was no reason to be concerned about intruders, and that no one wanted to intrude anyway, only to visit.

Stallman, speaking in an interview for the 1984 book *Hackers*, proudly noted that one-fifth of the LCS staff accepted this argument and employed the null-string password.[12]

Stallman's null-string campaign, and his resistance to security in general, would ultimately be defeated. By the early 1980s, even the AI Lab's machines were sporting password security systems. Even so, it represented a major milestone in terms of Stallman's personal and political maturation. Seen in the context of Stallman's later career, it represents a significant step in the development of the timid teenager, afraid to speak out even on issues of life-threatening importance, into the adult activist who would soon turn needling and cajoling into a full-time occupation.

In voicing his opposition to computer security, Stallman drew on many of the key ideas that had shaped his early life: hunger for knowledge, distaste for authority, and frustration over prejudice and secret rules that rendered some people outcasts. He would also draw on the ethical concepts that would shape his adult life: responsibility to the community, trust, and the hacker spirit of direct action. Expressed in software-computing terms, the null string represents the 1.0 version of the Richard Stallman political worldview – incomplete in a few places but, for the most part, fully mature.

Looking back, Stallman hesitates to impart too much significance to an event so early in his hacking career. "In that early stage there were a lot of people who shared my feelings," he says. "The large number of people who adopted the null string as their password was a sign that many people agreed that it was the proper thing to do. I was simply inclined to be an activist about it."

Stallman does credit the AI Lab for awakening that activist spirit, however. As a teenager, Stallman had observed political events with little idea as to how he could do or say anything of importance. As a young adult, Stallman was speaking out on matters in which he felt supremely confident, matters such as software design, responsibility to the community, and individual freedom. "I joined this community which had a way of life which involved respecting each other's freedom," he says. "It didn't take me long to figure out that that was a good thing. It took me longer to come to the conclusion that this was a moral issue."

Hacking at the AI Lab wasn't the only activity helping to boost Stallman's esteem. At the start of his junior year at Harvard, Stallman began participating in a recreational international folk dance group which had just been started in Currier House. He was not going to try it, considering himself incapable of dancing, but a friend pointed out, "You don't know you can't if you haven't tried." To his amazement, he was good at it and enjoyed it. What started as an experiment became another passion alongside hacking and studying; also, occasionally, a way to meet women, though it didn't lead to a date during his college career. While dancing, Stallman no longer felt like the awkward, uncoordinated 10-year-old whose attempts to play football had ended in frustration. He felt confident, agile, and alive. In the early 80s, Stallman went further and joined the MIT Folk Dance Performing Group. Dancing for audiences, dressed in an imitation of the traditional garb of a Balkan peasant, he found being in front of an audience fun, and discovered an aptitude for being on stage which later helped him in public speaking.

Although the dancing and hacking did little to improve Stallman's social standing, they helped him overcome the sense of exclusion that had clouded his pre-Harvard life. In 1977, attending a science-fiction convention for the first time, he came across Nancy the Buttonmaker, who makes calligraphic buttons saying whatever you wish. Excited,

Stallman ordered a button with the words "Impeach God" emblazoned on it.

For Stallman, the "Impeach God" message worked on many levels. An atheist since early childhood, Stallman first saw it as an attempt to start a "second front" in the ongoing debate on religion. "Back then everybody was arguing about whether a god existed," Stallman recalls. "'Impeach God' approached the subject from a completely different viewpoint. If a god was so powerful as to create the world and yet did nothing to correct the problems in it, why would we ever want to worship such a god? Wouldn't it be more just to put it on trial?"

At the same time, "Impeach God" was a reference to the the Watergate scandal of the 1970s, in effect comparing a tyrannical deity to Nixon. Watergate affected Stallman deeply. As a child, Stallman had grown up resenting authority. Now, as an adult, his mistrust had been solidified by the culture of the AI Lab hacker community. To the hackers, Watergate was merely a Shakespearean rendition of the daily power struggles that made life such a hassle for those without privilege. It was an outsized parable for what happened when people traded liberty and openness for security and convenience.

Buoyed by growing confidence, Stallman wore the button proudly. People curious enough to ask him about it received a well-prepared spiel. "My name is Jehovah," Stallman would say. "I have a secret plan to end injustice and suffering, but due to heavenly security reasons I can't tell you the workings of my plan. I see the big picture and you don't, and you know I'm good because I told you so. So put your faith in me and obey me without question. If you don't obey, that means you're evil, so I'll put you on my enemies list and throw you in a pit where the Infernal Revenue Service will audit your taxes every year for all eternity."

Those who interpreted the spiel as a parody of the Watergate hearings only got half the message. For Stallman, the other half of the message was something only his fellow hackers seemed to be hearing. One hundred years after Lord Acton warned about absolute power corrupting absolutely, Americans seemed to have forgotten the first part of Acton's truism: power, itself, corrupts. Rather than point out the numerous examples of petty corruption, Stallman felt content voicing his outrage toward an entire system that trusted power in the first place.

"I figured, why stop with the small fry," says Stallman, recalling the button and its message. "If we went after Nixon, why not go after Mr. Big? The way I see it, any being that has power and abuses it deserves to have that power taken away."

Endnotes

[1] See Michael Gross, "Richard Stallman: High School Misfit, Symbol of Free Software, MacArthur-certified Genius" (1999).

[2] Carmine DeSapio holds the dubious distinction of being the first Italian-American boss of Tammany Hall, the New York City political machine. For more information on DeSapio and the politics of post-war New York, see John Davenport, "Skinning the Tiger: Carmine DeSapio and the End of the Tammany Era," *New York Affairs* (1975): 3:1.

[3] Chess, another Columbia Science Honors Program alum, describes the protests as "background noise." "We were all political," he says, "but the SHP was important. We would never have skipped it for a demonstration."

[4] Stallman doubts this, however. "One of the reasons I moved from math and physics to programming is that I never learned how to discover anything new in the former two. I only learned to study what others had done. In programming, I could do something useful every day."

[5] See Steven Levy, *Hackers* (Penguin USA [paperback], 1984): 144.
Levy devotes about five pages to describing Gosper's fascination with LIFE, a math-based software game first created by British mathematician John Conway. I heartily recommend this book as a supplement, perhaps even a prerequisite, to this one.

[6] Gerald Sussman, an MIT faculty member and hacker whose work at the AI Lab predates Stallman's, disputes this story. According to Sussman, the hackers never broke any doors to retrieve terminals.

[7] *Ibid.*

[8] I apologize for the whirlwind summary of ITS' genesis, an operating system many hackers still regard as the epitome of the hacker ethos. For more information on the program's political significance, see Simson Garfinkel, *Architects of the Information Society: Thirty-Five Years of the Laboratory for Computer Science at MIT* (MIT Press, 1999).

[9] See Richard Stallman, "RMS lecture at KTH (Sweden)," (October 30, 1986), http://www.gnu.org/philosophy/stallman-kth.html.

[10] In an email shortly after this book went into its final edit cycle, Stallman says he drew political inspiration from the Harvard campus as well. "In my first year of Harvard, in a Chinese History class, I read the story of the first revolt against the Qin dynasty," he says. (That's the one whose cruel founder burnt all the books and was buried with the terra cotta warriors.) "The story is not reliable history, but it was very moving."

[11]See Richard Stallman (1986).

[12]See Steven Levy, *Hackers* (Penguin USA [paperback], 1984): 417.

.

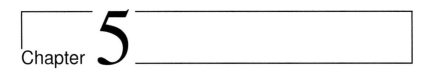

Chapter 5

Puddle of Freedom

[RMS: In this chapter, I have corrected statements about facts, including facts about my thoughts and feelings, and removed some gratuitous hostility in descriptions of events. I have preserved Williams' statements of his own impressions, except where noted.]

Ask anyone who's spent more than a minute in Richard Stallman's presence, and you'll get the same recollection: forget the long hair. Forget the quirky demeanor. The first thing you notice is the gaze. One look into Stallman's green eyes, and you know you're in the presence of a true believer.

To call the Stallman gaze intense is an understatement. Stallman's eyes don't just look at you; they look through you. Even when your own eyes momentarily shift away out of simple primate politeness, Stallman's eyes remain locked-in, sizzling away at the side of your head like twin photon beams.

Maybe that's why most writers, when describing Stallman, tend to go for the religious angle. In a 1998 *Salon.com* article titled "The Saint of Free Software," Andrew Leonard describes Stallman's green eyes as "radiating the power of an Old Testament prophet."[1] A 1999 *Wired* magazine article describes the Stallman beard as "Rasputin-like,"[2] while a *London Guardian* profile describes the Stallman smile as the smile of "a disciple seeing Jesus."[3]

Such analogies serve a purpose, but they ultimately fall short. That's because they fail to take into account the vulnerable side of the Stallman persona. Watch the Stallman gaze for an extended period of time, and you will begin to notice a subtle change. What appears at first to be an attempt to intimidate or hypnotize reveals itself upon second and third viewing as a frustrated attempt to build and maintain contact. If his personality has a touch or "shadow" of autism or Asperger's Syndrome, a possibility that Stallman has entertained from time to time, his eyes certainly confirm the diagnosis. Even at their most high-beam level of intensity, they have a tendency to grow cloudy and distant, like the eyes of a wounded animal preparing to give up the ghost.

My own first encounter with the legendary Stallman gaze dates back to the March, 1999, LinuxWorld Convention and Expo in San Jose, California. Billed as a "coming out party" for the "Linux" software community, the convention also stands out as the event that reintroduced Stallman to the technology media. Determined to push for his proper share of credit, Stallman used the event to instruct spectators and reporters alike on the history of the GNU Project and the project's overt political objectives.

As a reporter sent to cover the event, I received my own Stallman tutorial during a press conference announcing the release of GNOME 1.0, a free software graphic user interface. Unwittingly, I push an entire bank of hot buttons when I throw out my very first question to Stallman himself: "Do you think GNOME's maturity will affect the commercial popularity of the Linux operating system?"

"I ask that you please stop calling the operating system Linux," Stallman responds, eyes immediately zeroing in on mine. "The Linux kernel is just a small part of the operating system. Many of the software programs that make up the operating system you call Linux were not developed by Linus Torvalds at all. They were created by GNU Project volunteers, putting in their own personal time so that users might have a free operating system like the one we have today. To not acknowledge the contribution of those programmers is both impolite and a misrepresentation of history. That's why I ask that when you refer to the operating system, please call it by its proper name, GNU/Linux."

Taking the words down in my reporter's notebook, I notice an eerie silence in the crowded room. When I finally look up, I find Stallman's unblinking eyes waiting for me. Timidly, a second reporter throws out a question, making sure to use the term "GNU/Linux" instead of Linux. Miguel de Icaza, leader of the GNOME project, fields the question. It isn't until halfway through de Icaza's answer, however, that Stallman's eyes finally unlock from mine. As soon as they do, a mild shiver rolls down my back. When Stallman starts lecturing another reporter over a perceived error in diction, I feel a guilty tinge of relief. At least he isn't looking at me, I tell myself.

For Stallman, such face-to-face moments would serve their purpose. By the end of the first LinuxWorld show, most reporters know better than to use the term "Linux" in his presence, and Wired.com is running a story comparing Stallman to a pre-Stalinist revolutionary erased from the history books by hackers and entrepreneurs eager to downplay the GNU Project's overly political objectives.[4] Other articles follow, and while few reporters call the operating system GNU/Linux in print, most are quick to credit Stallman for launching the drive to build a free software operating system 15 years before.

I won't meet Stallman again for another 17 months. During the interim, Stallman will revisit Silicon Valley once more for the August, 1999 LinuxWorld show. Although not invited to speak, Stallman does manage to deliver the event's best line. Accepting the show's Linus Torvalds Award for Community Service – an award named after Linux creator Linus Torvalds – on behalf of the Free Software Foundation, Stallman wisecracks, "Giving the Linus Torvalds Award to the Free Software Foundation is a bit like giving the Han Solo Award to the Rebel Alliance."

This time around, however, the comments fail to make much of a media dent. Midway through the week, Red Hat, Inc., a prominent GNU/Linux vendor, goes public. The news merely confirms what many reporters such as myself already suspect: "Linux" has become a Wall Street buzzword, much like "e-commerce" and "dot-com" before it. With the stock market approaching the Y2K rollover like a hyperbola approaching its vertical asymptote, all talk of free software or open source as a political phenomenon falls by the wayside.

Maybe that's why, when LinuxWorld follows up its first two shows with a third LinuxWorld show in August, 2000, Stallman is conspicuously absent.

My second encounter with Stallman and his trademark gaze comes shortly after that third LinuxWorld show. Hearing that Stallman is going to be in Silicon Valley, I set up a lunch interview in Palo Alto, California. The meeting place seems ironic, not only because of his absence from the show but also because of the overall backdrop. Outside of Redmond, Washington, few cities offer a more direct testament to the economic value of proprietary software. Curious to see how Stallman, a man who has spent the better part of his life railing against our culture's predilection toward greed and selfishness, is coping in a city where even garage-sized bungalows run in the half-million-dollar price range, I make the drive down from Oakland.

I follow the directions Stallman has given me, until I reach the headquarters of Art.net, a nonprofit "virtual artists collective." Located in a hedge-shrouded house in the northern corner of the city, the Art.net headquarters are refreshingly run-down. Suddenly, the idea of Stallman lurking in the heart of Silicon Valley doesn't seem so strange after all.

I find Stallman sitting in a darkened room, tapping away on his gray laptop computer. He looks up as soon as I enter the room, giving me a full blast of his 200-watt gaze. When he offers a soothing "Hello," I offer a return greeting. Before the words come out, however, his eyes have already shifted back to the laptop screen.

"I'm just finishing an article on the spirit of hacking," Stallman says, fingers still tapping. "Take a look."

I take a look. The room is dimly lit, and the text appears as greenish-white letters on a black background, a reversal of the color scheme used by most desktop word-processing programs, so it takes my eyes a moment to adjust. When they do, I find myself reading Stallman's account of a recent meal at a Korean restaurant. Before the meal, Stallman makes an interesting discovery: the person setting the table has left six chopsticks instead of the usual two in front of Stallman's place setting. Where most restaurant goers would have ignored the redundant pairs, Stallman takes it as challenge: find a way to use all six chopsticks at once. Like many software hacks, the successful solution is both clever and silly at the same time. Hence Stallman's decision to use it as an illustration.

As I read the story, I feel Stallman watching me intently. I look over to notice a proud but child-like half smile on his face. When I praise the essay, my comment barely merits a raised eyebrow.

"I'll be ready to go in a moment," he says.

Stallman goes back to tapping away at his laptop. The laptop is gray and boxy, not like the sleek, modern laptops that seemed to be a programmer favorite at the recent LinuxWorld show. Above the keyboard rides a smaller, lighter keyboard, a testament to Stallman's aging hands. During the mid 1990s, the pain in Stallman's hands became so unbearable that he had to hire a typist. Today, Stallman relies on a keyboard whose keys require less pressure than a typical computer keyboard.

Stallman has a tendency to block out all external stimuli while working. Watching his eyes lock onto the screen and his fingers dance, one quickly gets the sense of two old friends locked in deep conversation.

The session ends with a few loud keystrokes and the slow disassembly of the laptop.

"Ready for lunch?" Stallman asks.

We walk to my car. Pleading a sore ankle, Stallman limps along slowly. Stallman blames the injury on a tendon in his left foot. The injury is three years old and has gotten so bad that Stallman, a huge fan of folk dancing, has been forced to give up all dancing activities. "I love folk dancing intensely," Stallman laments. "Not being able to dance has been a tragedy for me."

Stallman's body bears witness to the tragedy. Lack of exercise has left Stallman with swollen cheeks and a pot belly that was much less visible the year before. You can tell the weight gain has been dramatic, because when Stallman walks, he arches his back like a pregnant woman trying to accommodate an unfamiliar load.

The walk is further slowed by Stallman's willingness to stop and smell the roses, literally. Spotting a particularly beautiful blossom, he strokes the innermost petals against his nose, takes a deep sniff, and steps back with a contented sigh.

"Mmm, rhinophytophilia," he says, rubbing his back.[5]

The drive to the restaurant takes less than three minutes. Upon recommendation from Tim Ney, former executive director of the Free Software Foundation, I have let Stallman choose the restaurant. While some reporters zero in on Stallman's monk-like lifestyle, the truth is, Stallman is a committed epicure when it comes to food. One of the fringe benefits of being a traveling missionary for the free software cause is the ability to sample delicious food from around the world. "Visit almost any major city in the world, and chances are Richard knows the best restaurant in town," says Ney. "Richard also takes great pride in knowing what's on the menu and ordering for the entire the table." (If they are willing, that is.)

For today's meal, Stallman has chosen a Cantonese-style dim sum restaurant two blocks off University Avenue, Palo Alto's main drag. The choice is partially inspired by Stallman's recent visit to China, including a stop in Hong Kong, in addition to Stallman's personal aversion to spicier Hunanese and Szechuan cuisine. "I'm not a big fan of spicy," Stallman admits.

We arrive a few minutes after 11 a.m. and find ourselves already subject to a 20-minute wait. Given the hacker aversion to lost time, I hold my breath momentarily, fearing an outburst. Stallman, contrary to expectations, takes the news in stride.

"It's too bad we couldn't have found somebody else to join us," he tells me. "It's always more fun to eat with a group of people."

During the wait, Stallman practices a few dance steps. His moves are tentative but skilled. We discuss current events. Stallman says his only regret about not attending LinuxWorld was missing out on a press conference announcing the launch of the GNOME Foundation. Backed by Sun Microsystems and IBM, the foundation is in many ways a vindication for Stallman, who has long championed that free software and free-market economics need not be mutually exclusive. Nevertheless, Stallman remains dissatisfied by the message that came out.

"The way it was presented, the companies were talking about Linux with no mention of the GNU Project at all," Stallman says.

Such disappointments merely contrast the warm response coming from overseas, especially Asia, Stallman notes. A quick glance at the Stallman 2000 travel itinerary bespeaks the growing popularity of the free software message. Between recent visits to India, China, and

Brazil, Stallman has spent 12 of the last 115 days on United States soil. His travels have given him an opportunity to see how the free software concept translates into different languages of cultures.

"In India many people are interested in free software, because they see it as a way to build their computing infrastructure without spending a lot of money," Stallman says. "In China, the concept has been much slower to catch on. Comparing free software to free speech is harder to do when you don't have any free speech. Still, the level of interest in free software during my last visit was profound."

The conversation shifts to Napster, the San Mateo, California software company, which has become something of a media cause célèbre in recent months. The company markets a controversial software tool that lets music fans browse and copy the music files of other music fans. Thanks to the magnifying powers of the Internet, this so-called "peer-to-peer" program has evolved into a de facto online jukebox, giving ordinary music fans a way to listen to MP3 music files over the computer without paying a royalty or fee, much to record companies' chagrin.

Although based on proprietary software, the Napster system draws inspiration from the long-held Stallman contention that once a work enters the digital realm – in other words, once making a copy is less a matter of duplicating sounds or duplicating atoms and more a matter of duplicating information – the natural human impulse to share a work becomes harder to restrict. Rather than impose additional restrictions, Napster execs have decided to take advantage of the impulse. Giving music listeners a central place to trade music files, the company has gambled on its ability to steer the resulting user traffic toward other commercial opportunities.

The sudden success of the Napster model has put the fear in traditional record companies, with good reason. Just days before my Palo Alto meeting with Stallman, U.S. District Court Judge Marilyn Patel granted a request filed by the Recording Industry Association of America for an injunction against the file-sharing service. The injunction was subsequently suspended by the U.S. Ninth District Court of Appeals, but by early 2001, the Court of Appeals, too, would find the San Mateo-based company in breach of copyright law,[6] a decision RIAA spokesperson Hillary Rosen would later proclaim a "clear victory for the creative content community and the legitimate online marketplace."[7]

For hackers such as Stallman, the Napster business model is troublesome in different ways. The company's eagerness to appropriate time-worn hacker principles such as file sharing and communal information ownership, while at the same time selling a service based on proprietary software, sends a distressing mixed message. As a person who already has a hard enough time getting his own carefully articulated message into the media stream, Stallman is understandably reticent when it comes to speaking out about the company. Still, Stallman does admit to learning a thing or two from the social side of the Napster phenomenon.

"Before Napster, I thought it might be [sufficient] for people to privately redistribute works of entertainment," Stallman says. "The number of people who find Napster useful, however, tells me that the right to redistribute copies not only on a neighbor-to-neighbor basis, but to the public at large, is essential and therefore may not be taken away."

No sooner does Stallman say this than the door to the restaurant swings open and we are invited back inside by the host. Within a few seconds, we are seated in a side corner of the restaurant next to a large mirrored wall.

The restaurant's menu doubles as an order form, and Stallman is quickly checking off boxes before the host has even brought water to the table. "Deep-fried shrimp roll wrapped in bean-curd skin," Stallman reads. "Bean-curd skin. It offers such an interesting texture. I think we should get it."

This comment leads to an impromptu discussion of Chinese food and Stallman's recent visit to China. "The food in China is utterly exquisite," Stallman says, his voice gaining an edge of emotion for the first time this morning. "So many different things that I've never seen in the U.S., local things made from local mushrooms and local vegetables. It got to the point where I started keeping a journal just to keep track of every wonderful meal."

The conversation segues into a discussion of Korean cuisine. During the same June, 2000, Asian tour, Stallman paid a visit to South Korea. His arrival ignited a mini-firestorm in the local media thanks to a Korean software conference attended by Microsoft founder and chairman Bill Gates that same week. Next to getting his photo above Gates's photo on the front page of the top Seoul newspaper, Stallman says the best thing about the trip was the food. "I had a bowl of naeng myun, which is cold noodles," says Stallman. "These were a very interesting feeling noodle. Most places don't use quite the same kind of noodles for your naeng myun, so I can say with complete certainty that this was the most exquisite naeng myun I ever had."

The term "exquisite" is high praise coming from Stallman. I know this, because a few moments after listening to Stallman rhapsodize about naeng myun, I feel his laser-beam eyes singeing the top of my right shoulder.

"There is the most exquisite woman sitting just behind you," Stallman says.

I turn to look, catching a glimpse of a woman's back. The woman is young, somewhere in her mid-20s, and is wearing a white sequined dress. She and her male lunch companion are in the final stages of paying the check. When both get up from the table to leave the restaurant, I can tell without looking, because Stallman's eyes suddenly dim in intensity.

"Oh, no," he says. "They're gone. And to think, I'll probably never even get to see her again."

After a brief sigh, Stallman recovers. The moment gives me a chance to discuss Stallman's reputation vis-à-vis the fairer sex. The reputation is a bit contradictory at times. A number of hackers report Stallman's predilection for greeting females with a kiss on the back of the hand.[8] A May 26, 2000 *Salon.com* article, meanwhile, portrays Stallman as a bit of a hacker lothario. Documenting the free software-free love connection, reporter Annalee Newitz presents Stallman as rejecting traditional family values, telling her, "I believe in love, but not monogamy."[9]

Stallman lets his menu drop a little when I bring this up. "Well, most men seem to want sex and seem to have a rather contemptuous attitude towards women," he says. "Even women they're involved with. I can't understand it at all."

I mention a passage from the 1999 book *Open Sources* in which Stallman confesses to wanting to name the GNU kernel after a girlfriend at the time. The girlfriend's name was Alix, a name that fit perfectly with the Unix developer convention of putting an "x" at the

end names of operating systems and kernels – e.g., "Linux." Alix was a
Unix system administrator, and had suggested to her friends, "Someone should name a kernel after me." So Stallman decided to name the
GNU kernel "Alix" as a surprise for her. The kernel's main developer
renamed the kernel "Hurd," but retained the name "Alix" for part of
it. One of Alix's friends noticed this part in a source snapshot and
told her, and she was touched. A later redesign of the Hurd eliminated
that part.[10]

For the first time all morning, Stallman smiles. I bring up the hand
kissing. "Yes, I do do that," Stallman says. "I've found it's a way of
offering some affection that a lot of women will enjoy. It's a chance to
give some affection and to be appreciated for it."

Affection is a thread that runs clear through Richard Stallman's
life, and he is painfully candid about it when questions arise. "There
really hasn't been much affection in my life, except in my mind," he
says. Still, the discussion quickly grows awkward. After a few one-
word replies, Stallman finally lifts up his menu, cutting off the inquiry.

"Would you like some shu mai?" he asks.

When the food comes out, the conversation slaloms between the
arriving courses. We discuss the oft-noted hacker affection for Chinese
food, the weekly dinner runs into Boston's Chinatown district during
Stallman's days as a staff programmer at the AI Lab, and the underlying logic of the Chinese language and its associated writing system.
Each thrust on my part elicits a well-informed parry on Stallman's
part.

"I heard some people speaking Shanghainese the last time I was
in China," Stallman says. "It was interesting to hear. It sounded
quite different [from Mandarin]. I had them tell me some cognate
words in Mandarin and Shanghainese. In some cases you can see the
resemblance, but one question I was wondering about was whether
tones would be similar. They're not. That's interesting to me, because
there's a theory that the tones evolved from additional syllables that
got lost and replaced. Their effect survives in the tone. If that's true,
and I've seen claims that that happened within historic times, the
dialects must have diverged before the loss of these final syllables."

The first dish, a plate of pan-fried turnip cakes, has arrived. Both
Stallman and I take a moment to carve up the large rectangular cakes,

which smell like boiled cabbage but taste like potato latkes fried in bacon.

I decide to bring up the outcast issue again, wondering if Stallman's teenage years conditioned him to take unpopular stands, most notably his uphill battle since 1994 to get computer users and the media to replace the popular term "Linux" with "GNU/Linux."

"I believe [being an outcast] did help me [to avoid bowing to popular views]," Stallman says, chewing on a dumpling. "I have never understood what peer pressure does to other people. I think the reason is that I was so hopelessly rejected that for me, there wasn't anything to gain by trying to follow any of the fads. It wouldn't have made any difference. I'd still be just as rejected, so I didn't try."

Stallman points to his taste in music as a key example of his contrarian tendencies. As a teenager, when most of his high school classmates were listening to Motown and acid rock, Stallman preferred classical music. The memory leads to a rare humorous episode from Stallman's middle-school years. Following the Beatles' 1964 appearance on the Ed Sullivan Show, most of Stallman's classmates rushed out to purchase the latest Beatles albums and singles. Right then and there, Stallman says, he made a decision to boycott the Fab Four.

"I liked some of the pre-Beatles popular music," Stallman says. "But I didn't like the Beatles. I especially disliked the wild way people reacted to them. It was like: who was going to have a Beatles assembly to adulate the Beatles the most?"

When his Beatles boycott failed to take hold, Stallman looked for other ways to point out the herd-mentality of his peers. Stallman says he briefly considered putting together a rock band himself dedicated to satirizing the Liverpool group.

"I wanted to call it Tokyo Rose and the Japanese Beetles."

Given his current love for international folk music, I ask Stallman if he had a similar affinity for Bob Dylan and the other folk musicians of the early 1960s. Stallman shakes his head. "I did like Peter, Paul and Mary," he says. "That reminds me of a great filk."

When I ask for a definition of "filk," Stallman explains that the term is used in science fiction fandom to refer to the writing of new lyrics for songs. (In recent decades, some filkers write melodies too.) Classic filks include "On Top of Spaghetti," a rewrite of "On Top of

Old Smokey," and "Yoda," filk-master "Weird" Al Yankovic's Star
Wars-oriented rendition of the Kinks tune, "Lola."

Stallman asks me if I would be interested in hearing the filk. As
soon as I say yes, Stallman's voice begins singing in an unexpectedly
clear tone, using the tune of "Blowin' in the Wind":

> How much wood could a woodchuck chuck,
> If a woodchuck could chuck wood?
> How many poles could a polak lock,
> If a polak could lock poles?
> How many knees could a negro grow,
> If a negro could grow knees?
> The answer, my dear,
> is stick it in your ear.
> The answer is, stick it in your ear...

The singing ends, and Stallman's lips curl into another child-like
half smile. I glance around at the nearby tables. The Asian families
enjoying their Sunday lunch pay little attention to the bearded alto in
their midst.[11] After a few moments of hesitation, I finally smile too.

"Do you want that last cornball?" Stallman asks, eyes twinkling.
Before I can screw up the punch line, Stallman grabs the corn-encrusted
dumpling with his two chopsticks and lifts it proudly. "Maybe I'm the
one who should get the cornball," he says.

The food gone, our conversation assumes the dynamics of a normal
interview. Stallman reclines in his chair and cradles a cup of tea in his
hands. We resume talking about Napster and its relation to the free
software movement. Should the principles of free software be extended
to similar arenas such as music publishing? I ask.

"It's a mistake to transfer answers from one thing to another,"
says Stallman, contrasting songs with software programs. "The right
approach is to look at each type of work and see what conclusion you
get."

When it comes to copyrighted works, Stallman says he divides the
world into three categories. The first category involves "functional"
works – e.g., software programs, dictionaries, and textbooks. The
second category involves works that might best be described as "testi-
monial" – e.g., scientific papers and historical documents. Such works

serve a purpose that would be undermined if subsequent readers or authors were free to modify the work at will. It also includes works of personal expression – e.g., diaries, journals, and autobiographies. To modify such documents would be to alter a person's recollections or point of view, which Stallman considers ethically unjustifiable. The third category includes works of art and entertainment.

Of the three categories, the first should give users the unlimited right to make modified versions, while the second and third should regulate that right according to the will of the original author. Regardless of category, however, the freedom to copy and redistribute noncommercially should remain unabridged at all times, Stallman insists. If that means giving Internet users the right to generate a hundred copies of an article, image, song, or book and then email the copies to a hundred strangers, so be it. "It's clear that private occasional redistribution must be permitted, because only a police state can stop that," Stallman says. "It's antisocial to come between people and their friends. Napster has convinced me that we also need to permit, must permit, even noncommercial redistribution to the public for the fun of it. Because so many people want to do that and find it so useful."

When I ask whether the courts would accept such a permissive outlook, Stallman cuts me off.

"That's the wrong question," he says. "I mean now you've changed the subject entirely from one of ethics to one of interpreting laws. And those are two totally different questions in the same field. It's useless to jump from one to the other. How the courts would interpret the existing laws is mainly in a harsh way, because that's the way these laws have been bought by publishers."

The comment provides an insight into Stallman's political philosophy: just because the legal system currently backs up businesses' ability to treat copyright as the software equivalent of land title doesn't mean computer users have to play the game according to those rules. Freedom is an ethical issue, not a legal issue. "I'm looking beyond what the existing laws are to what they should be," Stallman says. "I'm not trying to draft legislation. I'm thinking about what should the law do? I consider the law prohibiting the sharing of copies with your friend the moral equivalent of Jim Crow. It does not deserve respect."

The invocation of Jim Crow prompts another question. How much influence or inspiration does Stallman draw from past political leaders? Like the civil-rights movement of the 1950s and 1960s, his attempt to drive social change is based on an appeal to timeless values: freedom, justice, and fair play.

Stallman divides his attention between my analogy and a particularly tangled strand of hair. When I stretch the analogy to the point where I'm comparing Stallman with Dr. Martin Luther King, Jr., Stallman, after breaking off a split end and popping it into his mouth, cuts me off.

"I'm not in his league, but I do play the same game," he says, chewing.

I suggest Malcolm X as another point of comparison. Like the former Nation of Islam spokesperson, Stallman has built up a reputation for courting controversy, alienating potential allies, and preaching a message favoring self-sufficiency over cultural integration.

Chewing on another split end, Stallman rejects the comparison. "My message is closer to King's message," he says. "It's a universal message. It's a message of firm condemnation of certain practices that mistreat others. It's not a message of hatred for anyone. And it's not aimed at a narrow group of people. I invite anyone to value freedom and to have freedom."

Many criticize Stallman for rejecting handy political alliances; some psychologize this and describe it as a character trait. In the case of his well-publicized distaste for the term "open source," the unwillingness to participate in recent coalition-building projects seems understandable. As a man who has spent the last two decades stumping on the behalf of free software, Stallman's political capital is deeply invested in the term. Still, comments such as the "Han Solo" comparison at the 1999 LinuxWorld have only reinforced Stallman's reputation, amongst those who believe virtue consists of following the crowd, as a disgruntled mossback unwilling to roll with political or marketing trends.

"I admire and respect Richard for all the work he's done," says Red Hat president Robert Young, summing up Stallman's paradoxical political conduct. "My only critique is that sometimes Richard treats his friends worse than his enemies."

[RMS: The term "friends" only partly fits people such as Young, and companies such as Red Hat. It applies to some of what they did, and do: for instance, Red Hat contributes to development of free software, including some GNU programs. But Red Hat does other things that work against the free software movement's goals – for instance, its versions of GNU/Linux contain nonfree software. Turning from deeds to words, referring to the whole system as "Linux" is unfriendly treatment of the GNU Project, and promoting "open source" instead of "free software" rejects our values. I could work with Young and Red Hat when we were going in the same direction, but that was not often enough to make them possible allies.]

Stallman's reluctance to ally the free software movement with other political causes is not due to lack of interest in them. Visit his offices at MIT, and you instantly find a clearinghouse of left-leaning news articles covering civil-rights abuses around the globe. Visit his personal web site, `stallman.org`, and you'll find attacks on the Digital Millennium Copyright Act, the War on Drugs, and the World Trade Organization. Stallman explains, "We have to be careful of entering the free software movement into alliances with other political causes that substantial numbers of free software supporters might not agree with. For instance, we avoid linking the free software movement with any political party because we do not want to drive away the supporters and elected officials of other parties."

Given his activist tendencies, I ask, why hasn't Stallman sought a larger voice? Why hasn't he used his visibility in the hacker world as a platform to boost his political voice? [RMS: But I do – when I see a good opportunity. That's why I started `stallman.org`.]

Stallman lets his tangled hair drop and contemplates the question for a moment. [RMS: My quoted response doesn't fit that question. It does fit a different question, "Why do you focus on free software rather than on the other causes you believe in?" I suspect the question I was asked was more like that one.]

"I hesitate to exaggerate the importance of this little puddle of freedom," he says. "Because the more well-known and conventional areas of working for freedom and a better society are tremendously important. I wouldn't say that free software is as important as they are. It's the responsibility I undertook, because it dropped in my lap and I saw a way I could do something about it. But, for example, to end police brutality, to end the war on drugs, to end the kinds of racism we still have, to help everyone have a comfortable life, to protect the rights of people who do abortions, to protect us from theocracy, these are tremendously important issues, far more important than what I do. I just wish I knew how to do something about them."

Once again, Stallman presents his political activity as a function of personal confidence. Given the amount of time it has taken him to develop and hone the free software movement's core tenets, Stallman is hesitant to believe he can advance the other causes he supports.

"I wish I knew how to make a major difference on those bigger issues, because I would be tremendously proud if I could, but they're very hard and lots of people who are probably better than I am have been working on them and have gotten only so far," he says. "But as I see it, while other people were defending against these big visible threats, I saw another threat that was unguarded. And so I went to defend against that threat. It may not be as big a threat, but I was the only one there [to oppose it]."

Chewing a final split end, Stallman suggests paying the check. Before the waiter can take it away, however, Stallman pulls out a white-colored dollar bill and throws it on the pile. The bill looks so clearly counterfeit, I can't help but pick it up and read it. Sure enough, it did not come from the US Mint. Instead of bearing the image of a George Washington or Abe Lincoln, the bill's front side bears the image of a cartoon pig. Instead of the United States of America, the banner above the pig reads, "Untied Status of Avarice." The bill is for zero dollars,[12] and when the waiter picks up the money, Stallman makes sure to tug on his sleeve.

"I added an extra zero to your tip," Stallman says, yet another half smile creeping across his lips.

The waiter, uncomprehending or fooled by the look of the bill, smiles and scurries away.

"I think that means we're free to go," Stallman says.

Endnotes

[1] See Andrew Leonard, "The Saint of Free Software," *Salon.com* (August 1998), http://www.salon.com/21st/feature/1998/08/cov_31feature.html.

[2] See Leander Kahney, "Linux's Forgotten Man," *Wired News* (March 5, 1999), http://www.wired.com/news/print/0,1294,18291,00.html.

[3]See "Programmer on moral high ground; Free software is a moral issue for Richard Stallman believes in freedom and free software," *London Guardian* (November 6, 1999), http://www.guardian.co.uk/uk/1999/nov/06/andrewbrown. These are just a small sampling of the religious comparisons. To date, the most extreme comparison has to go to Linus Torvalds, who, in his autobiography – see Linus Torvalds and David Diamond, *Just For Fun: The Story of an Accidental Revolutionary* (HarperCollins Publishers, Inc., 2001): 58 – writes, "Richard Stallman is the God of Free Software."

Honorable mention goes to Larry Lessig, who, in a footnote description of Stallman in his book – see Larry Lessig, *The Future of Ideas* (Random House, 2001): 270 – likens Stallman to Moses:

> ...as with Moses, it was another leader, Linus Torvalds, who finally carried the movement into the promised land by facilitating the development of the final part of the OS puzzle. Like Moses, too, Stallman is both respected and reviled by allies within the movement. He is [an] unforgiving, and hence for many inspiring, leader of a critically important aspect of modern culture. I have deep respect for the principle and commitment of this extraordinary individual, though I also have great respect for those who are courageous enough to question his thinking and then sustain his wrath.

In a final interview with Stallman, I asked him his thoughts about the religious comparisons. "Some people do compare me with an Old Testament prophet, and the reason is Old Testament prophets said certain social practices were wrong. They wouldn't compromise on moral issues. They couldn't be bought off, and they were usually treated with contempt."

[4]See Leander Kahney (1999).

[5]At the time, I thought Stallman was referring to the flower's scientific name. Months later, I would learn that *rhinophytophilia* was in fact a humorous reference to the activity – i.e., Stallman's sticking his nose into a flower and enjoying the moment – presenting it as the kinky practice of nasal sex with plants. For another humorous Stallman flower incident, visit: http://www.stallman.org/articles/texas.html.

[6]See Cecily Barnes and Scott Ard, "Court Grants Stay of Napster Injunction," *News.com* (July 28, 2000), http://news.cnet.com/news/0-1005-200-2376465.html.

[7]See "A Clear Victory for Recording Industry in Napster Case," RIAA press release (February 12, 2001), http://www.riaa.com/PR_story.cfm?id=372.

[8]See Mae Ling Mak, "A Mae Ling Story" (December 17, 1998), http://crackmonkey.org/pipermail/crackmonkey/1998-December/001777.html.

So far, Mak is the only person I've found willing to speak on the record in regard to this practice, although I've heard this from a few other female sources. Mak, despite expressing initial revulsion at it, later managed to put aside her misgivings and dance with Stallman at a 1999 LinuxWorld show.

[9]See Annalee Newitz, "If Code is Free Why Not Me?", *Salon.com* (May 26, 2000), http://www.salon.com/tech/feature/2000/05/26/free_love/print.html.

[10]See Richard Stallman, "The GNU Operating System and the Free Software Movement," *Open Sources* (O'Reilly & Associates, Inc., 1999): 65. [RMS: Williams interpreted this vignette as suggesting that I am a hopeless romantic, and that my

efforts were meant to impress some as-yet-unidentified woman. No MIT hacker
would believe this, since we learned quite young that most women wouldn't notice
us, let alone love us, for our programming. We programmed because it was fas-
cinating. Meanwhile, these events were only possible because I had a thoroughly
identified girlfriend at the time. If I was a romantic, at the time I was neither a
hopeless romantic nor a hopeful romantic, but rather temporarily a successful one.

On the strength of that naive interpretation, Williams went on to compare me
to Don Quijote.

For completeness' sake, here's a somewhat inarticulate quote from the first
edition: "I wasn't really trying to be romantic. It was more of a teasing thing. I
mean, it was romantic, but it was also teasing, you know? It would have been a
delightful surprise."]

[11] For Stallman's own filks, visit http://www.stallman.org/doggerel.html. To
hear Stallman singing "The Free Software Song," visit http://www.gnu.org/music/
free-software-song.html.

[12] RMS: Williams was mistaken to call this bill "counterfeit." It is legal tender,
worth zero dollars for payment of any debt. Any U.S. government office will convert
it into zero dollars' worth of gold.

Chapter **6**

The Emacs Commune

The AI Lab of the 1970s was by all accounts a special place. Cutting-edge projects and top-flight researchers gave it an esteemed position in the world of computer science. The internal hacker culture and its anarchic policies lent a rebellious mystique as well. Only later, when many of the lab's scientists and software superstars had departed, would hackers fully realize the unique and ephemeral world they had once inhabited.

"It was a bit like the Garden of Eden," says Stallman, summing up the lab and its software-sharing ethos in a 1998 *Forbes* article. "It hadn't occurred to us not to cooperate."[1]

Such mythological descriptions, while extreme, underline an important fact. The ninth floor of 545 Tech Square was more than a workplace for many. For hackers such as Stallman, it was home.

The word "home" is a weighted term in the Stallman lexicon. In a pointed swipe at his parents, Stallman, to this day, refuses to acknowledge any home before Currier House, the dorm he lived in during his days at Harvard. He has also been known to describe leaving that home in tragicomic terms. Once, while describing his years at Harvard, Stallman said his only regret was getting kicked out. It wasn't until I asked Stallman what precipitated his ouster, that I realized I had walked into a classic Stallman setup line.

"At Harvard they have this policy where if you pass too many classes they ask you to leave," Stallman says.

With no dorm and no desire to return to New York, Stallman followed a path blazed by Greenblatt, Gosper, Sussman, and the many other hackers before him. Enrolling at MIT as a grad student, Stallman rented a room in an apartment in nearby Cambridge but soon viewed the AI Lab itself as his de facto home. In a 1986 speech, Stallman recalled his memories of the AI Lab during this period:

> I may have done a little bit more living at the lab than most people, because every year or two for some reason or other I'd have no apartment and I would spend a few months living at the lab. And I've always found it very comfortable, as well as nice and cool in the summer. But it was not at all uncommon to find people falling asleep at the lab, again because of their enthusiasm; you stay up as long as you possibly can hacking, because you just don't want to stop. And then when you're completely exhausted, you climb over to the nearest soft horizontal surface. A very informal atmosphere.[2]

The lab's home-like atmosphere could be a problem at times. What some saw as a dorm, others viewed as an electronic opium den. In the 1976 book *Computer Power and Human Reason*, MIT researcher Joseph Weizenbaum offered a withering critique of the "computer bum," Weizenbaum's term for the hackers who populated computer rooms such as the AI Lab. "Their rumpled clothes, their unwashed hair and unshaved faces, and their uncombed hair all testify that they are oblivious to their bodies and to the world in which they move," Weizenbaum wrote. "[Computer bums] exist, at least when so engaged, only through and for the computers."[3]

Almost a quarter century after its publication, Stallman still bristles when hearing Weizenbaum's "computer bum" description, discussing it in the present tense as if Weizenbaum himself was still in the room. "He wants people to be just professionals, doing it for the money and wanting to get away from it and forget about it as soon as possible," Stallman says. "What he sees as a normal state of affairs, I see as a tragedy."

Hacker life, however, was not without tragedy. Stallman characterizes his transition from weekend hacker to full-time AI Lab denizen as a series of painful misfortunes that could only be eased through the euphoria of hacking. As Stallman himself has said, the first misfortune was his graduation from Harvard. Eager to continue his studies in physics, Stallman enrolled as a graduate student at MIT. The choice of schools was a natural one. Not only did it give Stallman the chance to follow the footsteps of great MIT alumni: William Shockley ('36), Richard P. Feynman ('39), and Murray Gell-Mann ('51), it also put him two miles closer to the AI Lab and its new PDP-10 computer. "My attention was going toward programming, but I still thought, well, maybe I can do both," Stallman says.

Toiling in the fields of graduate-level science by day and programming in the monastic confines of the AI Lab by night, Stallman tried to achieve a perfect balance. The fulcrum of this geek teeter-totter was his weekly outing with the Folk-Dance Club, his one social outlet that guaranteed at least a modicum of interaction with the opposite sex. Near the end of that first year at MIT, however, disaster struck. A knee injury forced Stallman to stop dancing. At first, Stallman viewed the injury as a temporary problem; he went to dancing and chatted with friends while listening to the music he loved. By the end of the summer, when the knee still ached and classes reconvened, Stallman began to worry. "My knee wasn't getting any better," Stallman recalls, "which meant I had to expect to be unable to dance, permanently. I was heartbroken."

With no dorm and no dancing, Stallman's social universe imploded. Dancing was the only situation in which he had found success in meeting women and occasionally even dating them. No more dancing ever was painful enough, but it also meant, it seemed, no more dates ever.

"I felt basically that I'd lost all my energy," Stallman recalls. "I'd lost my energy to do anything but what was most immediately tempting. The energy to do something else was gone. I was in total despair."

Stallman retreated from the world even further, focusing entirely on his work at the AI Lab. By October, 1975, he dropped out of MIT and out of physics, never to return to studies. Software hacking, once a hobby, had become his calling.

Looking back on that period, Stallman sees the transition from full-time student to full-time hacker as inevitable. Sooner or later, he believes, the siren's call of computer hacking would have overpowered his interest in other professional pursuits. "With physics and math, I could never figure out a way to contribute," says Stallman, recalling his struggles prior to the knee injury. "I would have been proud to advance either one of those fields, but I could never see a way to do that. I didn't know where to start. With software, I saw right away how to write things that would run and be useful. The pleasure of that knowledge led me to want to do it more."

Stallman wasn't the first to equate hacking with pleasure. Many of the hackers who staffed the AI Lab boasted similar, incomplete academic résumés. Most had come in pursuing degrees in math or electrical engineering only to surrender their academic careers and professional ambitions to the sheer exhilaration that came with solving problems never before addressed. Like St. Thomas Aquinas, the scholastic known for working so long on his theological summae that he sometimes achieved spiritual visions, hackers reached transcendent internal states through sheer mental focus and physical exhaustion. Although Stallman shunned drugs, like most hackers, he enjoyed the "high" that came near the end of a 20-hour coding bender.

Perhaps the most enjoyable emotion, however, was the sense of personal fulfillment. When it came to hacking, Stallman was a natural. A childhood's worth of late-night study sessions gave him the ability to work long hours with little sleep. As a social outcast since age 10, he had little difficulty working alone. And as a mathematician with a built-in gift for logic and foresight, Stallman possessed the ability to circumvent design barriers that left most hackers spinning their wheels.

"He was special," recalls Gerald Sussman, an AI Lab faculty member and (since 1985) board member of the Free Software Foundation. Describing Stallman as a "clear thinker and a clear designer," Sussman invited Stallman to join him in AI research projects in 1973 and 1975, both aimed at making AI programs that could analyze circuits the way human engineers do it. The project required an expert's command of Lisp, a programming language built specifically for AI applications, as well as understanding (supplied by Sussman) of how a human might approach the same task. The 1975 project pioneered an AI technique called dependency-directed backtracking or truth maintenance, which consists of positing tentative assumptions, noticing if they lead to contradictions, and reconsidering the pertinent assumptions if that occurs. When he wasn't working on official projects such as these, Stallman devoted his time to pet projects. It was in a hacker's best interest to improve the lab's software infrastructure, and one of Stallman's biggest pet projects during this period was the lab's editor program TECO.

The story of Stallman's work on TECO during the 1970s is inextricably linked with Stallman's later leadership of the free software movement. It is also a significant stage in the history of computer evolution, so much so that a brief recapitulation of that evolution is necessary. During the 1950s and 1960s, when computers were first appearing at universities, computer programming was an incredibly abstract pursuit. To communicate with the machine, programmers created a series of punch cards, with each card representing an individual software command. Programmers would then hand the cards over to a central system administrator who would then insert them, one by one, into the machine, waiting for the machine to spit out a new set of punch cards, which the programmer would then decipher as output. This process, known as "batch processing," was cumbersome and time consuming. It was also prone to abuses of authority. One of the motivating factors behind hackers' inbred aversion to centralization was the power held by early system operators in dictating which jobs held top priority.

In 1962, computer scientists and hackers involved in MIT's Project MAC, an early forerunner of the AI Lab, took steps to alleviate this frustration. Time-sharing, originally known as "time stealing," made it possible for multiple programs to take advantage of a machine's operational capabilities. Teletype interfaces also made it possible to communicate with a machine not through a series of punched holes but through actual text. A programmer typed in commands and read the line-by-line output generated by the machine.

During the late 1960s, interface design made additional leaps. In a famous 1968 lecture, Doug Engelbart, a scientist then working at the Stanford Research Institute, unveiled a prototype of the modern graphical interface. Rigging up a television set to the computer and adding a pointer device which Engelbart dubbed a "mouse," the scientist created a system even more interactive than the time-sharing system developed at MIT. Treating the video display like a high-speed printer, Engelbart's system gave a user the ability to move the cursor around the screen and see the cursor position updated by the computer in real time. The user suddenly had the ability to position text anywhere on the screen.

Such innovations would take another two decades to make their way into the commercial marketplace. Still, by the 1970s, video screens had started to replace teletypes as display terminals, creating the potential for full-screen – as opposed to line-by-line – editing capabilities.

One of the first programs to take advantage of this full-screen capability was the MIT AI Lab's TECO. Short for Text Editor and COrrector, the program had been upgraded by hackers from an old teletype line editor for the lab's PDP-6 machine.[4]

TECO was a substantial improvement over old editors, but it still had its drawbacks. To create and edit a document, a programmer had to enter a series of commands specifying each edit. It was an abstract process. Unlike modern word processors, which update text with each keystroke, TECO demanded that the user enter an extended series of editing instructions followed by an "end of command string" sequence just to change the text. Over time, a hacker grew proficient enough to make large changes elegantly in one command string, but as Stallman himself would later point out, the process required "a mental skill like that of blindfold chess."[5]

To facilitate the process, AI Lab hackers had built a system that displayed both the text and the command string on a split screen. Despite this innovative hack, editing with TECO still required skill and planning.

TECO wasn't the only full-screen editor floating around the computer world at this time. During a visit to the Stanford Artificial Intelligence Lab in 1976, Stallman encountered an edit program named E. The program contained an internal feature, which allowed a user to update display text after each command keystroke. In the language of 1970s programming, E was one of the first rudimentary WYSIWYG editors. Short for "what you see is what you get," WYSIWYG meant that a user could manipulate the file by moving through the displayed text, as opposed to working through a back-end editor program."[6]

Impressed by the hack, Stallman looked for ways to expand TECO's functionality in similar fashion upon his return to MIT. He found a TECO feature called Control-R, written by Carl Mikkelson and named after the two-key combination that triggered it. Mikkelson's hack switched TECO from its usual abstract command-execution mode to a more intuitive keystroke-by-keystroke mode. The only flaws were that it used just five lines of the screen and was too inefficient for real use. Stallman reimplemented the feature to use the whole screen efficiently, then extended it in a subtle but significant way. He made it possible to attach TECO command strings, or "macros," to keystrokes. Advanced TECO users already saved macros in files; Stallman's hack made it possible to call them up fast. The result was a user-programmable WYSI-WYG editor. "That was the real breakthrough," says Guy Steele, a fellow AI Lab hacker at the time.[7]

By Stallman's own recollection, the macro hack touched off an explosion of further innovation. "Everybody and his brother was writing his own collection of redefined screen-editor commands, a command for everything he typically liked to do," Stallman would later recall. "People would pass them around and improve them, making them more powerful and more general. The collections of redefinitions gradually became system programs in their own right."[8]

So many people found the macro innovations useful and had incorporated it into their own TECO programs that the TECO editor had become secondary to the macro mania it inspired. "We started to categorize it mentally as a programming language rather than as an editor," Stallman says. Users were experiencing their own pleasure tweaking the software and trading new ideas.[9]

Two years after the explosion, the rate of innovation began to exhibit inconvenient side effects. The explosive growth had provided an exciting validation of the collaborative hacker approach, but it had also led to incompatibility. "We had a Tower of Babel effect," says Guy Steele.

The effect threatened to kill the spirit that had created it, Steele says. Hackers had designed ITS to facilitate programmers' ability to share knowledge and improve each other's work. That meant being able to sit down at another programmer's desk, open up a programmer's work and make comments and modifications directly within the software. "Sometimes the easiest way to show somebody how to program or debug something was simply to sit down at the terminal and do it for them," explains Steele.

The macro feature, after its second year, began to foil this capability. In their eagerness to embrace the new full-screen capabilities, hackers had customized their versions of TECO to the point where a hacker sitting down at another hacker's terminal usually had to spend the first hour just figuring out what macro commands did what.

Frustrated, Steele took it upon himself to solve the problem. He gathered together the four different macro packages and began assembling a chart documenting the most useful macro commands. In the course of implementing the design specified by the chart, Steele says he attracted Stallman's attention.

"He started looking over my shoulder, asking me what I was doing," recalls Steele.

For Steele, a soft-spoken hacker who interacted with Stallman infrequently, the memory still sticks out. Looking over another hacker's shoulder while he worked was a common activity at the AI Lab. Stallman, the TECO maintainer at the lab, deemed Steele's work "interesting" and quickly set off to complete it.

"As I like to say, I did the first 0.001 percent of the implementation, and Stallman did the rest," says Steele with a laugh.

The project's new name, Emacs, came courtesy of Stallman. Short for "editing macros," it signified the evolutionary transcendence that had taken place during the macros explosion two years before. It also took advantage of a gap in the software programming lexicon. Noting a lack of programs on ITS starting with the letter "E," Stallman chose Emacs, making it natural to reference the program with a single letter. Once again, the hacker lust for efficiency had left its mark.[10]

Of course, not everyone switched to Emacs, or not immediately. Users were free to continue maintaining and running their own TECO-based editors as before. But most found it preferable to switch to Emacs, especially since Emacs was designed to make it easy to replace or add some parts while using others unchanged.

"On the one hand, we were trying to make a uniform command set again; on the other hand, we wanted to keep it open ended, because the programmability was important," recalls Steele.

Stallman now faced another conundrum: if users made changes but didn't communicate those changes back to the rest of the community, the Tower of Babel effect would simply emerge in other places. Falling back on the hacker doctrine of sharing innovation, Stallman embedded a statement within the source code that set the terms of use. Users were free to modify and redistribute the code on the condition that they gave back all the extensions they made. Stallman called this "joining the Emacs Commune." Just as TECO had become more than a simple editor, Emacs had become more than a simple software program. To Stallman, it was a social contract. In a 1981 memo documenting the project, Stallman spelled out the contract terms. "EMACS," he wrote, "was distributed on a basis of communal sharing, which means that all improvements must be given back to me to be incorporated and distributed." [11]

The original Emacs ran only on the PDP-10 computer, but soon users of other computers wanted an Emacs to edit with. The explosive innovation continued throughout the decade, resulting in a host of Emacs-like programs with varying degrees of cross-compatibility. The Emacs Commune's rules did not apply to them, since their code was separate. A few cited their relation to Stallman's original Emacs with humorously recursive names: Sine (Sine is not Emacs), Eine (Eine is not Emacs), and Zwei (Zwei was Eine initially). A true Emacs had to provide user-programmability like the original; editors with similar keyword commands but without the user-programmability were called "ersatz Emacs." One example was Mince (Mince is Not Complete Emacs).

While Stallman was developing Emacs in the AI Lab, there were other, unsettling developments elsewhere in the hacker community. Brian Reid's 1979 decision to embed "time bombs" in Scribe, making it possible for Unilogic to limit unpaid user access to the software, was a dark omen to Stallman. "He considered it the most Nazi thing he ever saw in his life," recalls Reid. Despite going on to later Internet fame as the co-creator of the Usenet *alt* hierarchy, Reid says he still has yet to live down that 1979 decision, at least in Stallman's eyes. "He said that all software should be free and the prospect of charging money for software was a crime against humanity." [12]

Although Stallman had been powerless to head off Reid's sale, he did possess the ability to curtail other forms of behavior deemed contrary to the hacker ethos. As central source-code maintainer for the original Emacs, Stallman began to wield his power for political effect. During his final stages of conflict with the administrators at the Laboratory for Computer Science over password systems, Stallman initiated a software "strike," refusing to send lab members the latest version of Emacs until they rejected the security system on the lab's computers.[13] This was more gesture than sanction, since nothing could stop them from installing it themselves. But it got the point across: putting passwords on an ITS system would lead to condemnation and reaction.

"A lot of people were angry with me, saying I was trying to hold them hostage or blackmail them, which in a sense I was," Stallman would later tell author Steven Levy. "I was engaging in violence against them because I thought they were engaging in violence to everyone at large."[14]

Over time, Emacs became a sales tool for the hacker ethic. The flexibility Stallman had built into the software not only encouraged collaboration, it demanded it. Users who didn't keep abreast of the latest developments in Emacs evolution or didn't contribute their contributions back to Stallman ran the risk of missing out on the latest breakthroughs. And the breakthroughs were many. Twenty years later, users of GNU Emacs (a second implementation started in 1984) have modified it for so many different uses – using it as a spreadsheet, calculator, database, and web browser – that later Emacs developers adopted an overflowing sink to represent its versatile functionality. "That's the idea that we wanted to convey," says Stallman. "The amount of stuff it has contained within it is both wonderful and awful at the same time."

Stallman's AI Lab contemporaries are more charitable. Hal Abelson, an MIT grad student who worked with Sussman during the 1970s and would later assist Stallman as a charter board member of the Free Software Foundation, describes Emacs as "an absolutely brilliant creation." In giving programmers a way to add new software libraries and features without messing up the system, Abelson says, Stallman paved the way for future large-scale collaborative software projects. "Its structure was robust enough that you'd have people all over the world who were loosely collaborating [and] contributing to it," Abelson says. "I don't know if that had been done before."[15]

Guy Steele expresses similar admiration. Currently a research scientist for Sun Microsystems, he remembers Stallman primarily as a "brilliant programmer with the ability to generate large quantities of relatively bug-free code." Although their personalities didn't exactly mesh, Steele and Stallman collaborated long enough for Steele to get a glimpse of Stallman's intense coding style. He recalls a notable episode in the late 1970s when the two programmers banded together to write the editor's "pretty print" feature. Originally conceived by Steele, pretty print was another keystroke-triggered feature that reformatted Emacs' source code so that it was both more readable and took up less space, further bolstering the program's WYSIWYG qualities. The feature was strategic enough to attract Stallman's active interest, and it wasn't long before Steele wrote that he and Stallman were planning an improved version.

"We sat down one morning," recalls Steele. "I was at the keyboard, and he was at my elbow," says Steele. "He was perfectly willing to let me type, but he was also telling me what to type.

The programming session lasted 10 hours. Throughout that entire time, Steele says, neither he nor Stallman took a break or made any small talk. By the end of the session, they had managed to hack the pretty print source code to just under 100 lines. "My fingers were on the keyboard the whole time," Steele recalls, "but it felt like both of our ideas were flowing onto the screen. He told me what to type, and I typed it."

The length of the session revealed itself when Steele finally left the AI Lab. Standing outside the building at 545 Tech Square, he was surprised to find himself surrounded by nighttime darkness. As a programmer, Steele was used to marathon coding sessions. Still, something about this session was different. Working with Stallman had forced Steele to block out all external stimuli and focus his entire mental energies on the task at hand. Looking back, Steele says he found the Stallman mind-meld both exhilarating and scary at the same time. "My first thought afterward was [that] it was a great experience, very intense, and that I never wanted to do it again in my life."

Endnotes

[1] See Josh McHugh, "For the Love of Hacking," *Forbes* (August 10, 1998), http://www.forbes.com/forbes/1998/0810/6203094a.html.

[2] See Stallman (1986).

[3] See Joseph Weizenbaum, *Computer Power and Human Reason: From Judgment to Calculation* (W. H. Freeman, 1976): 116.

[4] According to the *Jargon File*, TECO's name originally stood for Tape Editor and Corrector. See http://www.catb.org/jargon/html/T/TECO.html.

[5] See Richard Stallman, "EMACS: The Extensible, Customizable, Display Editor," AI Lab Memo (1979). An updated HTML version of this memo, from which I am quoting, is available at http://www.gnu.org/software/emacs/emacs-paper.html.

[6] See Richard Stallman, "Emacs the Full Screen Editor" (1987), http://www.lysator.liu.se/history/garb/txt/87-1-emacs.txt.

[7] *Ibid.*

[8] *Ibid.*

[9] *Ibid.*

[10] *Ibid.*

[11] See Stallman (1979): #SEC34.

[12] In a 1996 interview with online magazine *MEME*, Stallman cited Scribe's sale as irksome, but declined to mention Reid by name. "The problem was nobody censured or punished this student for what he did," Stallman said. "The result was other people got tempted to follow his example." See *MEME* 2.04, http://memex.org/meme2-04.html.

[13] See Steven Levy, *Hackers* (Penguin USA [paperback], 1984): 419.

[14] *Ibid.*

[15] In writing this chapter, I've elected to focus more on the social significance of Emacs than the software significance. To read more about the software side, I recommend Stallman's 1979 memo. I particularly recommend the section titled "Research Through Development of Installed Tools" (#SEC27). Not only is it accessible to the nontechnical reader, it also sheds light on how closely intertwined Stallman's political philosophies are with his software-design philosophies. A sample excerpt follows:

> EMACS could not have been reached by a process of careful design, because such processes arrive only at goals which are visible at the outset, and whose desirability is established on the bottom line at the outset. Neither I nor anyone else visualized an extensible editor until I had made one, nor appreciated its value until he had experienced it. EMACS exists because I felt free to make individually useful small improvements on a path whose end was not in sight.

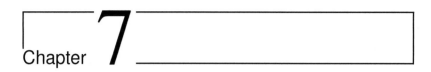

Chapter 7

A Stark Moral Choice

On September 27, 1983, computer programmers logging on to the Usenet newsgroup net.unix-wizards encountered an unusual message. Posted in the small hours of the morning, 12:30 a.m. to be exact, and signed by rms@mit-oz, the message's subject line was terse but attention-grabbing. "New UNIX implementation," it read. Instead of introducing a newly released version of Unix, however, the message's opening paragraph issued a call to arms:

> Starting this Thanksgiving I am going to write a complete Unix-compatible software system called GNU (for Gnu's Not Unix), and give it away free to everyone who can use it. Contributions of time, money, programs and equipment are greatly needed.[1]

To an experienced Unix developer, the message was a mixture of idealism and hubris. Not only did the author pledge to rebuild the already mature Unix operating system from the ground up, he also proposed to improve it in places. The new GNU system, the author predicted, would carry all the usual components – a text editor, a shell program to run Unix-compatible applications, a compiler, "and a few other things."[2] It would also contain many enticing features that other Unix systems didn't yet offer: a graphic user interface based on the

Lisp programming language, a crash-proof file system, and networking
protocols built according to MIT's internal networking system.

"GNU will be able to run Unix programs, but will not be identical
to Unix," the author wrote. "We will make all improvements that are
convenient, based on our experience with other operating systems."

Anticipating a skeptical response on some readers' part, the author made sure to follow up his operating-system outline with a brief
biographical sketch titled, "Who am I?":

> I am Richard Stallman, inventor of the original much-
> imitated EMACS editor, now at the Artificial Intelligence
> Lab at MIT. I have worked extensively on compilers, ed-
> itors, debuggers, command interpreters, the Incompatible
> Timesharing System and the Lisp Machine operating sys-
> tem. I pioneered terminal-independent display support in
> ITS. In addition I have implemented one crashproof file
> system and two window systems for Lisp machines.[3]

As fate would have it, Stallman's fanciful GNU Project missed its
Thanksgiving launch date. By January, 1984, however, Stallman made
good on his promise and fully immersed himself in the world of Unix
software development. For a software architect raised on ITS, it was
like designing suburban shopping malls instead of Moorish palaces.
Even so, building a Unix-like operating system had its hidden advantages. ITS had been powerful, but it also possessed an Achilles'
heel: MIT hackers had written it specifically to run on the powerful
DEC-built PDP-10 computer. When AI Lab administrators elected to
phase out the lab's PDP-10 machine in the early 1980s, the operating
system that hackers once likened to a vibrant city became an instant
ghost town. Unix, on the other hand, was designed for portability,
which made it immune to such dangers. Originally developed by junior scientists at AT&T, the program had slipped out under corporate-
management radar, finding a happy home in the cash-strapped world
of academic computer systems. With fewer resources than their MIT
brethren, Unix developers had customized the software to ride atop a
motley assortment of hardware systems, primarily the 16-bit PDP-11
– a machine considered fit for only small tasks by most AI Lab hackers
– but later also 32-bit mainframes such as the VAX 11/780. By 1983,

a few companies, most notably Sun Microsystems, were developing a more powerful generation of desktop computers, dubbed "workstations," to take advantage of that increasingly ubiquitous operating system on machines comparable in power to the much older PDP-10.

To facilitate portability, the developers of Unix had put an extra layer of abstraction between the software and the machine. Rather than writing it in the instructions of a specific machine type – as the AI Lab hackers had done with ITS and the PDP-10 – Unix developers wrote in a high-level language, called C. Focusing more on the interlocking interfaces and specifications that held the operating system's many subcomponents together, rather than the actual components themselves, they created a system that could be quickly modified to run on any machine. If a user disliked a certain component, the interface specifications made it possible to pull out an individual subcomponent and either fix it or replace it with something better. Simply put, the Unix approach promoted flexibility and economy, hence its rapid adoption.[4]

Stallman's decision to start developing the GNU system was triggered by the end of the ITS system that the AI Lab hackers had nurtured for so long. The demise of ITS, and the AI Lab hacker community which had sustained it, had been a traumatic blow to Stallman. If the Xerox laser printer episode had taught him to recognize the injustice of proprietary software, the community's death forced him to choose between surrendering to proprietary software and opposing it.

Like the software code that composed it, the roots of ITS' demise stretched way back. By 1980, most of the lab's hackers were working on developing the Lisp Machine and its operating system.

Created by artificial-intelligence research pioneer John McCarthy, a MIT artificial-intelligence researcher during the late 1950s, Lisp is an elegant language, well-suited for writing complex programs to operate on data with irregular structure. The language's name is a shortened version of LISt Processing. Following McCarthy's departure to the Stanford Artificial Intelligence Laboratory, MIT hackers refined the language into a local dialect dubbed MACLISP. The "MAC" stood for Project MAC, the DARPA-funded research project that gave birth to the AI Lab and the Laboratory for Computer Science. Led by AI Lab arch-hacker Richard Greenblatt, the AI Lab hackers during the late 1970s designed a computer specialized for running Lisp efficiently and conveniently, the Lisp Machine, then developed an entire Lisp-based operating system for it.

By 1980, two rival groups of hackers had formed two companies to manufacture and sell copies of the Lisp Machine. Greenblatt started Lisp Machines Incorporated. He planned to avoid outside investment and make a "hacker company." Most of the hackers joined Symbolics, a conventional startup. In 1982 they entirely ceased to work at MIT.

With few hackers left to mind the shop, programs and machines took longer to fix – or were not fixed at all. Even worse, Stallman says, the lab began to undergo a "demographic change." The hackers who had once formed a vocal minority within the AI Lab were almost gone while "the professors and the students who didn't really love the [PDP-10] were just as numerous as before."[5]

In 1982, the AI Lab received the replacement for its main computer, the PDP-10, which was over 12 years old. Digital's current model, the Decsystem 20, was compatible for user programs but would have required a drastic rewrite or "port" of ITS if hackers wanted to continue running the same operating system. Fearful that the lab had lost its critical mass of in-house programming talent, AI Lab faculty members pressed for Twenex, a commercial operating system developed by Digital. Outnumbered, the hackers had no choice but to comply.

"Without hackers to maintain the system, [faculty members] said, 'We're going to have a disaster; we must have commercial software,'" Stallman would recall a few years later. "They said, 'We can expect the company to maintain it.' It proved that they were utterly wrong, but that's what they did."[6]

At first, hackers viewed the Twenex system as yet another authoritarian symbol begging to be subverted. The system's name itself was a protest. Officially dubbed TOPS-20 by DEC, it was named as a successor to TOPS-10, a proprietary operating system DEC distributed for the PDP-10. But TOPS-20 was not based on TOPS-10. It was derived from the Tenex system which Bolt Beranek Newman had developed for the PDP-10.[7] Stallman, the hacker who coined the Twenex term, says he came up with the name as a way to avoid using the TOPS-20 name. "The system was far from tops, so there was no way I was going to call it that," Stallman recalls. "So I decided to insert a 'w' in the Tenex name and call it Twenex."

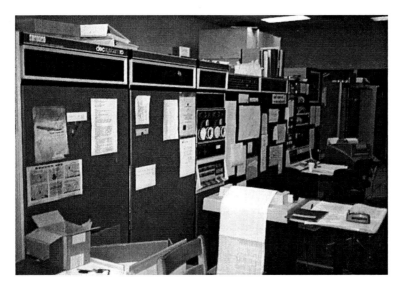

PDP-10 processor with KL-10 (a PDP-10 similar to that of the AI Lab), Stanford Artificial Intelligence Laboratory, 1979.

The machine that ran the Twenex/TOPS-20 system had its own derisive nickname: Oz. According to one hacker legend, the machine got its nickname because it required a smaller PDP-11 machine to power its terminal. One hacker, upon viewing the KL-10-PDP-11 setup for the first time, likened it to the wizard's bombastic onscreen introduction in the Wizard of Oz. "I am the great and powerful Oz," the hacker intoned. "Pay no attention to the PDP-11 behind that console."[8]

If hackers laughed when they first encountered the KL-10, their laughter quickly died when they encountered Twenex. Not only did Twenex boast built-in security, but the system's software engineers had designed the tools and applications with the security system in mind. What once had been a cat-and-mouse game over passwords in the case of the Laboratory for Computer Science's security system, now became an out-and-out battle over system management. System administrators argued that without security, the Oz system was more prone to accidental crashes. Hackers argued that crashes could be better prevented by overhauling the source code. Unfortunately, the number of hackers with the time and inclination to perform this sort of overhaul had dwindled to the point that the system-administrator argument prevailed.

The initial policy was that any lab member could have the "wheel privilege" to bypass security restrictions. But anyone who had the "wheel privilege" could take it away from anyone else, who would then be powerless to restore it. This state of affairs tempted a small group of hackers to try to seize total control by canceling the "wheel privilege" for all but themselves.

Cadging passwords, and applying the debugger during startup, Stallman successfully foiled these attempts. After the second foiled "*coup d'état,*" Stallman issued an alert to all the AI Lab personnel.[9]

"There has been another attempt to seize power," Stallman wrote. "So far, the aristocratic forces have been defeated." To protect his identity, Stallman signed the message "Radio Free OZ."

The disguise was a thin one at best. By 1982, Stallman's aversion to passwords and secrecy had become so well known that users outside the AI Laboratory were using his account from around the ARPAnet – the research-funded computer network that would serve as a foundation for today's Internet. One such "tourist" during the early 1980s was Don Hopkins, a California programmer who learned through the hacking grapevine that all an outsider needed to do to gain access to MIT's vaunted ITS system was to log in under the initials RMS and enter the same three-letter monogram when the system requested a password.

"I'm eternally grateful that MIT let me and many other people use their computers for free," says Hopkins. "It meant a lot to many people."

This so-called "tourist" policy, which had been openly tolerated by MIT management during the ITS years,[10] fell by the wayside when Oz became the lab's primary link to the ARPAnet. At first, Stallman continued his policy of repeating his login ID as a password so outside users could have access through his account. Over time, however, Oz's fragility prompted administrators to bar outsiders who, through sheer accident or malicious intent, might bring down the system. When those same administrators eventually demanded that Stallman stop publishing his password, Stallman, citing personal ethics, instead ceased using the Oz system altogether.[11]

"[When] passwords first appeared at the MIT AI Lab I [decided] to follow my belief that there should be no passwords," Stallman would later say. "Because I don't believe that it's really desirable to have security on a computer, I shouldn't be willing to help uphold the security regime."[12]

Stallman's refusal to bow before the great and powerful Oz symbolized the growing tension between hackers and AI Lab management during the early 1980s. This tension paled in comparison to the conflict that raged within the hacker community itself. By the time the Decsystem 20 arrived, the hacker community was divided into two camps, LMI and Symbolics.

Symbolics, with its outside investment, recruited various AI Lab hackers and set some of them working on improving parts of the Lisp Machine operating system outside the auspices of the AI Lab. By the end of 1980, the company had hired 14 AI Lab staffers as part-time consultants to develop its version of the Lisp Machine. The remaining few, apart from Stallman, worked for LMI.[13] Stallman, preferring the unpressured life at the AI Lab and not wishing to take a side, chose to join neither company.

At first, the other hackers continued spending some of their time at MIT, and contributed to MIT's Lisp Machine operating system. Both LMI and Symbolics had licensed this code from MIT. The license required them to return their changes to MIT, but did not require them to let MIT redistribute these changes. However, through 1981 they adhered to a gentleman's agreement to permit that, so all their system improvements were included in the MIT version and thus shared with all Lisp Machine users. This situation allowed those still at MIT to remain neutral.

On March 16, 1982, a date Stallman remembers well because it was his birthday, Symbolics executives ended the gentleman's agreement. The motive was to attack LMI. LMI had fewer hackers, and fewer staff in general, so the Symbolics executives thought that LMI was getting the main benefit of sharing the system improvements. By ending the sharing of system code, they hoped to wipe out LMI. So they decided to enforce the letter of the license. Instead of contributing their improvements to the MIT version of the system, which LMI could use, they provided MIT with a copy of the Symbolics version of the system for users at MIT to run. Anyone using it would provide the service of testing only to Symbolics, and if he made improvements, most likely they too would only be useful for Symbolics.

As the person responsible (with help from Greenblatt for the first couple of months) for keeping up the lab's Lisp Machine system, Stallman was incensed. The Symbolics hackers had left the system code with hundreds of half-made changes that caused errors. Viewing this announcement as an "ultimatum," he retaliated by disconnecting Symbolics' microwave communications link to the laboratory. He then vowed never to work on a Symbolics machine, and pledged to continue the development of MIT's system so as to defend LMI from Symbolics. "The way I saw it, the AI Lab was a neutral country, like Belgium in World War II," Stallman says. "If Germany invades Belgium, Belgium declares war on Germany and sides with Britain and France."

When Symbolics executives noticed that their latest features were still appearing in the MIT Lisp Machine system and, by extension, the LMI Lisp machine, they were not pleased. Stallman knew what copyright law required, and was rewriting the features from scratch. He took advantage of the opportunity to read the source code Symbolics supplied to MIT, so as to understand the problems and fixes, and then made sure to write his changes in a totally different way. But the Symbolics executives didn't believe this. They installed a "spy" program on Stallman's computer terminal looking for evidence against him. However, when they took their case to MIT administration, around the start of 1983, they had little evidence to present: a dozen places in the sources where both versions had been changed and appeared similar.

When the AI Lab administrators showed Stallman Symbolics' supposed evidence, he refuted it, showing that the similarities were actually held over from before the fork. Then he turned the logic around: if, after the thousands of lines he had written, Symbolics could produce no better evidence than this, it demonstrated that Stallman's diligent efforts to avoid copying were effective. The AI Lab approved Stallman's work, which he continued till the end of 1983.[14]

Stallman did make a change in his practices, though. "Just to be ultra safe, I no longer read their source code [for new features and major changes]. I used only the documentation and wrote the code from that." For the biggest new features, rather than wait for Symbolics to release documentation, he designed them on his own; later, when the Symbolics documentation appeared, he added compatibility with Symbolics' interface for the feature. Then he read Symbolics' source code changes to find minor bugs they had fixed, and fixed each of them differently.

The experience solidified Stallman's resolve. As Stallman designed replacements for Symbolics' new features, he also enlisted members of the AI Lab to keep using the MIT system, so as to provide a continuous stream of bug reports. MIT continued giving LMI direct access to the changes. "I was going to punish Symbolics if it was the last thing I did," Stallman says. Such statements are revealing. Not only do they shed light on Stallman's nonpacifist nature, they also reflect the intense level of emotion triggered by the conflict.

The level of despair owed much to what Stallman viewed as the "destruction" of his "home" – i.e., the demise of the AI Lab's close-knit hacker subculture. In a later email interview with Levy, Stallman would liken himself to the historical figure Ishi, the last surviving member of the Yahi, a Pacific Northwest tribe wiped out during the Indian wars of the 1860s and 1870s. The analogy casts Stallman's survival in epic, almost mythical, terms.[15] The hackers who worked for Symbolics saw it differently. Instead of seeing Symbolics as an exterminating force, many of Stallman's colleagues saw it as a belated bid for relevance. In commercializing the Lisp Machine, the company pushed hacker principles of engineer-driven software design out of the ivory-tower confines of the AI Lab and into the corporate marketplace where manager-driven design principles held sway. Rather than viewing Stallman as a holdout, many hackers saw him as the representative of an obsolete practice.

Personal hostilities also affected the situation. Even before Symbolics hired away most of the AI Lab's hacker staff, Stallman says many of the hackers who later joined Symbolics were shunning him. "I was no longer getting invited to go to Chinatown," Stallman recalls. "The custom started by Greenblatt was that if you went out to dinner, you went around or sent a message asking anybody at the lab if they also wanted to go. Sometime around 1980-1981, I stopped getting asked. They were not only not inviting me, but one person later confessed that he had been pressured to lie to me to keep their going away to dinner without me a secret."

Although Stallman felt hurt by this petty form of ostracism, there was nothing to be done about it. The Symbolics ultimatum changed the matter from a personal rejection to a broader injustice. When Symbolics excluded its source changes from redistribution, as a means to defeat its rival, Stallman determined to thwart Symbolics' goal. By holing up in his MIT offices and writing equivalents for each new software feature and fix, he gave users of the MIT system, including LMI customers, access to the same features as Symbolics users.

It also guaranteed Stallman's legendary status within the hacker community. Already renowned for his work with Emacs, Stallman's ability to match the output of an entire team of Symbolics programmers – a team that included more than a few legendary hackers itself – still stands as one of the major human accomplishments of the Information Age, or of any age for that matter. Dubbing it a "master hack" and Stallman himself a "virtual John Henry of computer code," author Steven Levy notes that many of his Symbolics-employed rivals had no choice but to pay their idealistic former comrade grudging respect. Levy quotes Bill Gosper, a hacker who eventually went to work for Symbolics in the company's Palo Alto office, expressing amazement over Stallman's output during this period:

> I can see something Stallman wrote, and I might decide it was bad (probably not, but somebody could convince me it was bad), and I would still say, "But wait a minute – Stallman doesn't have anybody to argue with all night over there. He's working alone! It's incredible anyone could do this alone!"[16]

For Stallman, the months spent playing catch up with Symbolics evoke a mixture of pride and profound sadness. As a dyed-in-the-wool liberal whose father had served in World War II, Stallman is no pacifist. In many ways, the Symbolics war offered the rite of passage toward which Stallman had been careening ever since joining the AI Lab staff a decade before. At the same time, however, it coincided with the traumatic destruction of the AI Lab hacker culture that had nurtured Stallman since his teenage years. One day, while taking a break from writing code, Stallman experienced a traumatic moment passing through the lab's equipment room. There, Stallman encountered the hulking, unused frame of the PDP-10 machine. Startled by the dormant lights, lights that once actively blinked out a silent code indicating the status of the internal program, Stallman says the emotional impact was not unlike coming across a beloved family member's well-preserved corpse.

"I started crying right there in the machine room," he says. "Seeing the machine there, dead, with nobody left to fix it, it all drove home how completely my community had been destroyed."

Stallman would have little opportunity to mourn. The Lisp Machine, despite all the furor it invoked and all the labor that had gone into making it, was merely a sideshow to the large battles in the technology marketplace. The relentless pace of computer miniaturization was bringing in newer, more powerful microprocessors that would soon incorporate the machine's hardware and software capabilities like a modern metropolis swallowing up an ancient desert village.

Riding atop this microprocessor wave were hundreds – thousands – of proprietary software programs, each protected by a patchwork of user licenses and nondisclosure agreements that made it impossible for hackers to review or share source code. The licenses were crude and ill-fitting, but by 1983 they had become strong enough to satisfy the courts and scare away would-be interlopers. Software, once a form of garnish most hardware companies gave away to make their expensive computer systems more flavorful, was quickly becoming the main dish. In their increasing hunger for new games and features, users were putting aside the traditional demand to review the recipe after every meal.

Nowhere was this state of affairs more evident than in the realm of personal computer systems. Companies such as Apple Computer and Commodore were minting fresh millionaires selling machines with built-in operating systems. Unaware of the hacker culture and its distaste for binary-only software, many of these users saw little need to protest when these companies failed to attach the accompanying source-code files. A few anarchic adherents of the hacker ethic helped propel that ethic into this new marketplace, but for the most part, the marketplace rewarded the programmers speedy enough to write new programs and savvy enough to write End User License Agreements to lock them up tight.

One of the most notorious of these programmers was Bill Gates, a Harvard dropout two years Stallman's junior. Although Stallman

didn't know it at the time, seven years before sending out his message
to thenet.unix-wizards newsgroup, Gates, a budding entrepreneur and
general partner with the Albuquerque-based software firm Micro-Soft,
later spelled as Microsoft, had sent out his own open letter to the
software-developer community. Written in response to the PC users
copying Micro-Soft's software programs, Gates' "Open Letter to Hobbyists" had excoriated the notion of communal software development.

"Who can afford to do professional work for nothing?" asked
Gates. "What hobbyist can put three man-years into programming,
finding all bugs, documenting his product, and distributing it for
free?" 17

Although few hackers at the AI Lab saw the missive, Gates' 1976
letter nevertheless represented the changing attitude toward software
both among commercial software companies and commercial software
developers. Why treat software as a zero-cost commodity when the
market said otherwise? As the 1970s gave way to the 1980s, selling
software became more than a way to recoup costs; it became a political
statement. At a time when the Reagan Administration was rushing
to dismantle many of the federal regulations and spending programs
that had been built up during the half century following the Great
Depression, more than a few software programmers saw the hacker
ethic as anticompetitive and, by extension, un-American. At best, it
was a throwback to the anticorporate attitudes of the late 1960s and
early 1970s. Like a Wall Street banker discovering an old tie-dyed shirt
hiding between French-cuffed shirts and double-breasted suits, many
computer programmers treated the hacker ethic as an embarrassing
reminder of an idealistic age.

For a man who had spent the entire 1960s as a throwback to the
1950s, Stallman didn't mind living out of step with his peers. As a
programmer used to working with the best machines and the best software, however, Stallman faced what he could only describe as a "stark
moral choice": either swallow his ethical objection for "proprietary"
software – the term Stallman and his fellow hackers used to describe
any program that carried copyright terms or an end-user license that
restricted copying and modification – or dedicate his life to building
an alternate, nonproprietary system of software programs. After his
two-year battle with Symbolics, Stallman felt confident enough to un-
dertake the latter option. "I suppose I could have stopped working

on computers altogether," Stallman says. "I had no special skills, but I'm sure I could have become a waiter. Not at a fancy restaurant, probably, but I could've been a waiter somewhere."

Being a waiter – i.e., dropping out of programming altogether – would have meant completely giving up an activity, computer programming, that had given him so much pleasure. Looking back on his life since moving to Cambridge, Stallman finds it easy to identify lengthy periods when software programming provided the only pleasure. Rather than drop out, Stallman decided to stick it out.

An Atheist, Stallman rejects notions such as fate, karma, or a divine calling in life. Nevertheless, he does feel that the decision to shun proprietary software and build an operating system to help others do the same was a natural one. After all, it was Stallman's own personal combination of stubbornness, foresight, and coding virtuosity that led him to consider a fork in the road most others didn't know existed. In his article, "The GNU Project," Stallman affirms agreement with the ideals encapsulated in the words of the Jewish sage Hillel:

> If I am not for myself, who will be for me? If I am only for myself, what am I? If not now, when?[18]

Speaking to audiences, Stallman avoids the religious route and expresses the decision in pragmatic terms. "I asked myself: what could I, an operating-system developer, do to improve the situation? It wasn't until I examined the question for a while that I realized an operating-system developer was exactly what was needed to solve the problem."

Once he recognized that, Stallman says, everything else "fell into place." In 1983, MIT was acquiring second-generation Lisp Machines from Symbolics, on which the MIT Lisp Machine system could not possibly run. Once most of the MIT machines were replaced, he would be unable to continue maintaining that system effectively for lack of users' bug reports. He would have to stop. But he also wanted to stop. The MIT Lisp Machine system was not free software: even though users could get the source code, they could not redistribute it freely. Meanwhile, the goal of continuing the MIT system had already been achieved: LMI had survived and was developing software on its own.

Stallman didn't want to spend his whole life punishing those who had destroyed his old community. He wanted to build a new one. He

decided to denounce software that would require him to compromise
his ethical beliefs, and devote his life to the creation of programs that
would make it easier for him and others to escape from it. Pledging
to build a free software operating system "or die trying – of old age,
of course," Stallman quips, he resigned from the MIT staff in January,
1984, to build GNU.

The resignation distanced Stallman's work from the legal auspices
of MIT. Still, Stallman had enough friends and allies within the AI Lab
to continue using the facilities, and later his own office. He also had
the ability to secure outside consulting gigs to underwrite the early
stages of the GNU Project. In resigning from MIT, however, Stallman
negated any debate about conflict of interest or Institute ownership of
the software. The man whose early adulthood fear of social isolation
had driven him deeper and deeper into the AI Lab's embrace was now
building a legal firewall between himself and that environment.

For the first few months, Stallman operated in isolation from the
Unix community as well. Although his announcement to the net.unix-
wizards group had attracted sympathetic responses, few volunteers
signed on to join the crusade in its early stages.

"The community reaction was pretty much uniform," recalls Rich
Morin, leader of a Unix user group at the time. "People said, 'Oh,
that's a great idea. Show us your code. Show us it can be done.'"

Aware that the job was enormous, Stallman decided to try to
reuse existing free software wherever possible. So he began looking for existing free programs and tools that could be converted into
GNU programs and tools. One of the first candidates was a compiler
named VUCK, which converted programs written in the popular C
programming language into machine-runnable code. Translated from
the Dutch, the program's acronym stood for the Free University Compiler Kit. Optimistic, Stallman asked the program's author if the program was free. When the author informed him that the words "Free
University" were a reference to the Vrije Universiteit in Amsterdam,
and that the program was not free, Stallman was chagrined.

"He responded derisively, stating that the university was free but
the compiler was not," recalls Stallman. He had not only refused
to help – he suggested Stallman drop his plan to develop GNU, and
instead write some add-ons to boost sales of VUCK, in return for a

share of the profits. "I therefore decided that my first program for the GNU Project would be a multi-language, multi-platform compiler."[19]

Instead of VUCK, Stallman found the Pastel compiler ("off-color Pascal"), written by programmers at Lawrence Livermore National Lab. According to what they said when they gave him a copy, the compiler was free to copy and modify. Unfortunately, the program was unsuitable for the job, because its memory requirements were enormous. It parsed the entire input file in core memory, then retained all the internal data until it finished compiling the file. On mainframe systems this design had been forgivable. On Unix systems it was a crippling barrier, since even 32-bit machines that ran Unix were often unable to provide so much memory to a program. Stallman made substantial progress at first, building a C-compatible frontend to the compiler and testing it on the larger Vax, whose system could handle large memory spaces. When he tried porting the system to the 68010, and investigated why it crashed, he discovered the memory size problem, and concluded he would have to build a totally new compiler from scratch. Stallman eventually did this, producing the GNU C Compiler or GCC. But it was not clear in 1984 what to do about the compiler, so he decided to let those plans gel while turning his attention to other parts of GNU.

In September of 1984, thus, Stallman began development of a GNU version of Emacs, the replacement for the program he had been supervising for a decade. Within the Unix community, the two native editor programs were vi, written by Sun Microsystems cofounder Bill Joy, and ed, written by Bell Labs scientist (and Unix cocreator) Ken Thompson. Both were useful and popular, but neither offered the endlessly expandable nature of Emacs.

Looking back, Stallman says he didn't view the decision in strategic terms. "I wanted an Emacs, and I had a good opportunity to develop one."

Once again, Stallman had found existing code with which he hoped to save time. In writing a Unix version of Emacs, Stallman was soon following the footsteps of Carnegie Mellon graduate student James Gosling, author of a C-based version dubbed Gosling Emacs or Gosmacs. Gosling's version of Emacs included an interpreter for a simplified offshoot of the Lisp language, called Mocklisp. Although Gosling had put Gosmacs under copyright and had sold the rights to UniPress, a privately held software company, Stallman received the assurances of a fellow developer who had participated in early Gosmacs development. According to the developer, Gosling, while a Ph.D. student at Carnegie Mellon, had given him permission by email to distribute his own version of Gosmacs in exchange for his contribution to the code.

At first Stallman thought he would change only the user-level commands, to implement full compatibility with the original PDP-10 Emacs. However, when he found how weak Mocklisp was in comparison with real Lisp, he felt compelled to replace it with a true Lisp system. This made it natural to rewrite most of the higher-level code of Gosmacs in a completely different way, taking advantage of the greater power and flexible data structures of Lisp. By mid-1985, in GNU Emacs as released on the Internet, only a few files still had code remaining from Gosmacs.

Then UniPress caught wind of Stallman's project, and denied that the other developer had received permission to distribute his own version of Gosmacs. He could not find a copy of the old email to defend his claim. Stallman eliminated this problem by writing replacements for the few modules that remained from Gosmacs.

Nevertheless, the notion of developers selling off software rights – indeed, the very notion of developers having such powers to sell in the first place – rankled Stallman. In a 1986 speech at the Swedish Royal Technical Institute, Stallman cited the UniPress incident as yet another example of the dangers associated with proprietary software.

"Sometimes I think that perhaps one of the best things I could do with my life is find a gigantic pile of proprietary software that was a trade secret, and start handing out copies on a street corner so it wouldn't be a trade secret any more," said Stallman. "Perhaps that would be a much more efficient way for me to give people new free software than actually writing it myself; but everyone is too cowardly to even take it."[20]

Despite the stress it generated, the dispute over Gosling's code would assist both Stallman and the free software movement in the long term. It would force Stallman to address the weaknesses of the Emacs Commune and the informal trust system that had allowed problematic offshoots to emerge. It would also force Stallman to sharpen the free software movement's political objectives. Following the release of GNU Emacs in 1985, Stallman issued *The GNU Manifesto*, an expansion of the original announcement posted in September, 1983. Stallman included within the document a lengthy section devoted to the many arguments used by commercial and academic programmers to justify the proliferation of proprietary software programs. One argument, "Don't programmers deserve a reward for their creativity," earned a response encapsulating Stallman's anger over the recent Gosling Emacs episode:

"If anything deserves a reward, it is social contribution," Stallman wrote. "Creativity can be a social contribution, but only in so far [sic] as society is free to use the results. If programmers deserve to be rewarded for creating innovative programs, by the same token they deserve to be punished if they restrict the use of these programs."[21]

With the release of GNU Emacs, the GNU Project finally had code to show. It also had the burdens of any software-based enterprise. As more and more Unix developers began playing with the software, money, gifts, and requests for tapes began to pour in. To address the business side of the GNU Project, Stallman drafted a few of his colleagues and formed the Free Software Foundation (FSF), a nonprofit organization dedicated to speeding the GNU Project towards its goal. With Stallman as president and various friends and hacker allies as board members, the FSF helped provide a corporate face for the GNU Project.

Robert Chassell, a programmer then working at Lisp Machines, Inc., became one of five charter board members at the Free Software Foundation following a dinner conversation with Stallman. Chassell also served as the organization's treasurer, a role that started small but quickly grew.

"I think in '85 our total expenses and revenue were something in the order of $23,000, give or take," Chassell recalls. "Richard had his office, and we borrowed space. I put all the stuff, especially the tapes, under my desk. It wasn't until sometime later LMI loaned us some space where we could store tapes and things of that sort."

In addition to providing a face, the Free Software Foundation provided a center of gravity for other disenchanted programmers. The Unix market that had seemed so collegial even at the time of Stallman's initial GNU announcement was becoming increasingly competitive. In an attempt to tighten their hold on customers, companies were starting to deny users access to Unix source code, a trend that only speeded the number of inquiries into ongoing GNU software projects.

The Unix wizards who once regarded Stallman as a noisy kook were now beginning to see him as a software prophet or a software Cassandra, according as they felt hope or despair over escaping the problems he identified.

"A lot of people don't realize, until they've had it happen to them, how frustrating it can be to spend a few years working on a software program only to have it taken away," says Chassell, summarizing the feelings and opinions of the correspondents writing in to the FSF during the early years. "After that happens a couple of times, you start to say to yourself, 'Hey, wait a minute.'"

For Chassell, the decision to participate in the Free Software Foundation came down to his own personal feelings of loss. Prior to LMI, Chassell had been working for hire, writing an introductory book on Unix for Cadmus, Inc., a Cambridge-area software company. When Cadmus folded, taking the rights to the book down with it, Chassell says he attempted to buy the rights back with no success.

"As far as I know, that book is still sitting on a shelf somewhere, unusable, uncopyable, just taken out of the system," Chassell says. "It was quite a good introduction if I may say so myself. It would have taken maybe three or four months to convert [the book] into a perfectly usable introduction to GNU/Linux today. The whole experience, aside from what I have in my memory, was lost."

Forced to watch his work sink into the mire while his erstwhile employer struggled through bankruptcy, Chassell says he felt a hint of the anger that drove Stallman to fits of apoplexy. "The main clarity, for me, was the sense that if you want to have a decent life, you don't want to have bits of it closed off," Chassell says. "This whole idea of having the freedom to go in and to fix something and modify it, whatever it may be, it really makes a difference. It makes one think happily that after you've lived a few years that what you've done is worthwhile. Because otherwise it just gets taken away and thrown out or abandoned or, at the very least, you no longer have any relation to it. It's like losing a bit of your life."

Endnotes

[1]See Richard Stallman, "Initial GNU Announcement" (September 1983).

[2]*Ibid.*

[3]*Ibid.*

[4]See Marshall Kirk McKusick, "Twenty Years of Berkeley Unix," *Open Sources* (O'Reilly & Associates, Inc., 1999): 38.

[5]See Richard Stallman (1986).

[6]*Ibid.*

[7]Multiple sources: see Richard Stallman interview, Gerald Sussman email, and *Jargon File 3.0.0* at http://catb.org/jargon/html/T/TWENEX.html.

[8]See http://www.as.cmu.edu/~geek/humor/See_Figure_1.txt.

[9]See Richard Stallman (1986).

[10]See "MIT AI Lab Tourist Policy," http://www.art.net/~hopkins/Don/text/tourist-policy.html.

[11]See Richard Stallman (1986).

[12]*Ibid.*

[13]See Steve Levy, *Hackers*, page 423.

[14]*The Brain Makers* by H. P. Newquist says inaccurately that the AI Lab told Stallman to stay away from the Lisp Machine project.

[15]Steven Levy in *Hackers* had this period in mind when he described Stallman as the "last of the true hackers," but his intended meaning was not what you might think. Levy used the term "true hackers" to distinguish the MIT hacker community from two other hacker communities described later in the book, to which he gave other names. When this community had dissolved, leaving only Stallman, he therefore became the last of the "true hackers." Levy did not mean that nobody else was truly a hacker, but people tend to interpret his words that way, especially those who see them without reading the explanations in Levy's book. Stallman has never described himself using those words of Levy's.

[16]See Steven Levy, *Hackers* (Penguin USA [paperback], 1984): 426

[17]See Bill Gates, "An Open Letter to Hobbyists" (February 3, 1976). To view an online copy of this letter, go to http://en.wikipedia.org/wiki/Open_Letter_to_Hobbyists.

[18]See http://www.gnu.org/gnu/the-gnu-project.html. Stallman adds his own footnote to this statement, writing, "As an Atheist, I don't follow any religious leaders, but I sometimes find I admire something one of them has said."

[19]See Richard Stallman, "The GNU Operating System and the Free Software Movement," *Open Sources* (O'Reilly & Associates, Inc., 1999): 65.

[20]See Richard Stallman (1986).

[21]See Richard Stallman, *The GNU Manifesto* (1985), http://www.gnu.org/gnu/manifesto.html.

Chapter 8

St. Ignucius

The Maui High Performance Computing Center is located in a single-story building in the dusty red hills just above the town of Kihei. Framed by million-dollar views and the multimillion dollar real estate of the Silversword Golf Course, the center seems like the ultimate scientific boondoggle. Far from the boxy, sterile confines of Tech Square or even the sprawling research metropolises of Argonne, Illinois and Los Alamos, New Mexico, the MHPCC seems like the kind of place where scientists spend more time on their tans than their post-doctoral research projects.

The image is only half true. Although researchers at the MH-PCC do take advantage of the local recreational opportunities, they also take their work seriously. According to Top500.org, a web site that tracks the most powerful supercomputers in the world, the IBM SP Power3 supercomputer housed within the MHPCC clocks in at 837 billion floating-point operations per second, making it one of 25 most powerful computers in the world. Co-owned and operated by the University of Hawaii and the U.S. Air Force, the machine divides its computer cycles between the number crunching tasks associated with military logistics and high-temperature physics research.

Simply put, the MHPCC is a unique place, a place where the brainy culture of science and engineering and the laid-back culture of the

Hawaiian islands coexist in peaceful equilibrium. A slogan on the lab's 2000 web site sums it up: "Computing in paradise."

It's not exactly the kind of place you'd expect to find Richard Stallman, a man who, when taking in the beautiful view of the nearby Maui Channel through the picture windows of a staffer's office, mutters a terse critique: "Too much sun." Still, as an emissary from one computing paradise to another, Stallman has a message to deliver, even if it means subjecting his hacker eyes to painful solar glare.

The conference room is already full by the time I arrive to catch Stallman's speech. The gender breakdown is a little better than at the New York speech, 85% male, 15% female, but not by much. About half of the audience members wear khaki pants and logo-encrusted golf shirts. The other half seems to have gone native. Dressed in the gaudy flower-print shirts so popular in this corner of the world, their faces are a deep shade of ochre. The only residual indication of geek status are the gadgets: Nokia cell phones, Palm Pilots, and Sony VAIO laptops.

Needless to say, Stallman, who stands in front of the room dressed in plain blue T-shirt, brown polyester slacks, and white socks, sticks out like a sore thumb. The fluorescent lights of the conference room help bring out the unhealthy color of his sun-starved skin.[1] His beard and hair are enough to trigger beads of sweat on even the coolest Hawaiian neck. Short of having the words "mainlander" tattooed on his forehead, Stallman couldn't look more alien if he tried. [RMS: Is there something bad about looking different from others?]

As Stallman putters around the front of the room, a few audience members wearing T-shirts with the logo of the Maui FreeBSD Users Group (MFUG) race to set up camera and audio equipment. FreeBSD, a free software offshoot of the Berkeley Software Distribution, the venerable 1970s academic version of Unix, is technically a competitor to the GNU/Linux operating system. Still, in the hacking world, Stallman speeches are documented with a fervor reminiscent of the Grateful Dead and its legendary army of amateur archivists. As the local free software heads, it's up to the MFUG members to make sure fellow programmers in Hamburg, Mumbai, and Novosibirsk don't miss out on the latest pearls of RMS wisdom.

The analogy to the Grateful Dead is apt. Often, when describing the business opportunities inherent within the free software model, Stallman has held up the Grateful Dead as an example. In refusing to restrict fans' ability to record live concerts, the Grateful Dead became more than a rock group. They became the center of a tribal community dedicated to Grateful Dead music. Over time, that tribal community became so large and so devoted that the band shunned record contracts and supported itself solely through musical tours and live appearances. In 1994, the band's last year as a touring act, the Grateful Dead drew $52 million in gate receipts alone.[2]

While few software companies have been able to match that success, the tribal aspect of the free software community is one reason many in the latter half of the 1990s started to accept the notion that publishing software source code might be a good thing. Hoping to build their own loyal followings, companies such as IBM, Sun Microsystems, and Hewlett Packard have come to accept the letter, if not the spirit, of the Stallman free software message. Describing the GPL as the information-technology industry's *Magna Carta*, ZDNet software columnist Evan Leibovitch sees the growing affection for all things GNU as more than just a trend. "This societal shift is letting users take back control of their futures," Leibovitch writes. "Just as the *Magna Carta* gave rights to British subjects, the GPL enforces consumer rights and freedoms on behalf of the users of computer software."[3]

The tribal aspect of the free software community also helps explain why 40-odd programmers, who might otherwise be working on physics projects or surfing the Web for windsurfing buoy reports, have packed into a conference room to hear Stallman speak.

Unlike the New York speech, Stallman gets no introduction. He also offers no self-introduction. When the FreeBSD people finally get their equipment up and running, Stallman simply steps forward, starts speaking, and steamrolls over every other voice in the room.

"Most of the time when people consider the question of what rules society should have for using software, the people considering it are from software companies, and they consider the question from a self-serving perspective," says Stallman, opening his speech. "What rules can we impose on everybody else so they have to pay us lots of money? I had the good fortune in the 1970s to be part of a community of programmers who shared software. And because of this I always like to look at the same issue from a different direction to ask: what kind of rules make possible a good society that is good for the people who are in it? And therefore I reach completely different answers."

Once again, Stallman quickly segues into the parable of the Xerox laser printer, taking a moment to deliver the same dramatic finger-pointing gestures to the crowd. He also devotes a minute or two to the GNU/Linux name.

"Some people say to me, 'Why make such a fuss about getting credit for this system? After all, the important thing is the job is done, not whether you get recognition for it.' Well, this would be wise advice if it were true. But the job wasn't to build an operating system; the job is to spread freedom to the users of computers. And to do that we have to make it possible to do everything with computers in freedom."[4]

Adds Stallman, "There's a lot more work to do."

For some in the audience, this is old material. For others, it's a little arcane. When a member of the golf-shirt contingent starts dozing off, Stallman stops the speech and asks somebody to wake the person up.

"Somebody once said my voice was so soothing, he asked if I was some kind of healer," says Stallman, drawing a quick laugh from the crowd. "I guess that probably means I can help you drift gently into a blissful, relaxing sleep. And some of you might need that. I guess I shouldn't object if you do. If you need to sleep, by all means do."

The speech ends with a brief discussion of software patents, a growing issue of concern both within the software industry and within the free software community. Like Napster, software patents reflect the awkward nature of applying laws and concepts written for the physical world to the frictionless universe of information technology.

Copyright law and patent law work differently, and have totally different effects in the software field. The copyright on a program controls the copying and adaptation of that program's code, and it belongs to the program's developer. But copyright does not cover ideas. In other words, a developer is free, under copyright, to implement in his own code features and commands he has seen in existing programs. Those aspects are ideas, not expression, and thus outside the scope of copyright law.

It is likewise lawful – though hard work – to decode how a binary program works, and then implement the same ideas and algorithms in different code. This practice is known as "reverse engineering."

Software patents work differently. According to the U.S. Patent Office, companies and individuals can obtain patents for computing ideas that are innovative (or, at least, unknown to the Patent Office). In theory, this allows the patent-holder to trade off disclosure of the technique for a specific monopoly lasting a minimum of 20 years after the patent filing. In practice, the disclosure is of limited value to the public, since the operation of the program is often self-evident, and could in any case be determined by reverse engineering. Unlike copyright, a patent gives its holder the power to forbid the independent development of software programs which use the patented idea.

In the software industry, where 20 years can cover the entire life cycle of a marketplace, patents take on a strategic weight. Where companies such as Microsoft and Apple once battled over copyright and the "look and feel" of various technologies, today's Internet companies use patents as a way to stake out individual applications and business models, the most notorious example being Amazon.com's 2000 attempt to patent the company's "one-click" online shopping process. For most companies, however, software patents have become a defensive tool, with cross-licensing deals balancing one set of corporate patents against another in a tense form of corporate detente. Still, in a few notable cases of computer encryption and graphic imaging algorithms, software vendors have successfully stifled rival developments. For instance, some font-rendering features are missing from free software because of patent threats from Apple.

For Stallman, the software-patent issue dramatizes the need for eternal hacker vigilance. It also underlines the importance of stressing the political benefits of free software programs over the competitive benefits. Stallman says competitive performance and price, two areas where free software operating systems such as GNU/Linux and FreeBSD already hold a distinct advantage over their proprietary counterparts, are side issues compared to the large issues of user and developer freedom.

This position is controversial within the community: open source advocates emphasize the utilitarian advantages of free software over the political advantages. Rather than stress the political significance of free software programs, open source advocates have chosen to stress the engineering integrity of the hacker development model. Citing the power of peer review, the open source argument paints programs such as GNU/Linux or FreeBSD as better built, better inspected and, by extension, more trustworthy to the average user.

That's not to say the term "open source" doesn't have its political implications. For open source advocates, the term open source serves two purposes. First, it eliminates the confusion associated with the word "free," a word many businesses interpret as meaning "zero cost." Second, it allows companies to examine the free software phenomenon on a technological, rather than ethical, basis. Eric Raymond, cofounder of the Open Source Initiative and one of the leading hackers to endorse the term, explained his refusal to follow Stallman's political path in a 1999 essay, titled "Shut Up and Show Them the Code":

> RMS's rhetoric is very seductive to the kind of people we are. We hackers are thinkers and idealists who readily resonate with appeals to "principle" and "freedom" and "rights." Even when we disagree with bits of his program, we want RMS's rhetorical style to work; we think it ought to work; we tend to be puzzled and disbelieving when it fails on the 95% of people who aren't wired like we are.[5]

Included among that 95%, Raymond writes, are the bulk of business managers, investors, and nonhacker computer users who, through sheer weight of numbers, tend to decide the overall direction of the commercial software marketplace. Without a way to win these people over, Raymond argues, programmers are doomed to pursue their ideology on the periphery of society:

> When RMS insists that we talk about "computer users' rights," he's issuing a dangerously attractive invitation to us to repeat old failures. It's one we should reject – not because his principles are wrong, but because that kind of language, applied to software, simply does not persuade anybody but us. In fact, it confuses and repels most people outside our culture.[6]

Stallman, however, rejects Raymond's premises:

Raymond's attempt to explain our failure is misleading because we have not failed. Our goal is large, and we have a long way to go, but we have also come a long way.

Raymond's pessimistic assertion about the values of non-hackers is an exaggeration. Many non-hackers are more concerned with the political issues we focus on than with the technical advantages that open source emphasizes. This often includes political leaders too, though not in all countries.

It was the ethical ideals of free software, not "better software," which persuaded the presidents of Ecuador and Brazil to move government agencies to free software. They are not geeks, but they understand freedom.

But the principal flaw in the open source argument, according to Stallman, is that it leads to weaker conclusions. It convinces many users to run some programs which are free, but does not offer them any reason to migrate entirely to free software. This partially gives them freedom, but does not teach them to recognize it and value it as such, so they remain likely to let it drop and lose it. For instance, what happens when the improvement of free software is blocked by a patent?

Most open source advocates are equally, if not more, vociferous as Stallman when it comes to opposing software patents. So too are most proprietary software developers, since patents threaten their projects too. However, pointing to software patents' tendency to put areas of software functionality off limits, Stallman contrasts what the free software idea and the open source idea imply about such cases.

"It's not because we don't have the talent to make better software," says Stallman. "It's because we don't have the right. Somebody has prohibited us from serving the public. So what's going to happen when users encounter these gaps in free software? Well, if they have been persuaded by the open source movement that these freedoms are good because they lead to more-powerful reliable software, they're likely to say, 'You didn't deliver what you promised. This software's not more powerful. It's missing this feature. You lied to me.' But if they have come to agree with the free software movement, that the freedom is important in itself, then they will say, 'How dare those people stop me from having this feature and my freedom too.' And with that kind of response, we may survive the hits that we're going to take as these patents explode."

Watching Stallman deliver his political message in person, it is hard to see anything confusing or repellent. Stallman's appearance may seem off-putting, but his message is logical. When an audience member asks if, in shunning proprietary software, free software proponents lose the ability to keep up with the latest technological advancements, Stallman answers the question in terms of his own personal beliefs. "I think that freedom is more important than mere technical advance," he says. "I would always choose a less advanced free program rather than a more advanced nonfree program, because I won't give up my freedom for something like that [advance]. My rule is, if I can't share it with you, I won't take it."

In the minds of those who assume ethics means religion, such answers reinforce the quasi-religious nature of the Stallman message. However, unlike a Jew keeping kosher or a Mormon refusing to drink alcohol, Stallman is not obeying a commandment, but simply refusing to cede his freedom. His speech explains the practical requisites for doing so: a proprietary program takes away your freedom, so if you want freedom, you need to reject the program.

Stallman paints his decision to use free software in place of proprietary in the color of a personal belief he hopes others will come to share. As software evangelists go, Stallman avoids forcing those beliefs down listeners' throats. Then again, a listener rarely leaves a Stallman speech not knowing where the true path to software righteousness lies.

As if to drive home this message, Stallman punctuates his speech with an unusual ritual. Pulling a black robe out of a plastic grocery bag, Stallman puts it on. Then he pulls out a reflective brown computer disk and places it on his head. The crowd lets out a startled laugh.

"I am St. IGNUcius of the Church of Emacs," says Stallman, raising his right hand in mock-blessing. "I bless your computer, my child."

The laughter turns into full-blown applause after a few seconds. As audience members clap, the computer disk on Stallman's head catches the glare of an overhead light, eliciting a perfect halo effect. In the blink of an eye, Stallman resembles a Russian religious icon.

Stallman dressed as St. IGNUcius. The photo was taken by Stian Eikeland in Bergen, Norway on February 19, 2009.

"Emacs was initially a text editor," says Stallman, explaining the getup. "Eventually it became a way of life for many and a religion for some. We call this religion the Church of Emacs."

The skit is a lighthearted moment of self-parody, a humorous return-jab at the many people who might see Stallman's form of software asceticism as religious fanaticism in disguise. It is also the sound of the other shoe dropping – loudly. It's as if, in donning his robe and halo, Stallman is finally letting listeners off the hook, saying, "It's OK to laugh. I know I'm weird." [RMS: To laugh at someone for being weird is boorish, and it is not my intention to excuse that. But I hope people will laugh at my St. IGNUcius comedy routine.]

Discussing the St. IGNUcius persona afterward, Stallman says he first came up with it in 1996, long after the creation of Emacs but well before the emergence of the "open source" term and the struggle for hacker-community leadership that precipitated it. At the time, Stallman says, he wanted a way to "poke fun at himself," to remind listeners that, though stubborn, Stallman was not the fanatic some made him out to be. It was only later, Stallman adds, that others seized the persona as a convenient way to play up his reputation as software ideologue, as Eric Raymond did in an 1999 interview with the Linux.com web site:

> When I say RMS calibrates what he does, I'm not belittling or accusing him of insincerity. I'm saying that like all good communicators he's got a theatrical streak. Sometimes it's conscious – have you ever seen him in his St. IGNUcius drag, blessing software with a disk platter on his head? Mostly it's unconscious; he's just learned the degree of ir-ritating stimulus that works, that holds attention without (usually) freaking people out.[7]

Stallman takes issue with the Raymond analysis. "It's simply my way of making fun of myself," he says. "The fact that others see it as anything more than that is a reflection of their agenda, not mine."

That said, Stallman does admit to being a ham. "Are you kid-ding?" he says at one point. "I love being the center of attention." To facilitate that process, Stallman says he once enrolled in Toastmas-ters, an organization that helps members bolster their public-speaking skills and one Stallman recommends highly to others. He possesses a stage presence that would be the envy of most theatrical performers and feels a link to vaudevillians of years past. A few days after the Maui High Performance Computing Center speech, I allude to the 1999 LinuxWorld performance and ask Stallman if he has a Groucho Marx complex – i.e., the unwillingness to belong to any club that would have him as a member.[8] Stallman's response is immediate: "No, but I admire Groucho Marx in a lot of ways and certainly have been in some things I say inspired by him. But then I've also been inspired in some ways by Harpo."

The Groucho Marx influence is certainly evident in Stallman's life-long fondness for punning. Then again, punning and wordplay are common hacker traits. Perhaps the most Groucho-like aspect of Stall-man's personality, however, is the deadpan manner in which the puns are delivered. Most come so stealthily – without even the hint of a raised eyebrow or upturned smile – you almost have to wonder if Stallman's laughing at his audience more than the audience is laughing at him.

Watching members of the Maui High Performance Computer Center laugh at the St. IGNUcius parody, such concerns evaporate. While not exactly a standup act, Stallman certainly possesses the chops to keep a roomful of engineers in stitches. "To be a saint in the Church of Emacs does not require celibacy, but it does require making a commitment to living a life of moral purity," he tells the Maui audience. "You must exorcise the evil proprietary operating systems from all your computers, and then install a wholly [holy] free operating system. And then you must install only free software on top of that. If you make this commitment and live by it, then you too will be a saint in the Church of Emacs, and you too may have a halo."

The St. IGNUcius skit ends with a brief inside joke. On most Unix systems and Unix-related offshoots, the primary competitor program to Emacs is vi, pronounced vee-eye, a text-editing program developed by former UC Berkeley student and current Sun Microsystems chief scientist, Bill Joy. Before doffing his "halo," Stallman pokes fun at the rival program. "People sometimes ask me if it is a sin in the Church of Emacs to use vi," he says. "Using a free version of vi is not a sin; it is a penance. So happy hacking."[9]

After a brief question-and-answer session, audience members gather around Stallman. A few ask for autographs. "I'll sign this," says Stallman, holding up one woman's print out of the GNU General Public License, "but only if you promise me to use the term GNU/Linux instead of Linux" (when referring to the system), "and tell all your friends to do likewise."

The comment merely confirms a private observation. Unlike other stage performers and political figures, Stallman has no "off" mode. Aside from the St. IGNUcius character, the ideologue you see onstage is the ideologue you meet backstage. Later that evening, during a dinner conversation in which a programmer mentions his affinity for "open source" programs, Stallman, between bites, upbraids his tablemate: "You mean free software. That's the proper way to refer to it."

During the question-and-answer session, Stallman admits to playing the pedagogue at times. "There are many people who say, 'Well, first let's invite people to join the community, and then let's teach them about freedom.' And that could be a reasonable strategy, but what we have is almost everybody's inviting people to join the community, and hardly anybody's teaching them about freedom once they come in."

The result, Stallman says, is something akin to a third-world city. "You have millions of people moving in and building shantytowns, but nobody's working on step two: getting them out of those shantytowns. If you think talking about software freedom is a good strategy, please join in doing step two. There are plenty working on step one. We need more people working on step two."

Working on "step two" means driving home the issue that freedom, not acceptance, is the root issue of the free software movement. Those who hope to reform the proprietary software industry from the inside are on a fool's errand. "Change from the inside is risky," Stallman stays. "Unless you're working at the level of a Gorbachev, you're going to be neutralized."

Hands pop up. Stallman points to a member of the golf shirt-wearing contingent. "Without patents, how would you suggest dealing with commercial espionage?"

"Well, those two questions have nothing to do with each other, really," says Stallman.

"But I mean if someone wants to steal another company's piece of software."

Stallman's recoils as if hit by a poisonous spray. "Wait a second," Stallman says. "Steal? I'm sorry, there's so much prejudice in that statement that the only thing I can say is that I reject that prejudice." Then he turns to the substance of the question. "Companies that develop nonfree software and other things keep lots and lots of trade secrets, and so that's not really likely to change. In the old days – even in the 1980s – for the most part programmers were not aware that there were even software patents and were paying no attention to them. What happened was that people published the interesting ideas, and if they were not in the free software movement, they kept secret the little details. And now they patent those broad ideas and keep secret the little details. So as far as what you're describing, patents really make no difference to it one way or another."

"But if it doesn't affect their publication," a new audience member jumps in, his voice trailing off almost as soon as he starts speaking.

"But it does," Stallman says. "Their publication is telling you that this is an idea that's off limits to the rest of the community for 20 years. And what the hell good is that? Besides, they've written it in such a hard way to read, both to obfuscate the idea and to make the patent as broad as possible, that it's basically useless looking at the published information [in the patent] to learn anything anyway. The only reason to look at patents is to see the bad news of what you can't do."

The audience falls silent. The speech, which began at 3:15, is now nearing the 5:00 whistle, and most listeners are already squirming in their seats, antsy to get a jump start on the weekend. Sensing the fatigue, Stallman glances around the room and hastily shuts things down. "So it looks like we're done," he says, following the observation with an auctioneer's "going, going, gone" to flush out any last-minute questioners. When nobody throws their hand up, Stallman signs off with a traditional exit line.

"Happy hacking," he says.

Endnotes

[1] RMS: The idea that skin can be "sun-starved" or that paleness is "unhealthy" is dangerous misinformation; staying out of the sun can't hurt you as long as you have enough Vitamin D. What damages the skin, and can even kill you, is excessive exposure to sunlight.

[2] See "Grateful Dead Time Capsule: 1985-1995 North American Tour Grosses," http://www.dead101.com/1197.htm.

[3] See Evan Leibovitch, "Who's Afraid of Big Bad Wolves," *ZDNet Tech Update* (December 15, 2000), http://www.zdnet.com/news/whos-afraid-of-the-big-bad-wolves/298394.

[4] For narrative purposes, I have hesitated to go in-depth when describing Stallman's full definition of software "freedom." The GNU Project web site lists four fundamental components:

- The freedom to run the program as you wish, for any purpose (freedom 0).

- The freedom to study the program's source code, and change it so that the program does what you wish (freedom 1).

- The freedom to redistribute copies of the program so you can help your neighbor (freedom 2).

- The freedom to distribute copies of your modified versions, so that the whole community can benefit from them (freedom 3).

For more information, please visit "The Free Software Definition" at `http://www.gnu.org/philosophy/free-sw.html`.

[5]See Eric Raymond, "Shut Up and Show Them the Code," online essay, (June 28, 1999), `http://www.catb.org/~esr/writings/shut-up-and-show-them.html`.

[6]*Ibid.*

[7]See "Guest Interview: Eric S. Raymond," *Linux.com* (May 18, 1999), `http://www.linux.com/interviews/19990518/8/`.

[8]RMS: Williams misinterprets Groucho's famous remark by treating it as psychological. It was intended as a jab at the overt antisemitism of many clubs, which was why they would refuse him as a member. I did not understand this either until my mother explained it to me. Williams and I grew up when bigotry had gone underground, and there was no need to veil criticism of bigotry in humor as Groucho did.

[9]The service of the Church of Emacs has developed further since 2001. Users can now join the Church by reciting the Confession of the Faith: "There is no system but GNU, and Linux is one of its kernels." Stallman sometimes mentions the religious ceremony known as the Foobar Mitzvah, the Great Schism between various rival versions of Emacs, and the cult of the Virgin of Emacs (which refers to any person that has not yet learned to use Emacs). In addition, "vi vi vi" has been identified as the Editor of the Beast.

Chapter 9

The GNU General Public License

By the spring of 1985, Richard Stallman had produced the GNU Project's first useful result – a Lisp-based version of Emacs for Unix-like operating systems. To make it available to others as free software, he had to develop the way to release it – in effect, the follow-on for the Emacs Commune.

The tension between the freedom to modify and authorial privilege had been building before Gosmacs. The Copyright Act of 1976 had overhauled U.S. copyright law, extending the legal coverage of copyright to software programs. According to Section 102(b) of the Act, individuals and companies could copyright the "expression" of a software program but not the "actual processes or methods embodied in the program."[1]

Translated, this treated a program much like an algebra textbook: its author can claim copyright on the text but not on the mathematical ideas of algebra or the pedagogical technique employed to explain it. Thus, regardless of what Stallman said about using the code of the original Emacs, other programmers were legally entitled to write their own implementations of the ideas and commands of Emacs, and they did. Gosmacs was one of 30-odd imitations of the original Emacs developed for various computer systems.

The Emacs Commune applied only to the code of the original Emacs program written by Stallman himself. Even if it had been legally enforced, it would not have applied to separately developed imitations such as Gosmacs. Making Gosmacs nonfree was unethical according to the ethical ideas of the free software movement, because (as proprietary software) it did not respect its users' freedom, but this issue had nothing to do with where the ideas in Gosmacs came from.

Under copyright, programmers who wanted to copy code from an existing program (even with changes) had to obtain permission from the original developer. The new law applied copyright even in the absence of copyright notices – though hackers generally did not know this – and the copyright notices too began appearing.

Stallman saw these notices as the flags of an invading, occupying army. Rare was the program that didn't borrow source code from past programs, and yet, with a single stroke of the president's pen, the U.S. government had given programmers and companies the legal power to forbid such reuse. Copyright also injected a dose of formality into what had otherwise been an informal system. Simply put, disputes that had once been settled hacker-to-hacker were now to be settled lawyer-to-lawyer. In such a system, companies, not hackers, held the automatic advantage. Some saw placing one's name in a copyright notice as taking responsibility for the quality of the code, but the copyright notice usually has a company's name, and there are other ways for individuals to say what code they wrote.

However, Stallman also noticed, in the years leading up to the GNU Project, that copyright allowed an author to grant permission for certain activities covered by copyright, and place conditions on them too. "I had seen email messages with copyright notices plus simple 'verbatim copying permitted' licenses," he recalls. "Those definitely were [an] inspiration." These licenses carried the condition not to remove the license. Stallman's idea was to take this a few steps further. For example, a permission notice could allow users to redistribute even modified versions, with the condition that these versions carry the same permission.

Thus Stallman concluded that use of copyright was not necessarily unethical. What was bad about software copyright was the way it was typically used, and designed to be used: to deny the user essential freedoms. Most authors imagined no other way to use it. But copyright could be used in a different way: to make a program free and assure its continued freedom.

By GNU Emacs 16, in early 1985, Stallman drafted a copyright-based license that gave users the right to make and distribute copies. It also gave users the right to make and distribute modified versions, but only under the same license. They could not exercise the unlimited power of copyright over those modified versions, so they could not make their versions proprietary as Gosmacs was. And they had to make the source code available. Those conditions closed the legal gap that would otherwise allow restricted, nonfree versions of GNU Emacs to emerge.

Although helpful in codifying the social contract of the Emacs Commune, the early GNU Emacs license remained too "informal" for its purpose, Stallman says. Soon after forming the Free Software Foundation he began working on a more airtight version, consulting with the other directors and with the attorneys who had helped to set it up.

Mark Fischer, a Boston copyright attorney who initially provided Stallman's legal advice, recalls discussing the license with Stallman during this period. "Richard had very strong views about how it should work," Fischer says, "He had two principles. The first was to make the software absolutely as open as possible." (By the time he said this, Fischer seems to have been influenced by open source supporters; Stallman never sought to make software "open.") "The second was to encourage others to adopt the same licensing practices." The requirements in the license were designed for the second goal.

The revolutionary nature of this final condition would take a while to sink in. At the time, Fischer says, he simply viewed the GNU Emacs license as a simple trade. It put a price tag on GNU Emacs' use. Instead of money, Stallman was charging users access to their own later modifications. That said, Fischer does remember the license terms as unique.

"I think asking other people to accept the price was, if not unique, highly unusual at that time," he says.

In fashioning the GNU Emacs license, Stallman made one major change to the informal tenets of the old Emacs Commune. Where he had once demanded that Commune members send him all the changes they wrote, Stallman now demanded only that they pass along source code and freedom whenever they chose to redistribute the program. In other words, programmers who simply modified Emacs for private use no longer needed to send the source-code changes back to Stallman. In a rare alteration of free software doctrine, Stallman slashed the "price tag" for free software. Users could innovate without Stallman looking over their shoulders, and distribute their versions only when they wished, just so long as all copies came with permission for their possessors to develop and redistribute them further.

Stallman says this change was fueled by his own dissatisfaction with the Big Brother aspect of the original Emacs Commune social contract. As much as he had found it useful for everyone to send him their changes, he came to feel that requiring this was unjust.

"It was wrong to require people to publish all changes," says Stallman. "It was wrong to require them to be sent to one privileged developer. That kind of centralization and privilege for one was not consistent with a society in which all had equal rights."

The GNU Emacs General Public License made its debut on a version of GNU Emacs in 1985. Following the release, Stallman welcomed input from the general hacker community on how to improve the license's language. One hacker to take up the offer was future software activist John Gilmore, then working as a consultant to Sun Microsystems. As part of his consulting work, Gilmore had ported Emacs over to SunOS, the company's in-house version of Unix. In the process of doing so, Gilmore had published the changed version under the GNU Emacs license. Instead of viewing the license as a liability, Gilmore saw it as clear and concise expression of the hacker ethos. "Up until then, most licenses were very informal," Gilmore recalls.

As an example of this informality, Gilmore cites the mid-1980s copyright license of trn, a news reader program written by Larry Wall, a hacker who could go onto later fame as the creator of both the Unix "patch" utility and the Perl scripting language. In the hope of striking a balance between common hacker courtesy and an author's right to dictate the means of commercial publication, Wall used the program's accompanying copyright notice as an editorial sounding board.

127

Copyright (c) 1985, Larry Wall
You may copy the trn kit in whole or in part as long as
you don't try to make money off it, or pretend that you
wrote it.[2]

Such statements, while reflective of the hacker ethic, also reflected
the difficulty of translating the loose, informal nature of that ethic
into the rigid, legal language of copyright. In writing the GNU Emacs
license, Stallman had done more than close up the escape hatch that
permitted proprietary offshoots. He had expressed the hacker ethic in
a manner understandable to both lawyer and hacker alike.

It wasn't long, Gilmore says, before other hackers began discussing
ways to "port" the GNU Emacs license over to their own programs.
Prompted by a conversation on Usenet, Gilmore sent an email to Stallman in November, 1986, suggesting modification:

You should probably remove "EMACS" from the license
and replace it with "SOFTWARE" or something. Soon,
we hope, Emacs will not be the biggest part of the GNU
system, and the license applies to all of it.[3]

Gilmore wasn't the only person suggesting a more general approach. By the end of 1986, Stallman himself was at work with GNU
Project's next major milestone, the source-code debugger GDB. To
release this, he had to modify the GNU Emacs license so it applied to
GDB instead of GNU Emacs. It was not a big job, but it was an opening for possible errors. In 1989, Stallman figured out how to remove
the specific references to Emacs, and express the connection between
the program code and the license solely in the program's source files.
This way, any developer could apply the license to his program without
changing the license. The GNU General Public License, GNU GPL
for short, was born. The GNU Project soon made it the official license
of all existing GNU programs.

In publishing the GPL, Stallman followed the software convention
of using decimal numbers to indicate versions with minor changes and
whole numbers to indicate versions with major changes. The first
version, in 1989, was labeled Version 1.0. The license contained a
preamble spelling out its political intentions:

The General Public License is designed to make sure that you have the freedom to give away or sell copies of free software, that you receive source code or can get it if you want it, that you can change the software or use pieces of it in new free programs; and that you know you can do these things.

To protect your rights, we need to make restrictions that forbid anyone to deny you these rights or to ask you to surrender the rights. These restrictions translate to certain responsibilities for you if you distribute copies of the software, or if you modify it.[4]

As hacks go, the GPL stands as one of Stallman's best. It created a system of communal ownership within the normally proprietary confines of copyright law. More importantly, it demonstrated the intellectual similarity between legal code and software code. Implicit within the GPL's preamble was a profound message: instead of viewing copyright law with suspicion, hackers should view it as a dangerous system that could be hacked.

"The GPL developed much like any piece of free software with a large community discussing its structure, its respect or the opposite in their observation, needs for tweaking and even to compromise it mildly for greater acceptance," says Jerry Cohen, another attorney who advised Stallman after Fischer departed. "The process worked very well and GPL in its several versions has gone from widespread skeptical and at times hostile response to widespread acceptance."

In a 1986 interview with *BYTE* magazine, Stallman summed up the GPL in colorful terms. In addition to proclaiming hacker values, Stallman said, readers should also "see it as a form of intellectual jujitsu, using the legal system that software hoarders have set up against them."[5] Years later, Stallman would describe the GPL's creation in less hostile terms. "I was thinking about issues that were in a sense ethical and in a sense political and in a sense legal," he says. "I had to try to do what could be sustained by the legal system that we're in. In spirit the job was that of legislating the basis for a new society, but since I wasn't a government, I couldn't actually change any laws. I had to try to do this by building on top of the existing legal system, which had not been designed for anything like this."

About the time Stallman was pondering the ethical, political, and legal issues associated with free software, a California hacker named Don Hopkins mailed him a manual for the 68000 microprocessor. Hopkins, a Unix hacker and fellow science-fiction buff, had borrowed the manual from Stallman a while earlier. As a display of gratitude, Hopkins decorated the return envelope with a number of stickers obtained at a local science-fiction convention. One sticker in particular caught Stallman's eye. It read, "Copyleft (L), All Rights Reversed." Stallman, inspired by the sticker, nicknamed the legal technique employed in the GNU Emacs license (and later in the GNU GPL) "Copyleft," jocularly symbolized by a backwards "C" in a circle. Over time, the nickname would become general Free Software Foundation terminology for any copyright license "making a program free software and requiring all modified and extended versions of the program to be free software as well."

The German sociologist Max Weber once proposed that all great religions are built upon the "routinization" or "institutionalization" of charisma. Every successful religion, Weber argued, converts the charisma or message of the original religious leader into a social, political, and ethical apparatus more easily translatable across cultures and time.

While not religious per se, the GNU GPL certainly qualifies as an interesting example of this "routinization" process at work in the modern, decentralized world of software development. Since its unveiling, programmers and companies who have otherwise expressed little loyalty or allegiance to Stallman have willingly accepted the GPL bargain at face value. Thousands have also accepted the GPL as a preemptive protective mechanism for their own software programs. Even those who reject the GPL conditions as too limiting still credit it as influential.

One hacker falling into this latter group was Keith Bostic, a University of California employee at the time of the GPL 1.0 release. Bostic's department, the Computer Systems Research Group (SRG), had been involved in Unix development since the late 1970s and was responsible for many key parts of Unix, including the TCP/IP networking protocol, the cornerstone of modern Internet communications. By the late 1980s, AT&T, the original owner of the Unix software, began to focus on commercializing Unix and began looking to the Berkeley

Software Distribution, or BSD, the academic version of Unix developed by Bostic and his Berkeley peers, as a key source of commercial technology.

The code written by Bostic and friends was off limits to nearly everyone, because it was intermixed with proprietary AT&T code. Berkeley distributions were therefore available only to institutions that already had a Unix source license from AT&T. As AT&T raised its license fees, this arrangement, which had at first seemed innocuous (to those who thought only of academia) became increasingly burdensome even there. To use Berkeley's code in GNU, Stallman would have to convince Berkeley to separate it from AT&T's code and release it as free software. In 1984 or 1985 he met with the leaders of the BSD effort, pointing out that AT&T was not a charity and that for a university to donate its work (in effect) to AT&T was not proper. He asked them to separate out their code and release it as free software.

Hired in 1986, Bostic had taken on the personal project of porting the latest version of BSD to the PDP-11 computer. It was during this period, Bostic says, that he came into close interaction with Stallman during Stallman's occasional forays out to the west coast. "I remember vividly arguing copyright with Stallman while he sat at borrowed workstations at CSRG," says Bostic. "We'd go to dinner afterward and continue arguing about copyright over dinner."

The arguments eventually took hold, although not in the way Stallman would have preferred. In June, 1989, Berkeley had separated its networking code from the rest of the AT&T-owned operating system and began distributing it under a copyright-based free license. The license terms were liberal. All a licensee had to do was give credit to the university in advertisements touting derivative programs.[6] In contrast to the GPL, this license permitted proprietary offshoots. One problem limited the use of the BSD Networking release: it wasn't a complete operating system, just the network-related parts of one. While the code would be a major contribution to any free operating system, it could only be run at that time in conjunction with other, proprietary-licensed code.

Over the next few years, Bostic and other University of California employees worked to replace the missing components and turn BSD into a complete, freely redistributable operating system. Although delayed by a legal challenge from Unix Systems Laboratories – the

AT&T spin-off that retained ownership of the Unix code – the effort would finally bear fruit in the early 1990s. Even before then, however, many of the Berkeley network utilities would make their way into Stallman's GNU system.

"I think it's highly unlikely that we ever would have gone as strongly as we did without the GNU influence," says Bostic, looking back. "It was clearly something where they were pushing hard and we liked the idea."

By the end of the 1980s, the GPL was beginning to exert a gravitational effect on the free software community. A program didn't have to carry the GPL to qualify as free software – witness the case of the BSD network utilities – but putting a program under the GPL sent a definite message. "I think the very existence of the GPL inspired people to think through whether they were making free software, and how they would license it," says Bruce Perens, creator of Electric Fence, a popular Unix utility, and future leader of the Debian GNU/Linux development team. A few years after the release of the GPL, Perens says he decided to discard Electric Fence's homegrown license in favor of Stallman's lawyer-vetted copyright. "It was actually pretty easy to do," Perens recalls.

Rich Morin, the programmer who had viewed Stallman's initial GNU announcement with a degree of skepticism, recalls being impressed by the software that began to gather under the GPL umbrella. As the leader of a SunOS user group, one of Morin's primary duties during the 1980s had been to send out distribution tapes containing the best freeware or free software utilities. The job often mandated calling up original program authors to verify whether their programs were copyrighted or whether they had been consigned to the public domain. Around 1989, Morin says, he began to notice that the best software programs typically fell under the GPL license. "As a software distributor, as soon as I saw the word GPL, I knew I was home free," recalls Morin.

To compensate for the prior hassles that went into compiling distribution tapes to the Sun User Group, Morin had charged recipients a convenience fee. Now, with programs moving over to the GPL, Morin was suddenly getting his tapes put together in half the time, turning a tidy profit in the process. Sensing a commercial opportunity, Morin rechristened his hobby as a business: Prime Time Freeware.

Such commercial exploitation was completely consistent with the free software agenda. "When we speak of free software, we are referring to freedom, not price," advised Stallman in the GPL's preamble. By the late 1980s, Stallman had refined it to a more simple mnemonic: "Don't think free as in free beer; think free as in free speech."

For the most part, businesses ignored Stallman's entreaties. Still, for a few entrepreneurs, the freedom associated with free software was the same freedom associated with free markets. Take software ownership out of the commercial equation, and you had a situation where even the smallest software company was free to compete against the IBMs and DECs of the world.

One of the first entrepreneurs to grasp this concept was Michael Tiemann, a software programmer and graduate student at Stanford University. During the 1980s, Tiemann had followed the GNU Project like an aspiring jazz musician following a favorite artist. It wasn't until the release of the GNU C Compiler, or GCC, in 1987, however, that he began to grasp the full potential of free software. Dubbing GCC a "bombshell," Tiemann says the program's own existence underlined Stallman's determination as a programmer.

"Just as every writer dreams of writing the great American novel, every programmer back in the 1980s talked about writing the great American compiler," Tiemman recalls. "Suddenly Stallman had done it. It was very humbling."

"You talk about single points of failure, GCC was it," echoes Bostic. "Nobody had a compiler back then, until GCC came along."

Rather than compete with Stallman, Tiemann decided to build on top of his work. The original version of GCC weighed in at 110,000 lines of code, but Tiemann recalls the program as surprisingly easy to understand. So easy in fact that Tiemann says it took less than five days to master and another week to port the software to a new hardware platform, National Semiconductor's 32032 microchip. Over the next year, Tiemann began playing around with the source code, creating the first "native" or direct compiler for the C++ programming language, by extending GCC to handle C++ as well as C. (The existing, proprietary implementation of the C++ language worked by converting the code to the C language, then feeding the result to a C compiler.) One day, while delivering a lecture on the program at Bell

Labs, Tiemann ran into some AT&T developers struggling to pull off the same thing.

"There were about 40 or 50 people in the room, and I asked how many people were working on the native code compiler," Tiemann recalls. "My host said the information was confidential but added that if I took a look around the room I might get a good general idea."

It wasn't long after, Tiemann says, that the light bulb went off in his head. "I had been working on that project for six months," Tiemann says. I just thought to myself, whether it's me or the code, this is a level of efficiency that the free market should be ready to reward."

Tiemann found added inspiration in the *GNU Manifesto*: while excoriating the greed of proprietary software vendors, it also encourages companies, as long as they respect users freedom, to use and redistribute free software in their commercial activities. By removing the power of monopoly from the commercial software question, the GPL makes it possible for even small companies to compete on the basis of service, which extends from simple tech support to training to extending free programs for specific clients' needs.

In a 1999 essay, Tiemann recalls the impact of Stallman's *Manifesto*. "It read like a socialist polemic, but I saw something different. I saw a business plan in disguise."[7]

This business plan was not new; Stallman supported himself in the late 80s by doing this on a small scale. But Tiemann intended to take it to a new level. Teaming up with John Gilmore and David Vinayak Wallace, Tiemann launched a software consulting service dedicated to customizing GNU programs. Dubbed Cygnus Support (informally, "Cygnus" was a recursive acronym for "Cygnus, Your GNU Support"), the company signed its first development contract in February, 1990. By the end of the year, the company had $725,000 worth of support and development contracts.

The complete GNU operating system Stallman envisioned required more than software development tools. In the 1990s, GNU also developed a command line interpreter or "shell," which was an extended replacement for the Bourne Shell (written by FSF employee Brian Fox, and christened by Stallman the Bourne Again Shell, or BASH), as well as the PostScript interpreter Ghostscript, the documentation browser platform Texinfo, the C Library which C programs need in order to run and talk to the system's kernel, the spreadsheet Oleo ("better for you than the more expensive spreadsheet"), and even a fairly good chess game. However, programmers were typically most interested in the GNU programming tools.

GNU Emacs, GDB, and GCC were the "big three" of developer-oriented tools, but they weren't the only ones developed by the GNU Project in the 80s. By 1990, GNU had also generated GNU versions of the build-controller Make, the parser-generator YACC (rechristened Bison), and awk (rechristened gawk); as well as dozens more. Like GCC, GNU programs were usually designed to run on multiple systems, not just a single vendor's platform. In the process of making programs more flexible, Stallman and his collaborators often made them more useful as well.

Recalling the GNU universalist approach, Prime Time Freeware's Morin points to a useless but vitally important software package called GNU Hello, which serves as an example to show programmers how to properly package a program for GNU. "It's the hello world program which is five lines of C, packaged up as if it were a GNU distribution," Morin says. "And so it's got the Texinfo stuff and the configure stuff. It's got all the other software engineering goo that the GNU Project has come up with to allow packages to port to all these different environments smoothly. That's tremendously important work, and it affects not only all of [Stallman's] software, but also all of the other GNU Project software."

According to Stallman, improving technically on the components of Unix was secondary to replacing them with free software. "With each piece I may or may not find a way to improve it," said Stallman to *BYTE*. "To some extent I am getting the benefit of reimplementation, which makes many systems much better. To some extent it's because I have been in the field a long time and worked on many other systems. I therefore have many ideas [which I learned from them] to bring to bear."[8]

Nevertheless, as GNU tools made their mark in the late 1980s, Stallman's AI Lab-honed reputation for design fastidiousness soon became legendary throughout the entire software-development community.

Jeremy Allison, a Sun user during the late 1980s and programmer destined to run his own free software project, Samba, in the 1990s, recalls that reputation with a laugh. During the late 1980s, Allison began using Emacs. Inspired by the program's community-development model, Allison says he sent in a snippet of source code only to have it rejected by Stallman.

"It was like the *Onion* headline," Allison says. "'Child's prayers to God answered: No.'"

As the GNU Project moved from success to success in creation of user-level programs and libraries, it postponed development of the kernel, the central "traffic cop" program that controls other programs' access to the processor and all machine resources.

As with several other major system components, Stallman sought a head-start on kernel development by looking for an existing program to adapt. A review of GNU Project "GNUsletters" of the late 1980s reveals that this approach, like the initial attempt to build GCC out of Pastel, had its problems. A January, 1987 GNUsletter reported the GNU Project's intention to overhaul TRIX, a kernel developed at MIT. However, Stallman never actually tried to do this, since he was working on GCC at the time; later he concluded that TRIX would require too much change to be a good starting point. By February of 1988, according to a newsletter published that month, the GNU Project had shifted its kernel plans to Mach, a lightweight "micro-kernel" developed at Carnegie Mellon. Mach was not then free software, but its developers privately said they would liberate it; when this occurred, in 1990, GNU Project kernel development could really commence.[9]

The delays in kernel development were just one of many concerns weighing on Stallman during this period. In 1989, Lotus Development Corporation filed suit against rival software companies, Paperback Software International and Borland, for copying menu commands from Lotus' popular 1-2-3 Spreadsheet program. Lotus' suit, coupled with the Apple-Microsoft "look and feel" battle, endangered the future of the GNU system. Although neither suit directly attacked the GNU Project, both threatened the right to develop software compatible with existing programs, as many GNU programs were. These lawsuits could impose a chilling effect on the entire culture of software development. Determined to do something, Stallman and a few professors put an ad in *The Tech* (the MIT student newspaper) blasting the lawsuits and calling for a boycott of both Lotus and Apple. He then followed up the ad by helping to organize a group to protest the corporations filing the suit. Calling itself the League for Programming Freedom, the group held protests outside the offices of Lotus, Inc. The protests were notable.[10]

They document the evolving nature of the software industry. Applications had quietly replaced operating systems as the primary corporate battleground. In its unfinished quest to build a free software operating system, the GNU Project seemed hopelessly behind the times to those whose primary values were fashion and success. Indeed, the very fact that Stallman had felt it necessary to put together an entirely new group dedicated to battling the "look and feel" lawsuits led some observers to think that the FSF was obsolete.

However, Stallman had a strategic reason to start a separate organization to fight the imposition of new monopolies on software development: so that proprietary software developers would join it too. Extending copyright to cover interfaces would threaten many proprietary software developers as well as many free software developers. These proprietary developers were unlikely to endorse the Free Software Foundation, but there was, intentionally, nothing in the League for Programming Freedom to drive them away. For the same reason, Stallman handed over leadership of LPF to others as soon as it was feasible.

In 1990, the John D. and Catherine T. MacArthur Foundation certified Stallman's genius status when it granted Stallman a MacArthur fellowship, the so-called "genius grant," amounting in this case to $240,000 over 5 years. Although the Foundation does not state a reason for its grants, this one was seen as an award for launching the GNU Project and giving voice to the free software philosophy. The grant relieved a number of short-term concerns for Stallman. For instance, it enabled him to cease the consulting work through which he had obtained his income in the 80s and devote more time to the free software cause.

The award also made it possible for Stallman to register normally to vote. In 1985 a fire in the house where Stallman lived left him without an official domicile. It also covered most of his books with ash, and cleaning these "dirty books" did not yield satisfying results. From that time he lived as a "squatter" at 545 Technology Square, and had to vote as a "homeless person."[11] "[The Cambridge Election Commission] didn't want to accept that as my address," Stallman would later recall. "A newspaper article about the MacArthur grant said that, and then they let me register."[12]

Most importantly, the MacArthur fellowship gave Stallman press attention and speaking invitations, which he used to spread the word about GNU, free software, and dangers such as "look and feel" lawsuits and software patents.

Interestingly, the GNU system's completion would stem from one of these trips. In April 1991, Stallman paid a visit to the Polytechnic University in Helsinki, Finland. Among the audience members was 21-year-old Linus Torvalds, who was just beginning to develop the Linux kernel – the free software kernel destined to fill the GNU system's main remaining gap.

A student at the nearby University of Helsinki at the time, Torvalds regarded Stallman with bemusement. "I saw, for the first time in my life, the stereotypical long-haired, bearded hacker type," recalls Torvalds in his 2001 autobiography *Just for Fun*. "We don't have much of them in Helsinki."[13]

While not exactly attuned to the "sociopolitical" side of the Stallman agenda, Torvalds nevertheless appreciated one aspect of the agenda's underlying logic: no programmer writes error-free code. Even when users have no wish to adapt a program to their specific preferences, any program can use improvement. By sharing software, hackers put a program's improvement ahead of individual motivations such as greed or ego protection.

Like many programmers of his generation, Torvalds had cut his teeth not on mainframe computers like the IBM 7094, but on a motley assortment of home-built computer systems. As a university student, Torvalds had made the step up from PC programming to Unix, using the university's MicroVAX. This ladder-like progression had given Torvalds a different perspective on the barriers to machine access. For Stallman, the chief barriers were bureaucracy and privilege. For Torvalds, the chief barriers were geography and the harsh Helsinki winter. Forced to trek across the University of Helsinki just to log in to his Unix account, Torvalds quickly began looking for a way to log in from the warm confines of his off-campus apartment.

Torvalds was using Minix, a lightweight nonfree system developed as an instructional example by Dutch university professor Andrew Tanenbaum.[14] It included the non-free Free University Compiler Kit, plus utilities of the sort that Tanenbaum had contemptuously invited Stallman in 1983 to write.[15]

Minix fit within the memory confines of Torvalds' 386 PC, but it was intended more to be studied than used. The Minix system also lacked the facility of terminal emulation, which would mimic a typical display terminal and thus enable Torvalds to log in to the MicroVAX from home.

Early in 1991, Torvalds began writing a terminal emulation program. He used Minix to develop his emulator, but the emulator didn't run on Minix; it was a stand-alone program. Then he gave it features to access disk files in Minix's file system. Around then, Torvalds referred to his evolving work as the "GNU/Emacs of terminal emulation programs."[16]

Since Minix lacked many important features, Torvalds began extending his terminal emulator into a kernel comparable to that of Minix, except that it was monolithic. Feeling ambitious, he solicited a Minix newsgroup for copies of the POSIX standards, the specifications for a Unix-compatible kernel.[17] A few weeks later, having put his kernel together with some GNU programs and adapted them to work with it, Torvalds was posting a message reminiscent of Stallman's original 1983 GNU posting:

Hello everybody out there using minix-

I'm doing a (free) operating system (just a hobby, won't be big and professional like gnu) for 386 (486) AT clones. This has been brewing since April, and is starting to get ready. I'd like any feedback on things people like/dislike in minix, as my OS resembles it somewhat (same physical layout of the file-system (due to practical reasons) among other things). I've currently ported bash (1.08) and gcc (1.40)...[18]

The posting drew a smattering of responses and within a month, Torvalds had posted a 0.01 version of his kernel – i.e., the earliest possible version fit for outside review – on an Internet FTP site. In the course of doing so, Torvalds had to come up with a name for the new kernel. On his own PC hard drive, Torvalds had saved the program as Linux, a name that paid its respects to the software convention of giving each Unix variant a name that ended with the letter X. Deeming the name too "egotistical," Torvalds changed it to Freax, only to have the FTP site manager change it back.

Torvalds said he was writing a free operating system, and his comparing it with GNU shows he meant a complete system. However, what he actually wrote was a kernel, pure and simple. Torvalds had no need to write more than the kernel because, as he knew, the other needed components were already available, thanks to the developers of GNU and other free software projects. Since the GNU Project wanted to use them all in the GNU system, it had perforce made them work together. While Torvalds continued developing the kernel, he (and later his collaborators) made those programs work with it too.

Initially, Linux was not free software: the license it carried did not qualify as free, because it did not allow commercial distribution. Torvalds was worried that some company would swoop in and take Linux away from him. However, as the growing GNU/Linux combination gained popularity, Torvalds saw that sale of copies would be useful for the community, and began to feel less worried about a possible takeover.[19] This led him to reconsider the licensing of Linux.

Neither compiling Linux with GCC nor running GCC with Linux required him legally to release Linux under the GNU GPL, but Torvalds' use of GCC implied for him a certain obligation to let other users borrow back. As Torvalds would later put it: "I had hoisted myself up on the shoulders of giants."[20] Not surprisingly, he began to think about what would happen when other people looked to him for similar support. A decade after the decision, Torvalds echoes the Free Software Foundation's Robert Chassell when he sums up his thoughts at the time:

> You put six months of your life into this thing and you want to make it available and you want to get something out of it, but you don't want people to take advantage of it. I wanted people to be able to see [Linux], and to make changes and improvements to their hearts' content. But I also wanted to make sure that what I got out of it was to

see what they were doing. I wanted to always have access to the sources so that if they made improvements, I could make those improvements myself.[21]

When it was time to release the 0.12 version of Linux, the first to operate fully with GCC, Torvalds decided to throw his lot in with the free software movement. He discarded the old license of Linux and replaced it with the GPL. Within three years, Linux developers were offering release 1.0 of Linux, the kernel; it worked smoothly with the almost complete GNU system, composed of programs from the GNU Project and elsewhere. In effect, they had completed the GNU operating system by adding Linux to it. The resulting system was basically GNU plus Linux. Torvalds and friends, however, referred to it confusingly as "Linux."

By 1994, the amalgamated system had earned enough respect in the hacker world to make some observers from the business world wonder if Torvalds hadn't given away the farm by switching to the GPL in the project's initial months. In the first issue of *Linux Journal*, publisher Robert Young sat down with Torvalds for an interview. When Young asked the Finnish programmer if he felt regret at giving up private ownership of the Linux source code, Torvalds said no. "Even with 20/20 hindsight," Torvalds said, he considered the GPL "one of the very best design decisions" made during the early stages of the Linux project.[22]

That the decision had been made with zero appeal or deference to Stallman and the Free Software Foundation speaks to the GPL's growing portability. Although it would take a couple of years to be recognized by Stallman, the explosiveness of Linux development conjured flashbacks of Emacs. This time around, however, the innovation triggering the explosion wasn't a software hack like Control-R but the novelty of running a Unix-like system on the PC architecture. The motives may have been different, but the end result certainly fit the ethical specifications: a fully functional operating system composed entirely of free software.

As his initial email message to the comp.os.minix newsgroup indicates, it would take a few months before Torvalds saw Linux as anything more than a holdover until the GNU developers delivered on the Hurd kernel. As far as Torvalds was concerned, he was simply the latest in a long line of kids taking apart and reassembling things just for fun. Nevertheless, when summing up the runaway success of a project that could have just as easily spent the rest of its days on an abandoned computer hard drive, Torvalds credits his younger self for having the wisdom to give up control and accept the GPL bargain.

"I may not have seen the light," writes Torvalds, reflecting on Stallman's 1991 Polytechnic University speech and his subsequent decision to switch to the GPL. "But I guess something from his speech sunk in." [23]

Endnotes

[1] See Hal Abelson, Mike Fischer, and Joanne Costello, "Software and Copyright Law," updated version (1997), http://groups.csail.mit.edu/mac/classes/6.805/articles/int-prop/software-copyright.html.

[2] See Trn Kit README, http://stuff.mit.edu/afs/sipb/project/trn/src/trn-3.6/README.

[3] See John Gilmore, quoted from email to author.

[4] See Richard Stallman, et al., "GNU General Public License: Version 1," (February, 1989), http://www.gnu.org/licenses/old-licenses/gpl-1.0.html.

[5] See David Betz and Jon Edwards, "Richard Stallman discusses his public-domain [*sic*] Unix-compatible software system with *BYTE* editors," *BYTE* (July, 1986). (Reprinted on the GNU Project web site: http://www.gnu.org/gnu/byte-interview.html.)

This interview offers an interesting, not to mention candid, glimpse at Stallman's political attitudes during the earliest days of the GNU Project. It is also helpful in tracing the evolution of Stallman's rhetoric.

Describing the purpose of the GPL, Stallman says, "I'm trying to change the way people approach knowledge and information in general. I think that to try to own knowledge, to try to control whether people are allowed to use it, or to try to stop other people from sharing it, is sabotage."

Contrast this with a statement to the author in August 2000: "I urge you not to use the term 'intellectual property' in your thinking. It will lead you to misunderstand things, because that term generalizes about copyrights, patents, and trademarks. And those things are so different in their effects that it is entirely foolish to try to talk about them at once. If you hear somebody saying something 'about intellectual property,' without [putting it in] quotes, then he's not thinking very clearly and you shouldn't join."

[RMS: The contrast it shows is that I've learned to be more cautious in generalizing. I probably wouldn't talk about "owning knowledge" today, since it's a very broad concept. But "owning knowledge" is not the same generalization as "intellectual property," and the difference between those three laws is crucial to understanding any legal issue about owning knowledge. Patents are direct monopolies over using specific knowledge; that really is one form of "owning knowledge."

Copyrights are one of the methods used to stop the sharing of works that embody or explain knowledge, which is a very different thing. Meanwhile, trademarks have very little to do with the subject of knowledge.]

[6]The University of California's "obnoxious advertising clause" would later prove to be a problem. Looking for a permissive alternative to the GPL, some hackers used the original BSD license, replacing "University of California" with their own names or the names of their institutions. The result: free software systems using many of these programs would have to cite dozens of names in advertisements. In 1999, after a few years of lobbying on Stallman's part, the University of California agreed to drop this clause. See "The BSD License Problem" at http://www.gnu.org/philosophy/bsd.html.

[7]See Michael Tiemann, "Future of Cygnus Solutions: An Entrepreneur's Account," *Open Sources* (O'Reilly & Associates, Inc., 1999): 139, http://www.oreilly.com/catalog/opensources/book/tiemans.html.

[8]See Richard Stallman, *BYTE* (1986).

[9]See "Hurd History," http://www.gnu.org/software/hurd/history.html.

[10]According to a League for Programming Freedom press release at http://progfree.org/Links/prep.ai.mit.edu/demo.final.release, the protests were notable for featuring the first hexadecimal protest chant:

> 1-2-3-4, toss the lawyers out the door
> 5-6-7-8, innovate don't litigate
> 9-A-B-C, 1-2-3 is not for me
> D-E-F-O, look and feel have got to go

[11]See Reuven Lerner, "Stallman wins $240,000 MacArthur award," MIT, *The Tech* (July 18, 1990), http://the-tech.mit.edu/V110/N30/rms.30n.html.

[12]See Michael Gross, "Richard Stallman: High School Misfit, Symbol of Free Software, MacArthur-certified Genius" (1999).

[13]See Linus Torvalds and David Diamond, *Just For Fun: The Story of an Accidentaly Revolutionary* (HarperCollins Publishers, Inc., 2001): 58-59. Although presumably accurate in regard to Torvalds' life, what the book says about Stallman is sometimes wrong. For instance, it says that Stallman "wants to make everything open source," and that he "complains about other people not using the GPL." In fact, Stallman advocates free software, not open source. He urges authors to choose the GNU GPL, in most circumstances, but says that all free software licenses are ethical.

[14]It was non-free in 1991. Minix is free software now.

[15]Tanenbaum describes Minix as an "operating system" in his book, *Operating System Design and Implementation*, but what the book discusses is only the part of the system that corresponds to the kernel of Unix. There are two customary usages of the term "operating system," and one of them is what is called the "kernel" in Unix terminology. But that's not the only terminological complication in the subject. That part of Minix consists of a microkernel plus servers that run on it, a design of the same kind as the GNU Hurd plus Mach. The microkernel plus servers are comparable to the kernel of Unix. but when that book says "the kernel," it refers to the microkernel only. See Andrew Tanenbaum, *Operating System Design and Implementation*, 1987.

[16] See Linus Torvalds and David Diamond, *Just For Fun: The Story of an Accidentaly Revolutionary* (HarperCollins Publishers, Inc., 2001): 78.

[17] POSIX was subsequently extended to include specifications for many command line features, but that did not exist in 1991.

[18] *Ibid, p. 85.*

[19] *Ibid, p. 94-95.*

[20] *Ibid, p. 95-97.*

[21] See Linus Torvalds and David Diamond, *Just For Fun: The Story of an Accidentaly Revolutionary* (HarperCollins Publishers, Inc., 2001): 94-95.

[22] See Robert Young, "Interview with Linus, the Author of Linux," *Linux Journal* (March 1, 1994), http://www.linuxjournal.com/article/2736.

[23] See Linus Torvalds and David Diamond, *Just For Fun: The Story of an Accidentaly Revolutionary* (HarperCollins Publishers, Inc., 2001): 59.

.

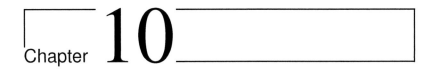

GNU/Linux

By 1993, the free software movement was at a crossroads. To the op-
timistically inclined, all signs pointed toward success for the hacker
culture. *Wired* magazine, a funky, new publication offering stories on
data encryption, Usenet, and software freedom, was flying off magazine racks. The Internet, once a slang term used only by hackers
and research scientists, had found its way into mainstream lexicon.
Even President Clinton was using it. The personal computer, once a
hobbyist's toy, had grown to full-scale respectability, giving a whole
new generation of computer users access to hacker-built software. And
while the GNU Project had not yet reached its goal of a fully intact,
free GNU operating system, users could already run the GNU/Linux
variant.

Any way you sliced it, the news was good, or so it seemed. After
a decade of struggle, hackers and hacker values were finally gaining
acceptance in mainstream society. People were getting it.

Or were they? To the pessimistically inclined, each sign of acceptance carried its own troubling countersign. Sure, being a hacker was
suddenly cool, but was cool good for a community that thrived on
alienation? Sure, the White House was saying nice things about the
Internet, even going so far as to register its own domain name, white-
house.gov, but it was also meeting with the companies, censorship ad-

vocates, and law-enforcement officials looking to tame the Internet's
Wild West culture. Sure, PCs were more powerful, but in commoditiz-
ing the PC marketplace with its chips, Intel had created a situation in
which proprietary software vendors now held the power. For every new
user won over to the free software cause via GNU/Linux, hundreds,
perhaps thousands, were booting up Microsoft Windows for the first
time. GNU/Linux had only rudimentary graphical interfaces, so it
was hardly user-friendly. In 1993, only an expert could use it. The
GNU Project's first attempt to develop a graphical desktop had been
abortive.

Then there was the political situation. Copyrighting of user interfaces was still a real threat – the courts had not yet rejected the
idea. Meanwhile, patents on software algorithms and features were a
growing danger that threatened to spread to other countries.

Finally, there was the curious nature of GNU/Linux itself. Unrestricted by legal disputes (such as BSD faced), GNU/Linux's high-
speed evolution had been so unplanned, its success so accidental, that
programmers closest to the software code itself didn't know what to
make of it. More compilation album than unified project, it was com-
prised of a hacker medley of greatest hits: everything from GCC,
GDB, and glibc (the GNU Project's newly developed C Library) to
X (a Unix-based graphic user interface developed by MIT's Laboratory for Computer Science) to BSD-developed tools such as BIND (the
Berkeley Internet Naming Daemon, which lets users substitute easy-
to-remember Internet domain names for numeric IP addresses) and
TCP/IP. In addition, it contained the Linux kernel – itself designed
as a replacement for Minix. Rather than developing a new operating
system, Torvalds and his rapidly expanding Linux development team
had plugged their work into this matrix. As Torvalds himself would
later translate it when describing the secret of his success: "I'm basically a very lazy person who likes to take credit for things other people
actually do."[1]

Such laziness, while admirable from an efficiency perspective, was
troubling from a political perspective. For one thing, it underlined
the lack of an ideological agenda on Torvalds' part. Unlike the GNU
developers, Torvalds hadn't built his kernel out of a desire to give
his fellow hackers freedom; he'd built it to have something he himself
could play with. So what exactly was the combined system, and which

philosophy would people associate it with? Was it a manifestation of the free software philosophy first articulated by Stallman in the *GNU Manifesto*? Or was it simply an amalgamation of nifty software tools that any user, similarly motivated, could assemble on his own home system?

By late 1993, a growing number of GNU/Linux users had begun to lean toward the latter definition and began brewing private variations on the theme. They began to develop various "distributions" of GNU/Linux and distribute them, sometimes gratis, sometimes for a price. The results were spotty at best.

"This was back before Red Hat and the other commercial distributions," remembers Ian Murdock, then a computer science student at Purdue University. "You'd flip through Unix magazines and find all these business card-sized ads proclaiming 'Linux.' Most of the companies were fly-by-night operations that saw nothing wrong with slipping a little of their own [proprietary] source code into the mix."

Murdock, a Unix programmer, remembers being "swept away" by GNU/Linux when he first downloaded and installed it on his home PC system. "It was just a lot of fun," he says. "It made me want to get involved." The explosion of poorly built distributions began to dampen his early enthusiasm, however. Deciding that the best way to get involved was to build a version free of additives, Murdock set about putting a list of the best free software tools available with the intention of folding them into his own distribution. "I wanted something that would live up to the Linux name," Murdock says.

In a bid to "stir up some interest," Murdock posted his intentions on the Internet, including Usenet's comp.os.linux newsgroup. One of the first responding email messages was from rms@ai.mit.edu. As a hacker, Murdock instantly recognized the address. It was Richard M. Stallman, founder of the GNU Project and a man Murdock knew even back then as "the hacker of hackers." Seeing the address in his mail queue, Murdock was puzzled. Why on Earth would Stallman, a person leading his own operating-system project, care about Murdock's gripes over "Linux" distributions?

Murdock opened the message.

"He said the Free Software Foundation was starting to look closely at Linux and that the FSF was interested in possibly doing a Linux [*sic*] system, too. Basically, it looked to Stallman like our goals were in line with their philosophy."

Not to overdramatize, the message represented a change in strategy on Stallman's part. Until 1993, Stallman had been content to keep his nose out of Linux affairs. After first hearing of the new kernel, Stallman asked a friend to check its suitability. Recalls Stallman, "He reported back that the software was modeled after System V, which was the inferior version of Unix. He also told me it wasn't portable."

The friend's report was correct. Built to run on 386-based machines, Linux was firmly rooted to its low-cost hardware platform. What the friend failed to report, however, was the sizable advantage Linux enjoyed as the only free kernel in the marketplace. In other words, while Stallman spent the next year and a half listening to progress reports from the Hurd developer, reporting rather slow progress, Torvalds was winning over the programmers who would later uproot and replant Linux and GNU onto new platforms.

By 1993, the GNU Project's failure to deliver a working kernel was leading to problems both within the GNU Project and in the free software movement at large. A March, 1993, *Wired* magazine article by Simson Garfinkel described the GNU Project as "bogged down" despite the success of the project's many tools.[2] Those within the project and its nonprofit adjunct, the Free Software Foundation, remember the mood as being even worse than Garfinkel's article let on. "It was very clear, at least to me at the time, that there was a window of opportunity to introduce a new operating system," says Chassell. "And once that window was closed, people would become less interested. Which is in fact exactly what happened."[3]

Much has been made about the GNU Project's struggles during the 1990-1993 period. While some place the blame on Stallman for those struggles, Eric Raymond, an old friend of Stallman's who supported the GNU Project lukewarmly, says the problem was largely institutional. "The FSF got arrogant," Raymond says. "They moved away from the goal of doing a production-ready operating system to doing operating-system research." Even worse, "They thought nothing outside the FSF could affect them."

Murdock adopts a more charitable view. "I think part of the problem is they were a little too ambitious and they threw good money after bad," he says. "Micro-kernels in the late 80s and early 90s were a hot topic. Unfortunately, that was about the time that the GNU Project started to design their kernel. They ended up with a lot of baggage and it would have taken a lot of backpedaling to lose it."

Stallman responds, "Although the emotions Raymond cites come from his imagination, he's right about one cause of the Hurd's delay: the Hurd developer several times redesigned and rewrote large parts of the code based on what he had learned, rather than trying to make the Hurd run as soon as possible. It was good design practice, but it wasn't the right practice for our goal: to get something working ASAP."

Stallman cites other issues that also caused delay. The Lotus and Apple lawsuits claimed much of his attention; this, coupled with hand problems that prevented him from typing for three years, mostly excluded Stallman from programming. Stallman also cites poor communication between various portions of the GNU Project. "We had to do a lot of work to get the debugging environment to work," he recalls. "And the people maintaining GDB at the time were not that cooperative." They had given priority to supporting the existing platforms of GDB's current users, rather than to the overall goal of a complete GNU system.

Most fundamentally, however, Stallman says he and the Hurd developers underestimated the difficulty of developing the Unix kernel facilities on top of the Mach microkernel. "I figured, OK, the [Mach] part that has to talk to the machine has already been debugged," Stallman says, recalling the Hurd team's troubles in a 2000 speech. "With that head start, we should be able to get it done faster. But instead, it turned out that debugging these asynchronous multithreaded programs was really hard. There were timing bugs that would clobber the files, and that's no fun. The end result was that it took many, many years to produce a test version."[4]

Over time, the growing success of GNU together with Linux made it clear that the GNU Project should get on the train that was leaving and not wait for the Hurd. Besides, there were weaknesses in the community surrounding GNU/Linux. Sure, Linux had been licensed under the GPL, but as Murdock himself had noted, the desire to treat GNU/Linux as a purely free software operating system was far from unanimous. By late 1993, the total GNU/Linux user population had grown from a dozen or so enthusiasts to somewhere between 20,000 and 100,000.[5] What had once been a hobby was now a marketplace ripe for exploitation, and some developers had no objection to exploiting it with nonfree software. Like Winston Churchill watching Soviet troops sweep into Berlin, Stallman felt an understandable set of mixed emotions when it came time to celebrate the GNU/Linux "victory."[6]

Although late to the party, Stallman still had clout. As soon as the FSF announced that it would lend its money and moral support to Murdock's software project, other offers of support began rolling in. Murdock dubbed the new project Debian – a compression of his and his wife, Deborah's, names – and within a few weeks was rolling out the first distribution. "[Richard's support] catapulted Debian almost overnight from this interesting little project to something people within the community had to pay attention to," Murdock says.

In January of 1994, Murdock issued the *Debian Manifesto*. Written in the spirit of Stallman's *GNU Manifesto* from a decade before, it explained the importance of working closely with the Free Software Foundation. Murdock wrote:

> The Free Software Foundation plays an extremely important role in the future of Debian. By the simple fact that they will be distributing it, a message is sent to the world that Linux [*sic*] is not a commercial product and that it never should be, but that this does not mean that Linux will never be able to compete commercially. For those of you who disagree, I challenge you to rationalize the success of GNU Emacs and GCC, which are not commercial software but which have had quite an impact on the commercial market regardless of that fact.
>
> The time has come to concentrate on the future of Linux [*sic*] rather than on the destructive goal of enriching oneself at the expense of the entire Linux community and its future. The development and distribution of Debian may not be the answer to the problems that I have outlined in the *Manifesto*, but I hope that it will at least attract enough attention to these problems to allow them to be solved.[7]

Shortly after the *Manifesto's* release, the Free Software Foundation made its first major request. Stallman wanted Murdock to call its distribution "GNU/Linux." At first, Stallman proposed the term "Lignux" – combining the names Linux and GNU – but the initial reaction was very negative, and this convinced Stallman to go with the longer but less criticized GNU/Linux.

Some dismissed Stallman's attempt to add the "GNU" prefix as a belated quest for credit, never mind whether it was due, but Murdock saw it differently. Looking back, Murdock saw it as an attempt to counteract the growing tension between the GNU Project's developers and those who adapted GNU programs to use with the Linux kernel. "There was a split emerging," Murdock recalls. "Richard was concerned."

By 1990, each GNU program had a designated maintainer-in-charge. Some GNU programs could run on many different systems, and users often contributed changes to port them to another system. Often these users knew only that one system, and did not consider how to keep the code clean for other systems. To add support for the new system while keeping the code comprehensible, so it could be maintained reliably for all systems, then required rewriting much of the changes. The maintainer-in-charge had the responsibility to critique the changes and tell their user-authors how to redo parts of the port. Generally they were eager to do this so that their changes would be integrated into the standard version. Then the maintainer-in-charge would edit in the reworked changes, and take care of them in future maintenance. For some GNU programs, this had happened dozens of times for dozens of different systems.

The programmers who adapted various GNU programs to work with the kernel Linux followed this common path: they considered only their own platform. But when the maintainers-in-charge asked them to help clean up their changes for future maintenance, several of them were not interested. They did not care about doing the correct thing, or about facilitating future maintenance of the GNU packages they had adapted. They cared only about their own versions and were inclined to maintain them as forks.

In the hacker world, forks are an interesting issue. Although the hacker ethic permits a programmer to do anything he wants with a given program's source code, it is considered correct behavior to offer to work with the original developer to maintain a joint version. Hackers usually find it useful, as well as proper, to pour their improvements into the program's principal version. A free software license gives every hacker the right to fork a program, and sometimes it is necessary, but doing so without need or cause is considered somewhat rude.

As leader of the GNU Project, Stallman had already experienced the negative effects of a software fork in 1991. Says Stallman, "Lucid hired several people to write improvements to GNU Emacs, meant to be contributions to it; but the developers did not inform me about the project. Instead they designed several new features on their own. As you might expect, I agreed with some of their decisions and disagreed with others. They asked me to incorporate all their code, but when I said I wanted to use about half of it, they declined to help me adapt that half to work on its own. I had to do it on my own." The fork had given birth to a parallel version, Lucid Emacs, and hard feelings all around.[8]

Now programmers had forked several of the principal GNU packages at once. At first, Stallman says he considered the forks to be a product of impatience. In contrast to the fast and informal dynamics of the Linux team, GNU source-code maintainers tended to be slower and more circumspect in making changes that might affect a program's long-term viability. They also were unafraid of harshly critiquing other people's code. Over time, however, Stallman began to sense that there was an underlying lack of awareness of the GNU Project and its objectives when reading Linux developers' emails.

"We discovered that the people who considered themselves 'Linux users' didn't care about the GNU Project," Stallman says. "They said, 'Why should I bother doing these things? I don't care about the GNU Project. It [the program]'s working for me. It's working for us Linux users, and nothing else matters to us.' And that was quite surprising, given that people were essentially using a variant of the GNU system, and they cared so little. They cared less than anybody else about GNU." Fooled by their own practice of calling the combination "Linux," they did not realize that their system was more GNU than Linux.

For the sake of unity, Stallman asked the maintainers-in-charge to do the work which normally the change authors should have done. In most cases this was feasible, but not in glibc. Short for GNU C Library, glibc is the package that all programs use to make "system calls" directed at the kernel, in this case Linux. User programs on a Unix-like system communicate with the kernel only through the C library.

The changes to make glibc work as a communication channel between Linux and all the other programs in the system were major and ad-hoc, written without attention to their effect on other platforms. For the glibc maintainer-in-charge, the task of cleaning them up was daunting. Instead the Free Software Foundation paid him to spend most of a year reimplementing these changes from scratch, to make glibc version 6 work "straight out of the box" in GNU/Linux.

Murdock says this was the precipitating cause that motivated Stallman to insist on adding the GNU prefix when Debian rolled out its software distribution. "The fork has since converged. Still, at the time, there was a concern that if the Linux community saw itself as a different thing as the GNU community, it might be a force for disunity."

While some viewed it as politically grasping to describe the combination of GNU and Linux as a "variant" of GNU, Murdock, already sympathetic to the free software cause, saw Stallman's request to call Debian's version GNU/Linux as reasonable. "It was more for unity than for credit," he says.

Requests of a more technical nature quickly followed. Although Murdock had been accommodating on political issues, he struck a firmer pose when it came to the design and development model of the actual software. What had begun as a show of solidarity soon became a running disagreement.

"I can tell you that I've had my share of disagreements with him," says Murdock with a laugh. "In all honesty Richard can be a fairly difficult person to work with." The principal disagreement was over debugging. Stallman wanted to include debugging information in all executable programs, to enable users to immediately investigate any bugs they might encounter. Murdock thought this would make the system files too big and interfere with distribution. Neither was willing to change his mind.

In 1996, Murdock, following his graduation from Purdue, decided to hand over the reins of the growing Debian project. He had already been ceding management duties to Bruce Perens, the hacker best known for his work on Electric Fence, a Unix utility released under the GPL. Perens, like Murdock, was a Unix programmer who had become enamored of GNU/Linux as soon as the operating system's Unix-like abilities became manifest. Like Murdock, Perens sympathized with the political agenda of Stallman and the Free Software Foundation, albeit from afar.

"I remember after Stallman had already come out with the *GNU Manifesto*, GNU Emacs, and GCC, I read an article that said he was working as a consultant for Intel," says Perens, recalling his first brush with Stallman in the late 1980s. "I wrote him asking how he could be advocating free software on the one hand and working for Intel on the other. He wrote back saying, 'I work as a consultant to produce free software.' He was perfectly polite about it, and I thought his answer made perfect sense."

As a prominent Debian developer, however, Perens regarded Murdock's design battles with Stallman with dismay. Upon assuming leadership of the development team, Perens says he made the command decision to distance Debian from the Free Software Foundation. "I decided we did not want Richard's style of micro-management," he says.

According to Perens, Stallman was taken aback by the decision but had the wisdom to roll with it. "He gave it some time to cool off and sent a message that we really needed a relationship. He requested that we call it GNU/Linux and left it at that. I decided that was fine. I made the decision unilaterally. Everybody breathed a sigh of relief."

Over time, Debian would develop a reputation as the hacker's version of GNU/Linux, alongside Slackware, another popular distribution founded during the same 1993-1994 period. However, Slackware contained some nonfree programs, and Debian after its separation from GNU began distributing non-free programs too.[9] Despite labeling them as "non-free" and saying that they were "not officially part of Debian," proposing these programs to the user implied a kind of endorsement for them. As the GNU Project became aware of these policies, it came to recognize that neither Slackware nor Debian was a GNU/Linux distro it could recommend to the public.

Outside the realm of hacker-oriented systems, however, GNU/Linux was picking up steam in the commercial Unix marketplace. In North Carolina, a Unix company billing itself as Red Hat was revamping its business to focus on GNU/Linux. The chief executive officer was Robert Young, the former *Linux Journal* editor who in 1994 had put the question to Linus Torvalds, asking whether he had any regrets about putting the kernel under the GPL. To Young, Torvalds' response had a "profound" impact on his own view toward GNU/Linux. Instead of looking for a way to corner the GNU/Linux market via traditional software tactics, Young began to consider what might happen if a company adopted the same approach as Debian – i.e., building an operating system completely out of free software parts. Cygnus Solutions, the company founded by Michael Tiemann and John Gilmore in 1990, was already demonstrating the ability to sell free software based on quality and customizability. What if Red Hat took the same approach with GNU/Linux?

"In the western scientific tradition we stand on the shoulders of giants," says Young, echoing both Torvalds and Sir Isaac Newton before him. "In business, this translates to not having to reinvent wheels as we go along. The beauty of [the GPL] model is you put your code into the public domain.[10] If you're an independent software vendor and you're trying to build some application and you need a modem-dialer, well, why reinvent modem dialers? You can just steal PPP off of Red Hat [GNU/]Linux and use that as the core of your modem-dialing tool. If you need a graphic tool set, you don't have to write your own graphic library. Just download GTK. Suddenly you have the ability to reuse the best of what went before. And suddenly your focus as an application vendor is less on software management and more on writing the applications specific to your customer's needs." However, Young was no free software activist, and readily included nonfree programs in Red Hat's GNU/Linux system.

Young wasn't the only software executive intrigued by the business efficiencies of free software. By late 1996, most Unix companies were starting to wake up and smell the brewing source code. The GNU/Linux sector was still a good year or two away from full commercial breakout mode, but those close enough to the hacker community could feel it: something big was happening. The Intel 386 chip, the Internet, and the World Wide Web had hit the marketplace like a set of monster waves; free software seemed like the largest wave yet.

For Ian Murdock, the wave seemed both a fitting tribute and a fitting punishment for the man who had spent so much time giving the free software movement an identity. Like many Linux aficionados, Murdock had seen the original postings. He'd seen Torvalds' original admonition that Linux was "just a hobby." He'd also seen Torvalds' admission to Minix creator Andrew Tanenbaum: "If the GNU kernel had been ready last spring, I'd not have bothered to even start my project."[11] Like many, Murdock knew that some opportunities had been missed. He also knew the excitement of watching new opportunities come seeping out of the very fabric of the Internet.

"Being involved with Linux in those early days was fun," recalls Murdock. "At the same time, it was something to do, something to pass the time. If you go back and read those old [comp.os.minix] exchanges, you'll see the sentiment: this is something we can play with until the Hurd is ready. People were anxious. It's funny, but in a lot of ways, I suspect that Linux would never have happened if the Hurd had come along more quickly."

By the end of 1996, however, such "what if" questions were already moot, because Torvalds' kernel had gained a critical mass of users. The 36-month window had closed, meaning that even if the GNU Project had rolled out its Hurd kernel, chances were slim anybody outside the hard-core hacker community would have noticed. Linux, by filling the GNU system's last gap, had achieved the GNU Project's goal of producing a Unix-like free software operating system. However, most of the users did not recognize what had happened: they thought the whole system was Linux, and that Torvalds had done it all. Most of them installed distributions that came with nonfree software; with Torvalds as their ethical guide, they saw no principled reason to reject it. Still, a precarious freedom was available for those that appreciated it.

Endnotes

[1] Torvalds has offered this quote in many different settings. To date, however, the quote's most notable appearance is in the Eric Raymond essay, "The Cathedral and the Bazaar" (May, 1997), http://www.catb.org/~esr/writings/cathedral-bazaar/.

[2] See Simson Garfinkel, "Is Stallman Stalled?" *Wired* (March, 1993).

[3] Chassell's concern about there being a 36-month "window" for a new operating system is not unique to the GNU Project. During the early 1990s, free software versions of the Berkeley Software Distribution were held up by Unix System Laboratories' lawsuit restricting the release of BSD-derived software. While many users consider BSD offshoots such as FreeBSD and OpenBSD to be demonstrably

superior to GNU/Linux both in terms of performance and security, the number of FreeBSD and OpenBSD users remains a fraction of the total GNU/Linux user population.

To view a sample analysis of the relative success of GNU/Linux in relation to other free software operating systems, see the essay by New Zealand hacker, Liam Greenwood, "Why is Linux Successful" (1999), http://www.freebsddiary. org/linux.php.

[4]See Maui High Performance Computing Center Speech.

In subsequent emails, I asked Stallman what exactly he meant by the term "timing bugs." Stallman said "timing errors" was a better way to summarize the problem and offered an elucidating technical information of how a timing error can hamper an operating system's performance:

> "Timing errors" occur in an asynchronous system where jobs done in parallel can theoretically occur in any order, and one particular order leads to problems.
>
> Imagine that program A does X, and program B does Y, where both X and Y are short routines that examine and update the same data structure. Nearly always the computer will do X before Y, or do Y before X, and then there will be no problem. On rare occasions, by chance, the scheduler will let program A run until it is in the middle of X, and then run B which will do Y. Thus, Y will be done while X is half-done. Since they are updating the same data structure, they will interfere. For instance, perhaps X has already examined the data structure, and it won't notice that there was a change. There will be an unreproducible failure, unreproducible because it depends on chance factors (when the scheduler decides to run which program and how long).
>
> The way to prevent such a failure is to use a lock to make sure X and Y can't run at the same time. Programmers writing asynchronous systems know about the general need for locks, but sometimes they overlook the need for a lock in a specific place or on a specific data structure. Then the program has a timing error.

[5]GNU/Linux user-population numbers are sketchy at best, which is why I've provided such a broad range. The 100,000 total comes from the Red Hat "Milestones" site, http://www.redhat.com/about/corporate/milestones.html.

[6]I wrote this Winston Churchill analogy before Stallman himself sent me his own unsolicited comment on Churchill:

> World War II and the determination needed to win it was a very strong memory as I was growing up. Statements such as Churchill's, "We will fight them in the landing zones, we will fight them on the beaches... we will never surrender," have always resonated for me.

[7]See Ian Murdock, *A Brief History of Debian,* (January 6, 1994): Appendix A, "The Debian Manifesto," http://www.debian.org/doc/manuals/project-history/ ap-manifesto.en.html.

[8]Jamie Zawinski, a former Lucid programmer who would go on to head the Mozilla development team, has a web site that documents the Lucid/GNU Emacs

fork, titled, "The Lemacs/FSFmacs Schism.", at http://www.jwz.org/doc/lemacs. html. Stallman's response to those accusations is in http://stallman.org/articles/ xemacs.origin.

[9]Debian Buzz in June 1996 contained non-free Netscape 3.01 in its Contrib section.

[10]Young uses the term "public domain" loosely here. Strictly speaking, it means "not copyrighted." Code released under the GNU GPL cannot be in the public domain, since it must be copyrighted in order for the GNU GPL to apply.

[11]This quote is taken from the much-publicized Torvalds-Tanenbaum "flame war" following the initial release of Linux. In the process of defending his choice of a nonportable monolithic kernel design, Torvalds says he started working on Linux as a way to learn more about his new 386 PC. "If the GNU kernel had been ready last spring, I'd not have bothered to even start my project." See Chris DiBona et al., *Open Sources* (O'Reilly & Associates, Inc., 1999): 224.

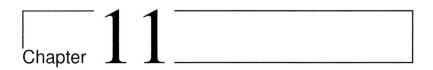

Chapter 11

Open Source

[RMS: In this chapter only, I have deleted some quotations. The material deleted was about open source and didn't relate to my life or my work.]

In November, 1995, Peter Salus, a member of the Free Software Foundation and author of the 1994 book, *A Quarter Century of Unix*, issued a call for papers to members of the GNU Project's "system-discuss" mailing list. Salus, the conference's scheduled chairman, wanted to tip off fellow hackers about the upcoming Conference on Freely Redistributable Software in Cambridge, Massachusetts. Slated for February, 1996, and sponsored by the Free Software Foundation, the event promised to be the first engineering conference solely dedicated to free software and, in a show of unity with other free software programmers, welcomed papers on "any aspect of GNU, Linux, NetBSD, 386BSD, FreeBSD, Perl, Tcl/tk, and other tools for which the code is accessible and redistributable." Salus wrote:

> Over the past 15 years, free and low-cost software has become ubiquitous. This conference will bring together implementers of several different types of freely redistributable software and publishers of such software (on various media). There will be tutorials and refereed papers, as well as keynotes by Linus Torvalds and Richard Stallman.[1]

Among the recipients of Salus' email was conference committee member Eric S. Raymond. Although not the leader of a project or company like the various other members of the list, Raymond had built a tidy reputation within the hacker community for some software projects and as editor of *The New Hacker's Dictionary*, a greatly enlarged version of *The Hacker's Dictionary* published a decade earlier by Guy Steele.

For Raymond, the 1996 conference was a welcome event. Although he did not thoroughly support the free software movement's ideas, he had contributed to some GNU programs, in particular to GNU Emacs. Those contributions stopped in 1992, when Raymond demanded authority to make changes in the official GNU version of GNU Emacs without discussing them with Stallman, who was directly in charge of Emacs development. Stallman rejected the demand, and Raymond accused Stallman of "micro-management." "Richard kicked up a fuss about my making unauthorized modifications when I was cleaning up the Emacs LISP libraries," Raymond recalls. "It frustrated me so much that I decided I didn't want to work with him anymore."

Despite the falling out, Raymond remained active in the free software community. So much so that when Salus suggested a conference pairing Stallman and Torvalds as keynote speakers, Raymond eagerly seconded the idea. With Stallman representing the older, wiser contingent of ITS/Unix hackers and Torvalds representing the younger, more energetic crop of Linux hackers, the pairing indicated a symbolic show of unity that could only be beneficial, especially to ambitious younger (i.e., below 40) hackers such as Raymond. "I sort of had a foot in both camps," Raymond says.

By the time of the conference, the tension between those two camps had become palpable. Both groups had one thing in common, though: the conference was their first chance to meet the Finnish *wunderkind* in the flesh. Surprisingly, Torvalds proved himself to be a charming, affable speaker. Possessing only a slight Swedish accent, Torvalds surprised audience members with his quick, self-effacing wit.[2]

Even more surprising, says Raymond, was Torvalds' equal willingness to take potshots at other prominent hackers, including the most prominent hacker of all, Richard Stallman. By the end of the conference, Torvalds' half-hacker, half-slacker manner was winning over older and younger conference-goers alike.

"It was a pivotal moment," recalls Raymond. "Before 1996, Richard was the only credible claimant to being the ideological leader of the entire culture. People who dissented didn't do so in public. The person who broke that taboo was Torvalds."

The ultimate breach of taboo would come near the end of the show. During a discussion on the growing market dominance of Microsoft Windows or some similar topic, Torvalds admitted to being a fan of Microsoft's PowerPoint slideshow software program. From the perspective of old-line software purists, it was like bragging about one's slaves at an abolitionist conference. From the perspective of Torvalds and his growing band of followers, it was simply common sense. Why shun convenient proprietary software programs just to make a point? They didn't agree with the point anyway. When freedom requires a sacrifice, those who don't care about freedom see the sacrifice as self-denial, rather than as a way to obtain something important. Being a hacker wasn't about self-denial, it was about getting the job done, and "the job," for them, was defined in practical terms.

"That was a pretty shocking thing to say," Raymond remembers. "Then again, he was able to do that, because by 1995 and 1996, he was rapidly acquiring clout."

Stallman, for his part, doesn't remember any tension at the 1996 conference; he probably wasn't present when Torvalds made that statement. But he does remember later feeling the sting of Torvalds' celebrated "cheekiness." "There was a thing in the Linux documentation which says print out the GNU coding standards and then tear them up," says Stallman, recalling one example. "When you look closely, what he disagreed with was the least important part of it, the recommendation for how to indent C code."

"OK, so he disagrees with some of our conventions. That's fine, but he picked a singularly nasty way of saying so. He could have just said, 'Here's the way I think you should indent your code.' Fine. There should be no hostility there."

For Raymond, the warm reception other hackers gave to Torvalds' comments confirmed a suspicion: the dividing line separating Linux developers from GNU developers was largely generational. Many Linux hackers, like Torvalds, had grown up in a world of proprietary software. They had begun contributing to free software without perceiving any injustice in nonfree software. For most of them, nothing was at stake beyond convenience. Unless a program was technically inferior, they saw little reason to reject it on licensing issues alone. Some day hackers might develop a free software alternative to PowerPoint. Until then, why criticize PowerPoint or Microsoft; why not use it?

This was an example of the growing dispute, within the free software community, between those who valued freedom as such, and those who mainly valued powerful, reliable software. Stallman referred to the two camps as political parties within the community, calling the former the "freedom party." The supporters of the other camp did not try to name it, so Stallman disparagingly called it the "bandwagon party" or the "success party," because many of them presented "more users" as the primary goal.

In the decade since launching the GNU Project, Stallman had built up a fearsome reputation as a programmer. He had also built up a reputation for intransigence both in terms of software design and people management. This was partly true, but the reputation provided a convenient excuse that anyone could cite if Stallman did not do as he wished. The reputation has been augmented by mistaken guesses.

For example, shortly before the 1996 conference, the Free Software Foundation experienced a full-scale staff defection. Brian Youmans, a current FSF staffer hired by Salus in the wake of the resignations, recalls the scene: "At one point, Peter [Salus] was the only staff member working in the office." The previous staff were unhappy with the executive director; as Bryt Bradley told her friends in December, 1995:

> [name omitted] (the Executive Director of the FSF) decided to come back from Medical/Political Leave last week. The office staff (Gena Bean, Mike Drain, and myself) decided we could not work with her as our supervisor because of the many mistakes she had made in her job tasks prior to her taking a leave. Also, there had been numerous instances where individuals were threatened with inappropriate firing and there were many instances of what we felt were verbal abuse from her to ALL members of the office staff. We requested (many times) that she not come back as our supervisor, but stated that we were willing to work with her as a co-worker. Our requests were ignored. We quit.

The executive director in question then gave Stallman an ultimatum: give her total autonomy in the office or she would quit. Stallman, as president of the FSF, declined to give her total control over its activities, so she resigned, and he recruited in Peter Salus to replace her.

When Raymond, an outsider, learned that these people had left the FSF, he presumed Stallman was at fault. This provided confirmation for his theory that Stallman's personality was the cause of any and all problems in the GNU Project.

Raymond had another theory: recent delays such as the Hurd and recent troubles such as the Lucid-Emacs schism reflected problems normally associated with software project management, not software code development.

Shortly after the Freely Redistributable Software Conference, Raymond began working on his own pet software project, a mail utility called "fetchmail." Taking a cue from Torvalds, Raymond issued his program with a tacked-on promise to update the source code as early and as often as possible. When users began sending in bug reports and feature suggestions, Raymond, at first anticipating a tangled mess, found the resulting software surprisingly sturdy. Analyzing the success of the Torvalds approach, Raymond issued a quick analysis: using the Internet as his "petri dish" and the harsh scrutiny of the hacker community as a form of natural selection, Torvalds had created an evolutionary model free of central planning.

What's more, Raymond decided, Torvalds had found a way around Brooks' Law. First articulated by Fred P. Brooks, manager of IBM's OS/360 project and author of the 1975 book, *The Mythical Man-Month*, Brooks' Law held that adding developers to a project only resulted in further project delays. Believing as most hackers that software, like soup, benefits from a limited number of cooks, Raymond sensed something revolutionary at work. In inviting more and more cooks into the kitchen, Torvalds had actually found a way to make the resulting software *better*.[3]

Raymond put his observations on paper. He crafted them into a speech, which he promptly delivered before a group of friends and neighbors in Chester County, Pennsylvania. Dubbed "The Cathedral and the Bazaar," the speech contrasted the "Bazaar" style originated by Torvalds with the "Cathedral" style generally used by everyone else.

Raymond says the response was enthusiastic, but not nearly as enthusiastic as the one he received during the 1997 Linux Kongress, a gathering of GNU/Linux users in Germany the next spring.

"At the Kongress, they gave me a standing ovation at the end of the speech," Raymond recalls. "I took that as significant for two reasons. For one thing, it meant they were excited by what they were hearing. For another thing, it meant they were excited even after hearing the speech delivered through a language barrier."

Eventually, Raymond would convert the speech into a paper, also titled "The Cathedral and the Bazaar." The paper drew its name from Raymond's central analogy. Previously, programs were "cathedrals," impressive, centrally planned monuments built to stand the test of time. Linux, on the other hand, was more like "a great babbling bazaar," a software program developed through the loose decentralizing dynamics of the Internet.

Raymond's paper associated the Cathedral style, which he and Stallman and many others had used, specifically with the GNU Project and Stallman, thus casting the contrast between development models as a comparison between Stallman and Torvalds. Where Stallman was his chosen example of the classic cathedral architect – i.e., a programming "wizard" who could disappear for 18 months and return with something like the GNU C Compiler – Torvalds was more like a genial dinner-party host. In letting others lead the Linux design discussion and stepping in only when the entire table needed a referee, Torvalds had created a development model very much reflective of his own laid-back personality. From Torvalds' perspective, the most important managerial task was not imposing control but keeping the ideas flowing.

Summarized Raymond, "I think Linus's cleverest and most consequential hack was not the construction of the Linux kernel itself, but rather his invention of the Linux development model."[4]

If the paper's description of these two styles of development was perceptive, its association of the Cathedral model specifically with Stallman (rather than all the others who had used it, including Raymond himself) was sheer calumny. In fact, the developers of some GNU packages including the GNU Hurd had read about and adopted

Torvalds' methods before Raymond tried them, though without analyzing them further and publicly championing them as Raymond's paper did. Thousands of hackers, reading Raymond's article, must have been led to a negative attitude towards GNU by this smear.

In summarizing the secrets of Torvalds' managerial success, Raymond attracted the attention of other members of the free software community for whom freedom was not a priority. They sought to interest business in the use and development of free software, and to do so, decided to cast the issue in terms of the values that appeal to business: powerful, reliable, cheap, advanced. Raymond became the best-known proponent of these ideas, and they reached the management of Netscape, whose proprietary browser was losing market share to Microsoft's equally proprietary Internet Explorer. Intrigued by a speech by Raymond, Netscape executives took the message back to corporate headquarters. A few months later, in January, 1998, the company announced its plan to publish the source code of its flagship Navigator web browser in the hopes of enlisting hacker support in future development.

When Netscape CEO Jim Barksdale cited Raymond's "Cathedral and the Bazaar" essay as a major influence upon the company's decision, the company instantly elevated Raymond to the level of hacker celebrity. He invited a few people including Larry Augustin, founder of VA Research which sold workstations with the GNU/Linux operating system preinstalled; Tim O'Reilly, founder of the publisher O'Reilly & Associates; and Christine Peterson, president of the Foresight Institute, a Silicon Valley think tank specializing in nanotechnology, to talk. "The meeting's agenda boiled down to one item: how to take advantage of Netscape's decision so that other companies might follow suit?"

Raymond doesn't recall the conversation that took place, but he does remember the first complaint addressed. Despite the best efforts of Stallman and other hackers to remind people that the word "free" in free software stood for freedom and not price, the message still wasn't getting through. Most business executives, upon hearing the term for the first time, interpreted the word as synonymous with "zero cost," tuning out any follow-up messages in short order. Until hackers found a way to get past this misunderstanding, the free software movement faced an uphill climb, even after Netscape.

Peterson, whose organization had taken an active interest in advancing the free software cause, offered an alternative: "open source."

Looking back, Peterson says she came up with the "open source" term while discussing Netscape's decision with a friend in the public relations industry. She doesn't remember where she came upon the term or if she borrowed it from another field, but she does remember her friend disliking the term.[5]

At the meeting, Peterson says, the response was dramatically different. "I was hesitant about suggesting it," Peterson recalls. "I had no standing with the group, so started using it casually, not highlighting it as a new term." To Peterson's surprise, the term caught on. By the end of the meeting, most of the attendees, including Raymond, seemed pleased by it.

Raymond says he didn't publicly use the term "open source" as a substitute for "free software" until a day or two after the Mozilla launch party, when O'Reilly had scheduled a meeting to talk about free software. Calling his meeting "the Freeware Summit," O'Reilly says he wanted to direct media and community attention to the other deserving projects that had also encouraged Netscape to release Mozilla. "All these guys had so much in common, and I was surprised they didn't all know each other," says O'Reilly. "I also wanted to let the world know just how great an impact the free software culture had already made. People were missing out on a large part of the free software tradition."

In putting together the invite list, however, O'Reilly made a decision that would have long-term political consequences. He decided to limit the list to west-coast developers such as Wall, Eric Allman, creator of sendmail, and Paul Vixie, creator of BIND. There were exceptions, of course: Pennsylvania-resident Raymond, who was already in town thanks to the Mozilla launch, earned an quick invite. So did Virginia-resident Guido van Rossum, creator of Python. "Frank Willison, my editor in chief and champion of Python within the company, invited him without first checking in with me," O'Reilly recalls. "I was happy to have him there, but when I started, it really was just a local gathering."

For some observers, the unwillingness to include Stallman's name on the list qualified as a snub. "I decided not to go to the event because of it," says Perens, remembering the summit. Raymond, who did go, says he argued for Stallman's inclusion to no avail. The snub rumor gained additional strength from the fact that O'Reilly, the event's host, had feuded publicly with Stallman over the issue of software-manual copyrights. Prior to the meeting, Stallman had argued that free software manuals should be as freely copyable and modifiable as free software programs. O'Reilly, meanwhile, argued that a value-added market for nonfree books increased the utility of free software by making it more accessible to a wider community. The two had also disputed the title of the event, with Stallman insisting on "Free Software" rather than "Freeware." The latter term most often refers to programs which are available gratis, but which are not free software because their source code is not released.

Looking back, O'Reilly doesn't see the decision to leave Stallman's name off the invite list as a snub. "At that time, I had never met Richard in person, but in our email interactions, he'd been inflexible and unwilling to engage in dialogue. I wanted to make sure the GNU tradition was represented at the meeting, so I invited John Gilmore and Michael Tiemann, whom I knew personally, and whom I knew were passionate about the value of the GPL but seemed more willing to engage in a frank back-and-forth about the strengths and weaknesses of the various free software projects and traditions. Given all the later brouhaha, I do wish I'd invited Richard as well, but I certainly don't think that my failure to do so should be interpreted as a lack of respect for the GNU Project or for Richard personally."

Snub or no snub, both O'Reilly and Raymond say the term "open source" won over just enough summit-goers to qualify as a success. The attendees shared ideas and experiences and brainstormed on how to improve free software's image. Of key concern was how to point out the successes of free software, particularly in the realm of Internet infrastructure, as opposed to playing up the GNU/Linux challenge to Microsoft Windows. But like the earlier meeting at VA, the discussion soon turned to the problems associated with the term "free software." O'Reilly, the summit host, remembers a comment from Torvalds, a summit attendee.

"Linus had just moved to Silicon Valley at that point, and he explained how only recently that he had learned that the word 'free' had two meanings – free as in 'libre' and free as in 'gratis' – in English."

Michael Tiemann, founder of Cygnus, proposed an alternative to the troublesome "free software" term: sourceware. "Nobody got too excited about it," O'Reilly recalls. "That's when Eric threw out the term 'open source.'"

Although the term appealed to some, support for a change in official terminology was far from unanimous. At the end of the one-day conference, attendees put the three terms – free software, open source, or sourceware – to a vote. According to O'Reilly, 9 out of the 15 attendees voted for "open source." Although some still quibbled with the term, all attendees agreed to use it in future discussions with the press. "We wanted to go out with a solidarity message," O'Reilly says.

The term didn't take long to enter the national lexicon. Shortly after the summit, O'Reilly shepherded summit attendees to a press conference attended by reporters from the *New York Times*, the *Wall Street Journal*, and other prominent publications. Within a few months, Torvalds' face was appearing on the cover of *Forbes* magazine, with the faces of Stallman, Perl creator Larry Wall, and Apache team leader Brian Behlendorf featured in the interior spread. Open source was open for business.

For summit attendees such as Tiemann, the solidarity message was the most important thing. Although his company had achieved a fair amount of success selling free software tools and services, he sensed the difficulty other programmers and entrepreneurs faced.

"There's no question that the use of the word free was confusing in a lot of situations," Tiemann says. "Open source positioned itself as being business friendly and business sensible. Free software positioned itself as morally righteous. For better or worse we figured it was more advantageous to align with the open source crowd."

Raymond called Stallman after the meeting to tell him about the new term "open source" and ask if he would use it. Raymond says Stallman briefly considered adopting the term, only to discard it. "I know because I had direct personal conversations about it," Raymond says.

Stallman's immediate response was, "I'll have to think about it." The following day he had concluded that the values of Raymond and O'Reilly would surely dominate the future discourse of "open source," and that the best way to keep the ideas of the free software movement in public view was to stick to its traditional term.

Later in 1998, Stallman announced his position: "open source," while helpful in communicating the technical advantages of free software also encouraged speakers to soft-pedal the issue of software freedom. It avoided the unintended meaning of "gratis software" and the intended meaning of "freedom-respecting software" equally. As a means for conveying the latter meaning, it was therefore no use. In effect, Raymond and O'Reilly had given a name to the nonidealistic political party in the community, the one Stallman did not agree with.

In addition, Stallman thought that the ideas of "open source" led people to put too much emphasis on winning the support of business. While such support in itself wasn't necessarily bad in itself, he expected that being too desperate for it would lead to harmful compromises. "Negotiation 101 would teach you that if you are desperate to get someone's agreement, you are asking for a bad deal," he says. "You need to be prepared to say no." Summing up his position at the 1999 LinuxWorld Convention and Expo, an event billed by Torvalds himself as a "coming out party" for the "Linux" community, Stallman implored his fellow hackers to resist the lure of easy compromise.

"Because we've shown how much we can do, we don't have to be desperate to work with companies or compromise our goals," Stallman said during a panel discussion. "Let them offer and we'll accept. We don't have to change what we're doing to get them to help us. You can take a single step towards a goal, then another and then more and more and you'll actually reach your goal. Or, you can take a half measure that means you don't ever take another step, and you'll never get there."

Even before the LinuxWorld show, however, Stallman was showing an increased willingness to alienate open source supporters. A few months after the Freeware Summit, O'Reilly hosted its second annual Perl Conference. This time around, Stallman was in attendance. During a panel discussion lauding IBM's decision to employ the free software Apache web server in its commercial offerings, Stallman, taking advantage of an audience microphone, made a sharp denunciation of panelist John Ousterhout, creator of the Tcl scripting language. Stallman branded Ousterhout a "parasite" on the free software community for marketing a proprietary version of Tcl via Ousterhout's startup company, Scriptics. Ousterhout had stated that Scriptics would contribute only the barest minimum of its improvements to the free version of Tcl, meaning it would in effect use that small contribution to win community approval for much a larger amount of nonfree software development. Stallman rejected this position and denounced Scriptics' plans. "I don't think Scriptics is necessary for the continued existence of Tcl," Stallman said to hisses from the fellow audience members.[6]

"It was a pretty ugly scene," recalls Prime Time Freeware's Rich Morin. "John's done some pretty respectable things: Tcl, Tk, Sprite. He's a real contributor." Despite his sympathies for Stallman and Stallman's position, Morin felt empathy for those troubled by Stallman's discordant words.

Stallman will not apologize. "Criticizing proprietary software isn't ugly – proprietary software is ugly. Ousterhout had indeed made real contributions in the past, but the point is that Scriptics was going to be nearly 100% a proprietary software company. In that conference, standing up for freedom meant disagreeing with nearly everyone. Speaking from the audience, I could only say a few sentences. The only way to raise the issue so it would not be immediately forgotten was to put it in strong terms."

"If people rebuke me for 'making a scene' when I state a serious criticism of someone's conduct, while calling Torvalds 'cheeky' for saying nastier things about trivial matters, that seems like a double standard to me."

Stallman's controversial criticism of Ousterhout momentarily alienated a potential sympathizer, Bruce Perens. In 1998, Eric Raymond proposed launching the Open Source Initiative, or OSI, an organization that would police the use of the term "open source" and provide a definition for companies interested in making their own programs. Raymond recruited Perens to draft the definition.[7]

Perens would later resign from the OSI, expressing regret that the organization had set itself up in opposition to Stallman and the FSF. Still, looking back on the need for a free software definition outside the Free Software Foundation's auspices, Perens understands why other hackers might still feel the need for distance. "I really like and admire Richard," says Perens. "I do think Richard would do his job better if Richard had more balance. That includes going away from free software for a couple of months."

Stallman's energies would do little to counteract the public-relations momentum of open source proponents. In August of 1998, when chipmaker Intel purchased a stake in GNU/Linux vendor Red Hat, an accompanying *New York Times* article described the company as the product of a movement "known alternatively as free software and open source."[8] Six months later, a John Markoff article on Apple Computer was proclaiming the company's adoption of the "open source" Apache server in the article headline.[9]

Such momentum would coincide with the growing momentum of companies that actively embraced the "open source" term. By August of 1999, Red Hat, a company that now eagerly billed itself as "open source," was selling shares on Nasdaq. In December, VA Linux – formerly VA Research – was floating its own IPO to historic effect. Opening at $30 per share, the company's stock price exploded past the $300 mark in initial trading only to settle back down to the $239 level. Shareholders lucky enough to get in at the bottom and stay until the end experienced a 698% increase in paper wealth, a Nasdaq record. Eric Raymond, as a board member, owned shares worth $36 million. However, these high prices were temporary; they tumbled when the dot-com boom ended.

The open source proponents' message was simple: all you need, to sell the free software concept, is to make it business-friendly. They saw Stallman and the free software movement as fighting the market; they sought instead to leverage it. Instead of playing the role of high-school outcasts, they had played the game of celebrity, magnifying their power in the process.

These methods won great success for open source, but not for the ideals of free software. What they had done to "spread the message" was to omit the most important part of it: the idea of freedom as an ethical issue. The effects of this omission are visible today: as of 2009, nearly all GNU/Linux distributions include proprietary programs, Torvalds' version of Linux contains proprietary firmware programs, and the company formerly called VA Linux bases its business on proprietary software. Over half of all the world's web servers run some version of Apache, and the usual version of Apache is free software, but many of those sites run a proprietary modified version distributed by IBM.

"On his worst days Richard believes that Linus Torvalds and I conspired to hijack his revolution," Raymond says. "Richard's rejection of the term open source and his deliberate creation of an ideological fissure in my view comes from an odd mix of idealism and territoriality. There are people out there who think it's all Richard's personal ego. I don't believe that. It's more that he so personally associates himself with the free software idea that he sees any threat to that as a threat to himself."

Stallman responds, "Raymond misrepresents my views: I don't think Torvalds 'conspired' with anyone, since being sneaky is not his way. However, Raymond's nasty conduct is visible in those statements themselves. Rather than respond to my views (even as he claims they are) on their merits, he proposes psychological interpretations for them. He attributes the harshest interpretation to unnamed others, then 'defends' me by proposing a slightly less derogatory one. He has often 'defended' me this way."

Ironically, the success of open source and open source advocates such as Raymond would not diminish Stallman's role as a leader – but it would lead many to misunderstand what he is a leader of. Since the free software movement lacks the corporate and media recognition of open source, most users of GNU/Linux do not hear that it exists, let alone what its views are. They have heard the ideas and values of open source, and they never imagine that Stallman might have different ones. Thus he receives messages thanking him for his advocacy of "open source," and explains in response that he has never been a supporter of that, using the occasion to inform the sender about free software.

Some writers recognize the term "free software" by using the term "FLOSS," which stands for "Free/Libre and Open Source Software." However, they often say there is a single "FLOSS" movement, which is like saying that the U.S. has a "Liberal/Conservative" movement, and the views they usually associate with this supposed single movement are the open source views they have heard.

Despite all these obstacles, the free software movement does make its ideas heard sometimes, and continues to grow in absolute terms. By sticking to its guns, and presenting its ideas in contrast to those of open source, it gains ground. "One of Stallman's primary character traits is the fact he doesn't budge," says Ian Murdock. "He'll wait up to a decade for people to come around to his point of view if that's what it takes."

Murdock, for one, finds that unbudgeable nature both refreshing and valuable. Stallman may no longer be the solitary leader of the free software movement, but he is still the polestar of the free software community. "You always know that he's going to be consistent in his views," Murdock says. "Most people aren't like that. Whether you agree with him or not, you really have to respect that."

Endnotes

[1] See Peter Salus, "FYI-Conference on Freely Redistributable Software, 2/2, Cambridge" (1995) (archived by Terry Winograd), http://bat8.inria.fr/~lang/hotlist/free/licence/fsf96/call-for-papers.html.

[2] Although Linus Torvalds is Finnish, his mother tongue is Swedish. "The Rampantly Unofficial Linus FAQ" at http://catb.org/~esr/faqs/linus/ offers a brief explanation:

> Finland has a significant (about 6%) Swedish-speaking minority population. They call themselves *finlandssvensk* or *finlandssvenskar* and consider themselves Finns; many of their families have lived in Finland for centuries. Swedish is one of Finland's two official languages.

[3] Brooks' Law is the shorthand summary of the following quote taken from Brooks' book:

> Since software construction is inherently a systems effort – an exercise in complex interrelationships – communication effort is great, and it quickly dominates the decrease in individual task time brought about by partitioning. Adding more men then lengthens, not shortens, the schedule.

See Fred P. Brooks, *The Mythical Man-Month* (Addison Wesley Publishing, 1995).

[4] See Eric Raymond, "The Cathedral and the Bazaar" (1997).

[5] See Malcolm Maclachlan, "Profit Motive Splits Open Source Movement," *TechWeb News* (August 26, 1998), http://www.techweb.com/article/showArticle?articleID=29102344.

[6] *Ibid.*

[7] See Bruce Perens et al., "The Open Source Definition," The Open Source Initiative (1998), http://www.opensource.org/docs/definition.html.

[8] See Amy Harmon, "For Sale: Free Operating System," *New York Times* (September 28, 1998), http://www.nytimes.com/library/tech/98/09/biztech/articles/28linux.html.

[9] See John Markoff, "Apple Adopts 'Open Source' for its Server Computers," *New York Times* (March 17, 1999), http://www.nytimes.com/library/tech/99/03/biztech/articles/17apple.html.

A Brief Journey through Hacker Hell

[RMS: In this chapter my only change is to add a few notes labeled like this one.]

Richard Stallman stares, unblinking, through the windshield of a rental car, waiting for the light to change as we make our way through downtown Kihei.

The two of us are headed to the nearby town of Pa'ia, where we are scheduled to meet up with some software programmers and their wives for dinner in about an hour or so.

It's about two hours after Stallman's speech at the Maui High Performance Center, and Kihei, a town that seemed so inviting before the speech, now seems profoundly uncooperative. Like most beach cities, Kihei is a one-dimensional exercise in suburban sprawl. Driving down its main drag, with its endless succession of burger stands, realty agencies, and bikini shops, it's hard not to feel like a steel-coated morsel passing through the alimentary canal of a giant commercial tapeworm. The feeling is exacerbated by the lack of side roads. With nowhere to go but forward, traffic moves in spring-like lurches. 200 yards ahead, a light turns green. By the time we are moving, the light is yellow again.

175

For Stallman, a lifetime resident of the east coast, the prospect of spending the better part of a sunny Hawaiian afternoon trapped in slow traffic is enough to trigger an embolism. [RMS: Since I was driving, I was also losing time to answer my email, and that's a real pain since I can barely keep up anyway.] Even worse is the knowledge that, with just a few quick right turns a quarter mile back, this whole situation easily could have been avoided. Unfortunately, we are at the mercy of the driver ahead of us, a programmer from the lab who knows the way and who has decided to take us to Pa'ia via the scenic route instead of via the nearby Pilani Highway.

"This is terrible," says Stallman between frustrated sighs. "Why didn't we take the other route?"

Again, the light a quarter mile ahead of us turns green. Again, we creep forward a few more car lengths. This process continues for another 10 minutes, until we finally reach a major crossroad promising access to the adjacent highway.

The driver ahead of us ignores it and continues through the intersection.

"Why isn't he turning?" moans Stallman, throwing up his hands in frustration. "Can you believe this?"

I decide not to answer either. I find the fact that I am sitting in a car with Stallman in the driver seat, in Maui no less, unbelievable enough. Until two hours ago, I didn't even know Stallman knew how to drive. Now, listening to Yo-Yo Ma's cello playing the mournful bass notes of "Appalachian Journey" on the car stereo and watching the sunset pass by on our left, I do my best to fade into the upholstery.

When the next opportunity to turn finally comes up, Stallman hits his right turn signal in an attempt to cue the driver ahead of us. No such luck. Once again, we creep slowly through the intersection, coming to a stop a good 200 yards before the next light. By now, Stallman is livid.

"It's like he's deliberately ignoring us," he says, gesturing and pantomiming like an air craft carrier landing-signals officer in a futile attempt to catch our guide's eye. The guide appears unfazed, and for the next five minutes all we see is a small portion of his head in the rearview mirror.

I look out Stallman's window. Nearby Kahoolawe and Lanai Islands provide an ideal frame for the setting sun. It's a breathtaking view, the kind that makes moments like this a bit more bearable if you're a Hawaiian native, I suppose. I try to direct Stallman's attention to it, but Stallman, by now obsessed by the inattentiveness of the driver ahead of us, blows me off.

When the driver passes through another green light, completely ignoring a "Pilani Highway Next Right," I grit my teeth. I remember an early warning relayed to me by BSD programmer Keith Bostic. "Stallman does not suffer fools gladly," Bostic warned me. "If somebody says or does something stupid, he'll look them in the eye and say, 'That's stupid.'"

Looking at the oblivious driver ahead of us, I realize that it's the stupidity, not the inconvenience, that's killing Stallman right now.

"It's as if he picked this route with absolutely no thought on how to get there efficiently," Stallman says.

The word "efficiently" hangs in the air like a bad odor. Few things irritate the hacker mind more than inefficiency. It was the inefficiency of checking the Xerox laser printer two or three times a day that triggered Stallman's initial inquiry into the printer source code. It was the inefficiency of rewriting software tools hijacked by commercial software vendors that led Stallman to battle Symbolics and to launch the GNU Project. If, as Jean Paul Sartre once opined, hell is other people, hacker hell is duplicating other people's stupid mistakes, and it's no exaggeration to say that Stallman's entire life has been an attempt to save mankind from these fiery depths.

This hell metaphor becomes all the more apparent as we take in the slowly passing scenery. With its multitude of shops, parking lots, and poorly timed street lights, Kihei seems less like a city and more like a poorly designed software program writ large. Instead of rerouting traffic and distributing vehicles through side streets and expressways, city planners have elected to run everything through a single main drag. From a hacker perspective, sitting in a car amidst all this mess is like listening to a CD rendition of nails on a chalkboard at full volume.

"Imperfect systems infuriate hackers," observes Steven Levy, another warning I should have listened to before climbing into the car with Stallman. "This is one reason why hackers generally hate driving cars – the system of randomly programmed red lights and oddly laid out one-way streets causes delays which are so goddamn *unnec-*

essary [Levy's emphasis] that the impulse is to rearrange signs, open up traffic-light control boxes . . . redesign the entire system."[1]

More frustrating, however, is the duplicity of our trusted guide. Instead of searching out a clever shortcut – as any true hacker would do on instinct – the driver ahead of us has instead chosen to play along with the city planners' game. Like Virgil in Dante's *Inferno*, our guide is determined to give us the full guided tour of this hacker hell whether we want it or not.

Before I can make this observation to Stallman, the driver finally hits his right turn signal. Stallman's hunched shoulders relax slightly, and for a moment the air of tension within the car dissipates. The tension comes back, however, as the driver in front of us slows down. "Construction Ahead" signs line both sides of the street, and even though the Pilani Highway lies less than a quarter mile off in the distance, the two-lane road between us and the highway is blocked by a dormant bulldozer and two large mounds of dirt.

It takes Stallman a few seconds to register what's going on as our guide begins executing a clumsy five-point U-turn in front of us. When he catches a glimpse of the bulldozer and the "No Through Access" signs just beyond, Stallman finally boils over.

"Why, why, why?" he whines, throwing his head back. "You should have known the road was blocked. You should have known this way wouldn't work. You did this deliberately." [RMS: I meant that he chose the slow road deliberately. As explained below, I think these quotes are not exact.]

The driver finishes the turn and passes us on the way back toward the main drag. As he does so, he shakes his head and gives us an apologetic shrug. Coupled with a toothy grin, the driver's gesture reveals a touch of mainlander frustration but is tempered with a protective dose of islander fatalism. Coming through the sealed windows of our rental car, it spells out a succinct message: "Hey, it's Maui; what are you gonna do?"

Stallman can take it no longer.

"Don't you fucking smile!" he shouts, fogging up the glass as he does so. "It's your fucking fault. This all could have been so much easier if we had just done it my way." [RMS: These quotes appear to be inaccurate, because I don't use "fucking" as an adverb. This was not an interview, so Williams would not have had a tape recorder running. I'm sure things happened overall as described, but these quotations probably reflect his understanding rather than my words.]

Stallman accents the words "my way" by gripping the steering wheel and pulling himself towards it twice. The image of Stallman's lurching frame is like that of a child throwing a temper tantrum in a car seat, an image further underlined by the tone of Stallman's voice. Halfway between anger and anguish, Stallman seems to be on the verge of tears.

Fortunately, the tears do not arrive. Like a summer cloudburst, the tantrum ends almost as soon as it begins. After a few whiny gasps, Stallman shifts the car into reverse and begins executing his own U-turn. By the time we are back on the main drag, his face is as impassive as it was when we left the hotel 30 minutes earlier.

It takes less than five minutes to reach the next cross-street. This one offers easy highway access, and within seconds, we are soon speeding off toward Pa'ia at a relaxing rate of speed. The sun that once loomed bright and yellow over Stallman's left shoulder is now burning a cool orange-red in our rearview mirror. It lends its color to the gauntlet wili wili trees flying past us on both sides of the highway.

For the next 20 minutes, the only sound in our vehicle, aside from the ambient hum of the car's engine and tires, is the sound of a cello and a violin trio playing the mournful strains of an Appalachian folk tune.

Endnotes

[1] See Steven Levy, *Hackers* (Penguin USA [paperback], 1984): 40.

Chapter 13

Continuing the Fight

For Richard Stallman, time may not heal all wounds, but it does provide a convenient ally.

Four years after "The Cathedral and the Bazaar," Stallman still chafes over the Raymond critique. He also grumbles over Linus Torvalds' elevation to the role of world's most famous hacker. He recalls a popular T-shirt that began showing at Linux tradeshows around 1999. Designed to mimic the original promotional poster for Star Wars, the shirt depicted Torvalds brandishing a lightsaber like Luke Skywalker, while Stallman's face rides atop R2D2. The shirt still grates on Stallman's nerves not only because it depicts him as Torvalds' sidekick, but also because it elevates Torvalds to the leadership role in the free software community, a role even Torvalds himself is loath to accept. "It's ironic," says Stallman mournfully. "Picking up that sword is exactly what Linus refuses to do. He gets everybody focusing on him as the symbol of the movement, and then he won't fight. What good is it?"

Then again, it is that same unwillingness to "pick up the sword," on Torvalds' part, that has left the door open for Stallman to bolster his reputation as the hacker community's ethical arbiter. Despite his grievances, Stallman has to admit that the last few years have been quite good, both to himself and to his organization. Relegated to the periphery by the ironic success of the GNU/Linux system because users thought of it as "Linux," Stallman has nonetheless successfully recaptured the initiative. His speaking schedule between January 2000 and December 2001 included stops on six continents and visits to countries where the notion of software freedom carries heavy overtones – China and India, for example.

Outside the bully pulpit, Stallman has taken advantage of the leverage of the GNU General Public License (GPL), of which he remains the steward. During the summer of 2000, while the air was rapidly leaking out of the 1999 Linux IPO bubble, Stallman and the Free Software Foundation scored two major victories. In July, 2000, Trolltech, a Norwegian software company and developer of Qt, a graphical interface library that ran on the GNU/Linux operating system, announced it was licensing its software under the GPL. A few weeks later, Sun Microsystems, a company that, until then, had been warily trying to ride the open source bandwagon without actually contributing its code, finally relented and announced that it, too, was dual licensing its new OpenOffice[1] application suite under the Lesser GNU Public License (LGPL) and the Sun Industry Standards Source License (SISSL).

In the case of Trolltech, this victory was the result of a protracted effort by the GNU Project. The nonfreeness of Qt was a serious problem for the free software community because KDE, a free graphical desktop environment that was becoming popular, depended on it. Qt was non-free software but Trolltech had invited free software projects (such as KDE) to use it gratis. Although KDE itself was free software, users that insisted on freedom couldn't run it, since they had to reject Qt. Stallman recognized that many users would want a graphical desktop on GNU/Linux, and most would not value freedom enough to reject the temptation of KDE, with Qt hiding within. The danger was that GNU/Linux would become a motor for the installation of KDE, and therefore also of non-free Qt. This would undermine the freedom which was the purpose of GNU.

To deal with this danger, Stallman recruited people to launch two parallel counterprojects. One was GNOME, the GNU free graphical desktop environment. The other was Harmony, a compatible free replacement for Qt. If GNOME succeeded, KDE would not be necessary; if Harmony succeeded, KDE would not need Qt. Either way, users would be able to have a graphical desktop on GNU/Linux without nonfree Qt.

In 1999, these two efforts were making good progress, and the management of Trolltech were starting to feel the pressure. So Trolltech released Qt under its own free software license, the QPL. The QPL qualified as a free license, but Stallman pointed out the drawback of incompatibility with the GPL: in general, combining GPL-covered code with Qt in one program was impossible without violating one license or the other. Eventually the Trolltech management recognized that the GPL would serve their purposes equally well, and released Qt with dual licensing: the same Qt code, in parallel, was available under the GNU GPL and under the QPL. After three years, this was victory.

Once Qt was free, the motive for developing Harmony (which wasn't complete enough for actual use) had disappeared, and the developers abandoned it. GNOME had acquired substantial momentum, so its development continued, and it remains the main GNU graphical desktop.

Sun desired to play according to the Free Software Foundation's conditions. At the 1999 O'Reilly Open Source Conference, Sun Microsystems cofounder and chief scientist Bill Joy defended his company's "community source" license, essentially a watered-down compromise letting users copy and modify Sun-owned software but not sell copies of said software without negotiating a royalty agreement with Sun. (With this restriction, the license did not qualify as free, nor for that matter as open source.) A year after Joy's speech, Sun Microsystems vice president Marco Boerries was appearing on the same stage spelling out the company's new licensing compromise in the case of OpenOffice, an office-application suite designed specifically for the GNU/Linux operating system.

"I can spell it out in three letters," said Boerries. "GPL."

At the time, Boerries said his company's decision had little to do with Stallman and more to do with the momentum of GPL-protected programs. "What basically happened was the recognition that different products attracted different communities, and the license you use depends on what type of community you want to attract," said Boerries. "With [OpenOffice], it was clear we had the highest correlation

with the GPL community."[2] Alas, this victory was incomplete, since
OpenOffice recommends the use of nonfree plug-ins.

Such comments point out the under-recognized strength of the
GPL and, indirectly, the political genius of the man who played the
largest role in creating it. "There isn't a lawyer on earth who would
have drafted the GPL the way it is," says Eben Moglen, Columbia
University law professor and Free Software Foundation general counsel. "But it works. And it works because of Richard's philosophy of
design."

A former professional programmer, Moglen traces his pro bono
work with Stallman back to 1990 when Stallman requested Moglen's
legal assistance on a private affair. Moglen, then working with encryption expert Phillip Zimmerman during Zimmerman's legal battles
with the federal government, says he was honored by the request.[3]

"I told him I used Emacs every day of my life, and it would take
an awful lot of lawyering on my part to pay off the debt."

Since then, Moglen, perhaps more than any other individual, has
had the best chance to observe the crossover of Stallman's hacker
philosophies into the legal realm. Moglen says Stallman's approach
to legal code and his approach to software code are largely the same.
"I have to say, as a lawyer, the idea that what you should do with a
legal document is to take out all the bugs doesn't make much sense,"
Moglen says. "There is uncertainty in every legal process, and what
most lawyers want to do is to capture the benefits of uncertainty for
their client. Richard's goal is the complete opposite. His goal is to
remove uncertainty, which is inherently impossible. It is inherently
impossible to draft one license to control all circumstances in all legal
systems all over the world. But if you were to go at it, you would have
to go at it his way. And the resulting elegance, the resulting simplicity
in design almost achieves what it has to achieve. And from there a
little lawyering will carry you quite far."

As the person charged with pushing the Stallman agenda, Moglen
understands the frustration of would-be allies. "Richard is a man
who does not want to compromise over matters that he thinks of as
fundamental," Moglen says, "and he does not take easily the twisting
of words or even just the seeking of artful ambiguity, which human
society often requires from a lot of people."

In addition to helping the Free Software Foundation, Moglen has provided legal aid to other copyright defendants, such as Dmitry Sklyarov, and distributors of the DVD decryption program deCSS. Sklyarov had written and released a program to break digital copyprotection on Adobe e-Books, in Russia where there was no law against it, as an employee of a Russian company. He was then arrested while visiting the US to give a scientific paper about his work. Stallman eagerly participated in protests condemning Adobe for having Sklyarov arrested, and the Free Software Foundation denounced the Digital Millennium Copyright Act as "censorship of software," but it could not intervene in favor of Sklyarov's program because that was nonfree. Thus, Moglen worked for Sklyarov's defense through the Electronic Frontier Foundation. The FSF avoided involvement in the distribution of deCSS, since that was illegal, but Stallman condemned the U.S. government for prohibiting deCSS, and Moglen worked as direct counsel for the defendants.

Following the FSF's decision not to involve itself in those cases, Moglen has learned to appreciate the value of Stallman's stubbornness. "There have been times over the years where I've gone to Richard and said, 'We have to do this. We have to do that. Here's the strategic situation. Here's the next move. Here's what he have to do.' And Richard's response has always been, 'We don't have to do anything.' Just wait. What needs doing will get done."

"And you know what?" Moglen adds. "Generally, he's been right."

Such comments disavow Stallman's own self-assessment: "I'm not good at playing games," Stallman says, addressing the many unseen critics who see him as a shrewd strategist. "I'm not good at looking ahead and anticipating what somebody else might do. My approach has always been to focus on the foundation [of ideas], to say 'Let's make the foundation as strong as we can make it.'"

The GPL's expanding popularity and continuing gravitational strength are the best tributes to the foundation laid by Stallman and his GNU colleagues. While Stallman was never the sole person in the world releasing free software, he nevertheless can take sole credit for building the free software movement's ethical framework. Whether or not other modern programmers feel comfortable working inside that framework is immaterial. The fact that they even have a choice at all is Stallman's greatest legacy.

Discussing Stallman's legacy at this point seems a bit premature. Stallman, 48 at the time of this writing, still has a few years left to add to or subtract from that legacy. Still, the momentum of the free software movement makes it tempting to examine Stallman's life outside the day-to-day battles of the software industry and within a more august, historical setting.

To his credit, Stallman refuses all opportunities to speculate about this. "I've never been able to work out detailed plans of what the future was going to be like," says Stallman, offering his own premature epitaph. "I just said 'I'm going to fight. Who knows where I'll get?'"

There's no question that in picking his fights, Stallman has alienated the very people who might otherwise have been his greatest champions, had he been willing to fight for their views instead of his own. It is also a testament to his forthright, ethical nature that many of Stallman's erstwhile political opponents still manage to put in a few good words for him when pressed. The tension between Stallman the ideologue and Stallman the hacker genius, however, leads a biographer to wonder: how will people view Stallman when Stallman's own personality is no longer there to get in the way?

In early drafts of this book, I dubbed this question the "100 year" question. Hoping to stimulate an objective view of Stallman and his work, I asked various software-industry luminaries to take themselves out of the current timeframe and put themselves in a position of a historian looking back on the free software movement 100 years in the future. From the current vantage point, it is easy to see similarities between Stallman and past Americans who, while somewhat marginal during their lifetime, have attained heightened historical importance in relation to their age. Easy comparisons include Henry David Thoreau, transcendentalist philosopher and author of *Civil Disobedience*, and John Muir, founder of the Sierra Club and progenitor of the modern environmental movement. It is also easy to see similarities in men like William Jennings Bryan, a.k.a. "The Great Commoner," leader of the populist movement, enemy of monopolies, and a man who, though powerful, seems to have faded into historical insignificance.

Although not the first person to view software as public property, Stallman is guaranteed a footnote in future history books thanks to the GPL. Given that fact, it seems worthwhile to step back and examine Richard Stallman's legacy outside the current time frame. Will the

GPL still be something software programmers use in the year 2102, or will it have long since fallen by the wayside? Will the term "free software" seem as politically quaint as "free silver" does today, or will it seem eerily prescient in light of later political events?

Predicting the future is risky sport. Stallman refuses, saying that asking what people will think in 100 years presumes we have no influence over it. The question he prefers is, "What should we do to make a better future?" But most people, when presented with the predictive question, seemed eager to bite.

"One hundred years from now, Richard and a couple of other people are going to deserve more than a footnote," says Moglen. "They're going to be viewed as the main line of the story."

The "couple of other people" Moglen nominates for future textbook chapters include John Gilmore, who beyond contributing in various ways to free software has founded the Electronic Frontier Foundation, and Theodor Holm Nelson, a.k.a. Ted Nelson, author of the 1982 book, *Literary Machines*. Moglen says Stallman, Nelson, and Gilmore each stand out in historically significant, nonoverlapping ways. He credits Nelson, commonly considered to have coined the term "hypertext," for identifying the predicament of information ownership in the digital age. Gilmore and Stallman, meanwhile, earn notable credit for identifying the negative political effects of information control and building organizations – the Electronic Frontier Foundation in the case of Gilmore and the Free Software Foundation in the case of Stallman – to counteract those effects. Of the two, however, Moglen sees Stallman's activities as more personal and less political in nature.

"Richard was unique in that the ethical implications of unfree software were particularly clear to him at an early moment," says Moglen. "This has a lot to do with Richard's personality, which lots of people will, when writing about him, try to depict as epiphenomenal or even a drawback in Richard Stallman's own life work."

Gilmore, who describes his inclusion between the erratic Nelson and the irascible Stallman as something of a "mixed honor," nevertheless seconds the Moglen argument. Writes Gilmore:

My guess is that Stallman's writings will stand up as well as Thomas Jefferson's have; he's a pretty clear writer and also clear on his principles... Whether Richard will be as

influential as Jefferson will depend on whether the abstractions we call "civil rights" end up more important a hundred years from now than the abstractions that we call
"software" or "technically imposed restrictions."

Another element of the Stallman legacy not to be overlooked,
Gilmore writes, is the collaborative software-development model pioneered by the GNU Project. Although flawed at times, the model has
nevertheless evolved into a standard within the software-development
industry. All told, Gilmore says, this collaborative software-development
model may end up being even more influential than the GNU Project,
the GPL License, or any particular software program developed by
Stallman:

> Before the Internet, it was quite hard to collaborate over
> distance on software, even among teams that know and
> trust each other. Richard pioneered collaborative develop-
> ment of software, particularly by disorganized volunteers
> who seldom meet each other. Richard didn't build any of
> the basic tools for doing this (the TCP protocol, email lists,
> diff and patch, tar files, RCS or CVS or remote-CVS), but
> he used the ones that were available to form social groups
> of programmers who could effectively collaborate.

Stallman thinks that evaluation, though positive, misses the point.
"It emphasizes development methods over freedom, which reflects the
values of open source rather than free software. If that is how future
users look back on the GNU Project, I fear it will lead to a world in
which developers maintain users in bondage, and let them aid development occasionally as a reward, but never take the chains off them."

Lawrence Lessig, Stanford law professor and author of the 2001
book, *The Future of Ideas*, is similarly bullish. Like many legal scholars, Lessig sees the GPL as a major bulwark of the current so-called
"digital commons," the vast agglomeration of community-owned software programs, network and telecommunication standards that have
triggered the Internet's exponential growth over the last three decades.
Rather than connect Stallman with other Internet pioneers, men such
as Vannevar Bush, Vinton Cerf, and J. C. R. Licklider who convinced

others to see computer technology on a wider scale, Lessig sees Stallman's impact as more personal, introspective, and, ultimately, unique:

> [Stallman] changed the debate from "is" to "ought." He
> made people see how much was at stake, and he built a
> device to carry these ideals forward... That said, I don't
> quite know how to place him in the context of Cerf or
> Licklider. The innovation is different. It is not just about
> a certain kind of code, or enabling the Internet. [It's] much
> more about getting people to see the value in a certain kind
> of Internet. I don't think there is anyone else in that class,
> before or after.

Not everybody sees the Stallman legacy as set in stone, of course.
Eric Raymond, the open source proponent who feels that Stallman's
leadership role has diminished significantly since 1996, sees mixed signals when looking into the 2102 crystal ball:

> I think Stallman's artifacts (GPL, Emacs, GCC) will be
> seen as revolutionary works, as foundation-stones of the
> information world. I think history will be less kind to some
> of the theories from which RMS operated, and not kind at
> all to his personal tendency towards territorial, cult-leader
> behavior.

As for Stallman himself, he, too, sees mixed signals:

> What history says about the GNU Project, twenty years
> from now, will depend on who wins the battle of freedom to
> use public knowledge. If we lose, we will be just a footnote.
> If we win, it is uncertain whether people will know the role
> of the GNU operating system – if they think the system is
> "Linux," they will build a false picture of what happened
> and why.

> But even if we win, what history people learn a hundred
> years from now is likely to depend on who dominates po-
> litically.

Searching for his own 19th-century historical analogy, Stallman
summons the figure of John Brown, the militant abolitionist regarded

as a hero on one side of the Mason Dixon line and a madman on the other.

John Brown's slave revolt never got going, but during his subsequent trial he effectively roused national demand for abolition. During the Civil War, John Brown was a hero; 100 years after, and for much of the 1900s, history textbooks taught that he was crazy. During the era of legal segregation, while bigotry was shameless, the U.S. partly accepted the story that the South wanted to tell about itself, and history textbooks said many untrue things about the Civil War and related events.

Such comparisons document both the self-perceived peripheral nature of Stallman's current work and the binary nature of his current reputation. It's hard to see Stallman's reputation falling to the same level of infamy as Brown's did during the post-Reconstruction period. Stallman, despite his occasional war-like analogies, has done little to inspire violence. Still, it is easy to envision a future in which Stallman's ideas wind up on the ash-heap.[4]

Then again, it is that very will that may someday prove to be Stallman's greatest lasting legacy. Moglen, a close observer over the last decade, warns those who mistake the Stallman personality as counter-productive or epiphenomenal to the "artifacts" of Stallman's life. Without that personality, Moglen says, there would be precious few artifacts to discuss. Says Moglen, a former Supreme Court clerk:

> Look, the greatest man I ever worked for was Thurgood Marshall. I knew what made him a great man. I knew why he had been able to change the world in his possible way. I would be going out on a limb a little bit if I were to make a comparison, because they could not be more different: Thurgood Marshall was a man in society, representing an outcast society to the society that enclosed it, but still a man in society. His skill was social skills. But he was all of a piece, too. Different as they were in every other respect, the person I now most compare him to in that sense – of a piece, compact, made of the substance that makes stars, all the way through – is Stallman.

In an effort to drive that image home, Moglen reflects on a shared moment in the spring of 2000. The success of the VA Linux IPO was still resonating in the business media, and a half dozen issues related to free software were swimming through the news. Surrounded by a swirling hurricane of issues and stories each begging for comment, Moglen recalls sitting down for lunch with Stallman and feeling like a castaway dropped into the eye of the storm. For the next hour, he says, the conversation calmly revolved around a single topic: strengthening the GPL.

"We were sitting there talking about what we were going to do about some problems in Eastern Europe and what we were going to do when the problem of the ownership of content began to threaten free software," Moglen recalls. "As we were talking, I briefly thought about how we must have looked to people passing by. Here we are, these two little bearded anarchists, plotting and planning the next steps. And, of course, Richard is plucking the knots from his hair and dropping them in the soup and behaving in his usual way. Anybody listening in on our conversation would have thought we were crazy, but I knew: I knew the revolution's right here at this table. This is what's making it happen. And this man is the person making it happen."

Moglen says that moment, more than any other, drove home the elemental simplicity of the Stallman style.

"It was funny," recalls Moglen. "I said to him, 'Richard, you know, you and I are the two guys who didn't make any money out of this revolution.' And then I paid for the lunch, because I knew he didn't have the money to pay for it."[5]

Endnotes

[1]Sun was compelled by a trademark complaint to use the clumsy name "OpenOffice.org."

[2]Marco Boerries, interview with author (July, 2000).

[3]For more information on Zimmerman's legal travails, read Steven Levy's *Crypto*, p. 287-288. In the original book version of *Free as in Freedom*, I reported that Moglen helped defend Zimmerman against the National Security Agency. According to Levy's account, Zimmerman was investigated by the U.S. Attorney's office and U.S. Customs, not the NSA.

[4]RMS: Sam Williams' further words here, "In fashioning the free software cause not not as a mass movement but as a collection of private battles against the forces of proprietary temptation," do not fit the facts. Ever since the first announcement of the GNU Project, I have asked the public to support the cause. The free software movement aims to be a mass movement, and the only question is whether it has

enough supporters to qualify as "mass." As of 2009, the Free Software Foundation
has some 3000 members that pay the hefty dues, and over 20,000 subscribers to
its monthly e-mail newsletter.

[5]RMS: I never refuse to let people treat me to a meal, since my pride is not
based on picking up the check. But I surely did have the money to pay for lunch.
My income, which comes from around half the speeches I give, is much less than a
law professor's salary, but I'm not poor.

Epilogue from Sam Williams: Crushing Loneliness

[RMS: Because this chapter is so personally from Sam Williams, I have indicated all changes to the text with square brackets or ellipses, and I have made such changes only to clear up technical or legal points, and to remove passages that I found to be hostile and devoid of information. I have also added notes labeled 'RMS:' to respond to certain points. Williams has also changed the text of this chapter; changes made by Williams are not explicitly indicated.]

Writing the biography of a living person is a bit like producing a play. The drama in front of the curtain often pales in comparison to the drama backstage.

In *The Autobiography of Malcolm X*, Alex Haley gives readers a rare glimpse of that backstage drama. Stepping out of the ghostwriter role, Haley delivers the book's epilogue in his own voice. The epilogue explains how a freelance reporter originally dismissed as a "tool" and "spy" by the Nation of Islam spokesperson managed to work through personal and political barriers to get Malcolm X's life story on paper.

While I hesitate to compare this book with *The Autobiography of Malcolm X*, I do owe a debt of gratitude to Haley for his candid epilogue. Over the last 12 months, it has served as a sort of instruction manual on how to deal with a biographical subject who has built an entire career on being disagreeable. [RMS: I have built my career on saying no to things others accept without much question, but if I sometimes seem or am disagreeable, it is not through specific intention.] From the outset, I envisioned closing this biography with

193

a similar epilogue, both as an homage to Haley and as a way to let readers know how this book came to be.

The story behind this story starts in an Oakland apartment, winding its way through the various locales mentioned in the book – Silicon Valley, Maui, Boston, and Cambridge. Ultimately, however, it is a tale of two cities: New York, New York, the book-publishing capital of the world, and Sebastopol, California, the book-publishing capital of Sonoma County.

The story starts in April, 2000. At the time, I was writing stories for the ill-fated web site BeOpen.com. One of my first assignments was a phone interview with Richard M. Stallman. The interview went well, so well that Slashdot (`http://www.slashdot.org`), the popular "news for nerds" site owned by VA Software, Inc. (formerly VA Linux Systems and before that, VA Research), gave it a link in its daily list of feature stories. Within hours, the web servers at BeOpen were heating up as readers clicked over to the site.

For all intents and purposes, the story should have ended there. Three months after the interview, while attending the O'Reilly Open Source Conference in Monterey, California, I received the following email message from Tracy Pattison, foreign-rights manager at a large New York publishing house:

To: `sam@BeOpen.com`
Subject: RMS Interview
Date: Mon, 10 Jul 2000 15:56:37 -0400

Dear Mr. Williams,

I read your interview with Richard Stallman on BeOpen with great interest. I've been intrigued by RMS and his work for some time now and was delighted to find your piece which I really think you did a great job of capturing some of the spirit of what Stallman is trying to do with GNU-Linux and the Free Software Foundation.

What I'd love to do, however, is read more - and I don't think I'm alone. Do you think there is more information and/or sources out there to expand and update your interview and adapt it into more of a profile of Stallman? Perhaps including some more anecdotal information about his personality and background that might really interest and enlighten readers outside the more hardcore programming scene?

Tracy ended the email with a request that I give her a call to discuss the idea further. I did just that. Tracy told me her company was launching a new electronic book line, and it wanted stories that appealed to an early-adopter audience. The e-book format was 30,000 words, about 100 pages, and she had pitched her bosses on the idea of profiling a major figure in the hacker community. Her bosses liked the idea, and in the process of searching for interesting people to profile, she had come across my BeOpen interview with Stallman. Hence her email to me.

That's when Tracy asked me: would I be willing to expand the interview into a full-length feature profile?

My answer was instant: yes. Before accepting it, Tracy suggested I put together a story proposal she could show her superiors. Two days later, I sent her a polished proposal. A week later, Tracy sent me a follow up email. Her bosses had given it the green light.

I have to admit, getting Stallman to participate in an e-book project was an afterthought on my part. As a reporter who covered the open source beat, I knew Stallman was a stickler. I'd already received a half dozen emails at that point upbraiding me for the use of "Linux" instead of "GNU/Linux."

Then again, I also knew Stallman was looking for ways to get his message out to the general public. Perhaps if I presented the project to him that way, he would be more receptive. If not, I could always rely upon the copious amounts of documents, interviews, and recorded online conversations Stallman had left lying around the Internet and do an unauthorized biography.

During my research, I came across an essay titled "Freedom – Or Copyright?" Written by Stallman and published in the June, 2000, edition of the MIT *Technology Review*, the essay blasted e-books for an assortment of software sins. Not only did readers have to use proprietary software programs to read them, Stallman lamented, but the methods used to prevent unauthorized copying were overly harsh. Instead of downloading a transferable HTML or PDF file, readers downloaded an encrypted file. In essence, purchasing an e-book meant purchasing a nontransferable key to unscramble the encrypted content. Any attempt to open a book's content without an authorized key constituted a criminal violation of the Digital Millennium Copyright Act, the 1998 law designed to bolster copyright enforcement on the Internet. Similar penalties held for readers who converted a book's content into an open file format, even if their only intention was to read the book on a different computer in their home. Unlike a normal book, the reader no longer held the right to lend, copy, or resell an e-book. They only had the right to read it on an authorized machine, warned Stallman:

> We still have the same old freedoms in using paper books. But if e-books replace printed books, that exception will do little good. With "electronic ink," which makes it possible to download new text onto an apparently printed piece of paper, even newspapers could become ephemeral. Imagine: no more used book stores; no more lending a book to your friend; no more borrowing one from the public library – no more "leaks" that might give someone a chance to read without paying. (And judging from the ads for Microsoft Reader, no more anonymous purchasing of books either.) This is the world publishers have in mind for us.[1]

Needless to say, the essay caused some concern. Neither Tracy nor I had discussed the software her company would use nor had we discussed the type of copyright [license] that would govern the e-book's usage. I mentioned the *Technology Review* article and asked if she could give me information on her company's e-book policies. Tracy promised to get back to me.

Eager to get started, I decided to call Stallman anyway and mention the book idea to him. When I did, he expressed immediate interest and immediate concern. "Did you read my essay on e-books?" he asked.

When I told him, yes, I had read the essay and was waiting to hear back from the publisher, Stallman laid out two conditions: he didn't want to lend support to an e-book licensing mechanism he fundamentally opposed, and he didn't want to come off as lending support. "I don't want to participate in anything that makes me look like a hypocrite," he said.

For Stallman, the software issue was secondary to the copyright issue. He said he was willing to ignore whatever software the publisher or its third-party vendors employed just so long as the company specified within the copyright that readers were free to make and distribute verbatim copies of the e-book's content. Stallman pointed to Stephen King's *The Plant* as a possible model. In June, 2000, King announced on his official web site that he was self-publishing *The Plant* in serial form. According to the announcement, the book's total cost would be $13, spread out over a series of $1 installments. As long as at least 75% of the readers paid for each chapter, King promised to continue releasing new installments. By August, the plan seemed to be working, as King had published the first two chapters with a third on the way.

"I'd be willing to accept something like that," Stallman said. "As long as it also permitted verbatim copying." [RMS: As I recall, I also raised the issue of encryption; the text two paragraphs further down confirms this. I would not have agreed to publish the book in a way that *required* a nonfree program to read it.]

I forwarded the information to Tracy. Feeling confident that she and I might be able to work out an equitable arrangement, I called up Stallman and set up the first interview for the book. Stallman agreed to the interview without making a second inquiry into the status issue. Shortly after the first interview, I raced to set up a second interview (this one in Kihei), squeezing it in before Stallman headed off on a 14-day vacation to Tahiti. [RMS: That was not a pure vacation; I gave a speech there too.]

It was during Stallman's vacation that the bad news came from Tracy. Her company's legal department didn't want to adjust its [license] notice on the e-books. Readers who wanted to make their books transferable would [first have to crack the encryption code, to be able to convert the book to a free, public format such as HTML. This would be illegal and they might face criminal penalties.]

With two fresh interviews under my belt, I didn't see any way to write the book without resorting to the new material. I quickly set up a trip to New York to meet with my agent and with Tracy to see if there was a compromise solution.

When I flew to New York, I met my agent, Henning Guttman. It was our first face-to-face meeting, and Henning seemed pessimistic about our chances of forcing a compromise, at least on the publisher's end. The large, established publishing houses already viewed the e-book format with enough suspicion and weren't in the mood to experiment with copyright language that made it easier for readers to avoid payment. As an agent who specialized in technology books, however, Henning was intrigued by the novel nature of my predicament. I told him about the two interviews I'd already gathered and the promise not to publish the book in a way that made Stallman "look like a hypocrite." Agreeing that I was in an ethical bind, Henning suggested we make that our negotiating point.

Barring that, Henning said, we could always take the carrot-and-stick approach. The carrot would be the publicity that came with publishing an e-book that honored the hacker community's internal ethics. The stick would be the risks associated with publishing an e-book that didn't. Nine months before Dmitry Sklyarov became an Internet *cause célèbre*, we knew it was only a matter of time before an enterprising programmer revealed how to hack e-books. We also knew that a major publishing house releasing an [encrypted] e-book on Richard M. Stallman was the software equivalent of putting "Steal This E-Book" on the cover.

After my meeting with Henning, I called Stallman. Hoping to make the carrot more enticing, I discussed a number of potential compromises. What if the publisher released the book's content under a [dual] license, something similar to what Sun Microsystems had done with OpenOffice, the free software desktop applications suite? The publisher could then release DRM-restricted[2] versions of the e-book under [its usual] format, taking advantage of all the bells and whistles that went with the e-book software, while releasing the copyable version under a less aesthetically pleasing HTML format.

Stallman told me he didn't mind the [dual-license] idea, but he did dislike the idea of making the freely copyable version inferior to the restricted version. Besides, he said [on second thought, this case was different precisely because he had] a way to control the outcome. He could refuse to cooperate.

[RMS: The question was whether it would be wrong for me to agree to the restricted version. I can endorse the free version of Sun's OpenOffice, because it is free software and much better than nothing, while at the same time I reject the nonfree version. There is no self-contradiction here, because Sun didn't need or ask my approval for the non-free version; I was not responsible for its existence. In this case, if I had said yes to the non-freely-copyable version, the onus would fall on me.]

I made a few more suggestions with little effect. About the only thing I could get out of Stallman was a concession [RMS: i.e., a further compromise] that the e-book's [license] restrict all forms of file sharing to "noncommercial redistribution."

Before I signed off, Stallman suggested I tell the publisher that I'd promised Stallman that the work would be [freely sharable]. I told Stallman I couldn't agree to that statement [RMS: though it was true, since he had accepted my conditions at the outset] but that I did view the book as unfinishable without his cooperation. Seemingly satisfied, Stallman hung up with his usual sign-off line: "Happy hacking."

Henning and I met with Tracy the next day. Tracy said her company was willing to publish copyable excerpts in a unencrypted format but would limit the excerpts to 500 words. Henning informed her that this wouldn't be enough for me to get around my ethical obligation to Stallman. Tracy mentioned her own company's contractual obligation to online vendors such as Amazon.com. Even if the company decided to open up its e-book content this one time, it faced the risk of its partners calling it a breach of contract. Barring a change of heart in the executive suite or on the part of Stallman, the decision was up to me. I could use the interviews and go against my earlier agreement with Stallman, or I could plead journalistic ethics and back out of the verbal agreement to do the book.

Following the meeting, my agent and I relocated to a pub on Third Ave. I used his cell phone to call Stallman, leaving a message when nobody answered. Henning left for a moment, giving me time to collect my thoughts. When he returned, he was holding up the cell phone.

"It's Stallman," Henning said.

The conversation got off badly from the start. I relayed Tracy's comment about the publisher's contractual obligations.

"So," Stallman said bluntly. "Why should I give a damn about their contractual obligations?"

Because asking a major publishing house to risk a legal battle with its vendors over a 30,000-word e-book is a tall order, I suggested.

[RMS: His unstated premise was that I couldn't possibly refuse this deal for mere principle.]

"Don't you see?" Stallman said. "That's exactly why I'm doing this. I want a signal victory. I want them to make a choice between freedom and business as usual."

As the words "signal victory" echoed in my head, I felt my attention wander momentarily to the passing foot traffic on the sidewalk. Coming into the bar, I had been pleased to notice that the location was less than half a block away from the street corner memorialized in the 1976 Ramones song, "53rd and 3rd," a song I always enjoyed playing in my days as a musician. Like the perpetually frustrated street hustler depicted in that song, I could feel things falling apart as quickly as they had come together. The irony was palpable. After weeks of gleefully recording other people's laments, I found myself in the position of trying to pull off the rarest of feats: a Richard Stallman compromise. When I continued hemming and hawing, pleading the publisher's position and revealing my growing sympathy for it, Stallman, like an animal smelling blood, attacked.

"So that's it? You're just going to screw me? You're just going to bend to their will?"

[RMS: The quotations show that Williams' interpretation of this conversation was totally wrong. He compares me to a predator, but I was only saying no to the deal he was badgering me to accept. I had already made several compromises, some described above; I just refused to compromise my principles entirely away. I often do this; people who aren't satisfied say I "refused to compromise at all," but that is an exaggeration; see http://www.gnu.org/philosophy/compromise.html. Then I feared he was going to disregard the conditions he had previously agreed to, and publish the book with DRM despite my refusal. What I smelled was not his "blood" but possible betrayal.]

I brought up the issue of a dual-copyright again.

"You mean license," Stallman said curtly.

"Yeah, license. Copyright. Whatever," I said, feeling suddenly like a wounded tuna trailing a rich plume of plasma in the water.

"Aw, why didn't you just fucking do what I told you to do!" he shouted. [RMS: I think this quotation was garbled, both because using "fucking" as an adverb was never part of my speech pattern, and because the words do not fit the circumstances. The words he quotes are a rebuke to a disobedient subordinate. I felt he had an ethical obligation, but he was not my subordinate, and I would not have spoken to him as one. Using notes rather than a recorder, he could not reliably retain the exact words.]

I must have been arguing on behalf of the publisher to the very end, because in my notes I managed to save a final Stallman chestnut: "I don't care. What they're doing is evil. I can't support evil. Goodbye." [RMS: It sounds like I had concluded that he would never take no for an answer, and the only way to end the conversation without accepting his proposition was to hang up on him.]

As soon as I put the phone down, my agent slid a freshly poured Guinness to me. "I figured you might need this," he said with a laugh. "I could see you shaking there towards the end."

I was indeed shaking. The shaking wouldn't stop until the Guinness was more than halfway gone. It felt weird, hearing myself characterized as an emissary of "evil." [RMS: My words as quoted criticize the publisher, not Williams personally. If he took it personally, perhaps that indicates he was starting to take ethical responsibility for the deal he had pressed me to accept.] It felt weirder still, knowing that three months before, I was sitting in an Oakland apartment trying to come up with my next story idea. Now, I was sitting in a part of the world I'd only known through rock songs, taking meetings with publishing executives and drinking beer with an agent I'd never even laid eyes on until the day before. It was all too surreal, like watching my life reflected back as a movie montage.

About that time, my internal absurdity meter kicked in. The initial shaking gave way to convulsions of laughter. To my agent, I must have looked like a another fragile author undergoing an untimely emotional breakdown. To me, I was just starting to appreciate the cynical beauty of my situation. Deal or no deal, I already had the makings of a pretty good story. It was only a matter of finding a place to tell it. When my laughing convulsions finally subsided, I held up my drink in a toast.

"Welcome to the front lines, my friend," I said, clinking pints with my agent. "Might as well enjoy it."

If this story really were a play, here's where it would take a momentary, romantic interlude. Disheartened by the tense nature of our meeting, Tracy invited Henning and me to go out for drinks with her and some of her coworkers. We left the bar on Third Ave., headed down to the East Village, and caught up with Tracy and her friends.

Once there, I spoke with Tracy, careful to avoid shop talk. Our conversation was pleasant, relaxed. Before parting, we agreed to meet the next night. Once again, the conversation was pleasant, so pleasant that the Stallman e-book became almost a distant memory.

When I got back to Oakland, I called around to various journalist friends and acquaintances. I recounted my predicament. Most upbraided me for giving up too much ground to Stallman in the preinterview negotiation. [RMS: Those who have read the whole book know that I would never have dropped the conditions.] A former j-school professor suggested I ignore Stallman's "hypocrite" comment and just write the story. Reporters who knew of Stallman's media-savviness expressed sympathy but uniformly offered the same response: it's your call.

I decided to put the book on the back burner. Even with the interviews, I wasn't making much progress. Besides, it gave me a chance to speak with Tracy without running things past Henning first. By Christmas we had traded visits: she flying out to the west coast once, me flying out to New York a second time. The day before New Year's Eve, I proposed. Deciding which coast to live on, I picked New York. By February, I packed up my laptop computer and all my research notes related to the Stallman biography, and we winged our way to JFK Airport. Tracy and I were married on May 11. So much for failed book deals.

During the summer, I began to contemplate turning my interview notes into a magazine article. Ethically, I felt in the clear doing so, since the original interview terms said nothing about traditional print media. To be honest, I also felt a bit more comfortable writing about Stallman after eight months of radio silence. Since our telephone conversation in September, I'd only received two emails from Stallman. Both chastised me for using "Linux" instead of "GNU/Linux" in a pair of articles for the web magazine *Upside Today*. Aside from that, I had enjoyed the silence. In June, about a week after the New York University speech, I took a crack at writing a 5,000-word magazine-length story about Stallman. This time, the words flowed. The distance had helped restore my lost sense of emotional perspective, I suppose.

In July, a full year after the original email from Tracy, I got a call from Henning. He told me that O'Reilly & Associates, a publishing house out of Sebastopol, California, was interested in the running the Stallman story as a biography. [RMS: I have a vague memory that I suggested contacting O'Reilly, but I can't be sure after all these years.] The news pleased me. Of all the publishing houses in the world, O'Reilly, the same company that had published Eric Raymond's *The Cathedral and the Bazaar*, seemed the most sensitive to the issues that had killed the earlier e-book. As a reporter, I had relied heavily on the O'Reilly book *Open Sources* as a historical reference. I also knew that various chapters of the book, including a chapter written by Stallman, had been published with [license] notices that permitted redistribution. Such knowledge would come in handy if the issue of electronic publication ever came up again.

Sure enough, the issue did come up. I learned through Henning that O'Reilly intended to publish the biography both as a book and as part of its new Safari Tech Books Online subscription service. The Safari user license would involve special restrictions,[3] Henning warned, but O'Reilly was willing to allow for a copyright that permitted users to copy and share the book's text regardless of medium. Basically, as author, I had the choice between two licenses: the Open Publication License or the GNU Free Documentation License.

I checked out the contents and background of each license. The Open Publication License (OPL)[4] gives readers the right to reproduce and distribute a work, in whole or in part, in any medium "physical or electronic," provided the copied work retains the Open Publication License. It also permits modification of a work, provided certain conditions are met. Finally, the Open Publication License includes a number of options, which, if selected by the author, can limit the creation of "substantively modified" versions or book-form derivatives without prior author approval.

The GNU Free Documentation License (GFDL), meanwhile, permits the copying and distribution of a document in any medium, provided the resulting work carries the same license.[5] It also permits the modification of a document provided certain conditions. Unlike the OPL, however, it does not give authors the option to restrict certain modifications. It also does not give authors the right to reject modifications that might result in a competitive book product. It does require certain forms of front- and back-cover information if a party other than the copyright holder wishes to publish more than 100 copies of a protected work, however.

In the course of researching the licenses, I also made sure to visit the GNU Project web page titled "Various Licenses and Comments About Them."[6] On that page, I found a Stallman critique of the Open Publication License. Stallman's critique related to the creation of modified works and the ability of an author to select either one of the OPL's options to restrict modification. If an author didn't want to select either option, it was better to use the GFDL instead, Stallman noted, since it minimized the risk of the nonselected options popping up in modified versions of a document.

The importance of modification in both licenses was a reflection of their original purpose – namely, to give software-manual owners a chance to improve their manuals and publicize those improvements to the rest of the community. Since my book wasn't a manual, I had little concern about the modification clause in either license. My only concern was giving users the freedom to exchange copies of the book or make copies of the content, the same freedom they would have enjoyed if they purchased a hardcover book. Deeming either license suitable for this purpose, I signed the O'Reilly contract when it came to me.

Still, the notion of unrestricted modification intrigued me. In my early negotiations with Tracy, I had pitched the merits of a GPL-style license for the e-book's content. At worst, I said, the license would guarantee a lot of positive publicity for the e-book. At best, it would encourage readers to participate in the book-writing process. As an author, I was willing to let other people amend my work just so long as my name always got top billing. Besides, it might even be interesting to watch the book evolve. I pictured later editions looking much like online versions of the *Talmud*, my original text in a central column surrounded by illuminating, third-party commentary in the margins.

My idea drew inspiration from Project Xanadu (`http://www.xanadu.com`), the legendary software concept originally conceived by Ted Nelson in 1960. During the O'Reilly Open Source Conference in 1999, I had seen the first demonstration of the project's [free] offshoot Udanax and had been wowed by the result. In one demonstration sequence, Udanax displayed a parent document and a derivative work in a similar two-column, plain-text format. With a click of the button, the program introduced lines linking each sentence in the parent to its conceptual offshoot in the derivative. An e-book biography of Richard M. Stallman didn't have to be Udanax-enabled, but given such technological possibilities, why not give users a chance to play around?[7]

When Laurie Petrycki, my editor at O'Reilly, gave me a choice between the OPL or the GFDL, I indulged the fantasy once again. By September of 2001, the month I signed the contract, e-books had become almost a dead topic. Many publishing houses, Tracy's included, were shutting down their e-book imprints for lack of interest. I had to wonder. If these companies had treated e-books not as a form of publication but as a form of community building, would those imprints have survived?

After I signed the contract, I notified Stallman that the book project was back on. I mentioned the choice O'Reilly was giving me between the Open Publication License and the GNU Free Documentation License. I told him I was leaning toward the OPL, if only for the fact I saw no reason to give O'Reilly's competitors a chance to print the same book under a different cover. Stallman wrote back, arguing in favor of the GFDL, noting that O'Reilly had already used it several times in the past. Despite the events of the past year, I suggested a deal. I would choose the GFDL if it gave me the possibility to do more interviews and if Stallman agreed to help O'Reilly publicize the book. Stallman agreed to participate in more interviews but said that his participation in publicity-related events would depend on the content of the book. Viewing this as only fair, I set up an interview for December 17, 2001 in Cambridge.

I set up the interview to coincide with a business trip my wife Tracy was taking to Boston. Two days before leaving, Tracy suggested I invite Stallman out to dinner.

"After all," she said, "he is the one who brought us together."

I sent an email to Stallman, who promptly sent a return email accepting the offer. When I drove up to Boston the next day, I met Tracy at her hotel and hopped the T to head over to MIT. When we got to Tech Square, I found Stallman in the middle of a conversation just as we knocked on the door.

"I hope you don't mind," he said, pulling the door open far enough so that Tracy and I could just barely hear Stallman's conversational counterpart. It was a youngish woman, mid-20s I'd say, named Sarah.

"I took the liberty of inviting somebody else to have dinner with us," Stallman said, matter-of-factly, giving me the same cat-like smile he gave me back in that Palo Alto restaurant.

To be honest, I wasn't too surprised. The news that Stallman had a new female friend had reached me a few weeks before, courtesy of Stallman's mother. "In fact, they both went to Japan last month when Richard went over to accept the Takeda Award," Lippman told me at the time.[8]

On the way over to the restaurant, I learned the circumstances of Sarah and Richard's first meeting. Interestingly, the circumstances were very familiar. Working on her own fictional book, Sarah said she heard about Stallman and what an interesting character he was. She promptly decided to create a character in her book on Stallman and, in the interests of researching the character, set up an interview with Stallman. Things quickly went from there. The two had been dating since the beginning of 2001, she said.

"I really admired the way Richard built up an entire political movement to address an issue of profound personal concern," Sarah said, explaining her attraction to Stallman.

My wife immediately threw back the question: "What was the issue?"

"Crushing loneliness."

During dinner, I let the women do the talking and spent most of the time trying to detect clues as to whether the last 12 months had softened Stallman in any significant way. I didn't see anything to suggest they had. Although more flirtatious than I remembered, Stallman retained the same general level of prickliness. At one point, my wife uttered an emphatic "God forbid" only to receive a typical Stallman rebuke.

"I hate to break it to you, but there is no God," Stallman said. [RMS: I must have been too deadpan. He could justly accuse me of being a wise guy, but not of rebuking.]

Afterwards, when the dinner was complete and Sarah had departed, Stallman seemed to let his guard down a little. As we walked to a nearby bookstore, he admitted that the last 12 months had dramatically changed his outlook on life. "I thought I was going to be alone forever," he said. "I'm glad I was wrong."

Before parting, Stallman handed me his "pleasure card," a business card listing Stallman's address, phone number, and favorite pastimes ("sharing good books, good food and exotic music and dance") so that I might set up a final interview.

The next day, over another meal of dim sum, Stallman seemed even more lovestruck than the night before. Recalling his debates with Currier House dorm maters over the benefits and drawbacks of an immortality serum, Stallman expressed hope that scientists might some day come up with the key to immortality. "Now that I'm finally starting to have happiness in my life, I want to have [a longer life]," he said.

When I mentioned Sarah's "crushing loneliness" comment, Stallman failed to see a connection between loneliness on a physical or spiritual level and loneliness on a hacker level. "The impulse to share code is about friendship but friendship at a much lower level," he said. Later, however, when the subject came up again, Stallman did admit that loneliness, or the fear of perpetual loneliness [RMS: at the hacker-to-hacker, community level, that is], had played a major role in fueling his determination during the earliest days of the GNU Project.

"My fascination with computers was not a consequence of anything else," he said. "I wouldn't have been less fascinated with computers if I had been popular and all the women flocked to me. However, it's certainly true the experience of feeling I didn't have a home, finding one and losing it, finding another and having it destroyed, affected me deeply. The one I lost was the dorm. The one that was destroyed was the AI Lab. The precariousness of not having any kind of home or community was very powerful. It made me want to fight to get it back."

After the interview, I couldn't help but feel a certain sense of emotional symmetry. Hearing Sarah describe what attracted her to Stallman and hearing Stallman himself describe the emotions that prompted him to take up the free software cause, I was reminded of my own reasons for writing this book. Since July, 2000, I have learned to appreciate both the seductive and the repellent sides of the Richard Stallman persona. Like Eben Moglen before me, I feel that dismissing that persona as epiphenomenal or distracting in relation to the overall free software movement would be a grievous mistake. In many ways the two are so mutually defining as to be indistinguishable.

[RMS: Williams objectifies his reactions, both positive and negative, as parts of me, but they are functions also of his own attitudes about appearance, conformity, and business success.]

While I'm sure not every reader feels the same level of affinity for Stallman... I'm sure most will agree [that] few individuals offer as singular a human portrait as Richard M. Stallman. It is my sincere hope that, with this initial portrait complete and with the help of the GFDL, others will feel a similar urge to add their own perspective to that portrait.

Endnotes

[1] See "Freedom – Or Copyright?" (May, 2000), http://www.technologyreview.com/articles/stallman0500.asp.

[2] RMS: Williams wrote "commercial" here, but that is a misnomer, since it means "connected with business." All these versions would be commercial if a company published them.

[3] See "Safari Tech Books Online; Subscriber Agreement: Terms of Service" http://my.safaribooksonline.com/termsofservice. As of December, 2009, these e-books require nonfree reader software, so people should refuse to use them.

[4] See "The Open Publication License: Draft v1.0" (June 8, 1999), http://opencontent.org/openpub/.

[5] See "The GNU Free Documentation License: Version 1.3" (November, 2008), http://www.gnu.org/copyleft/fdl.html.

[6] See http://www.gnu.org/philosophy/license-list.html.

[7] Anybody willing to "port" this book over to Udanax, the free software version of Xanadu, will receive enthusiastic support from me. To find out more about this intriguing technology, visit http://www.udanax.com.

[8] Alas, I didn't find out about the Takeda Foundation's decision to award Stallman, along with Linus Torvalds and Ken Sakamura, with its first-ever award for "Techno-Entrepreneurial Achievement for Social/Economic Well-Being" until after Stallman had made the trip to Japan to accept the award. For more information about the award and its accompanying $1 million prize, visit the Takeda site, http://www.takeda-foundation.jp.

Appendix A – Hack, Hackers, and Hacking

To understand the full meaning of the word "hacker," it helps to examine the word's etymology over the years.

The New Hacker Dictionary, an online compendium of software-programmer jargon, officially lists nine different connotations of the word "hack" and a similar number for "hacker." Then again, the same publication also includes an accompanying essay that quotes Phil Agre, an MIT hacker who warns readers not to be fooled by the word's perceived flexibility. "Hack has only one meaning," argues Agre. "An extremely subtle and profound one which defies articulation." Richard Stallman tries to articulate it with the phrase, "Playful cleverness."

Regardless of the width or narrowness of the definition, most modern hackers trace the word back to MIT, where the term bubbled up as popular item of student jargon in the early 1950s. In 1990 the MIT Museum put together a journal documenting the hacking phenomenon. According to the journal, students who attended the institute during the fifties used the word "hack" the way a modern student might use the word "goof." Hanging a jalopy out a dormitory window was a "hack," but anything harsh or malicious – e.g., egging a rival dorm's windows or defacing a campus statue – fell outside the bounds. Implicit within the definition of "hack" was a spirit of harmless, creative fun.

This spirit would inspire the word's gerund form: "hacking." A 1950s student who spent the better part of the afternoon talking on the phone or dismantling a radio might describe the activity as "hacking."

Again, a modern speaker would substitute the verb form of "goof" – "goofing" or "goofing off" – to describe the same activity.

As the 1950s progressed, the word "hack" acquired a sharper, more rebellious edge. The MIT of the 1950s was overly competitive, and hacking emerged as both a reaction to and extension of that competitive culture. Goofs and pranks suddenly became a way to blow off steam, thumb one's nose at campus administration, and indulge creative thinking and behavior stifled by the Institute's rigorous undergraduate curriculum. With its myriad hallways and underground steam tunnels, the Institute offered plenty of exploration opportunities for the student undaunted by locked doors and "No Trespassing" signs. Students began to refer to their off-limits explorations as "tunnel hacking." Above ground, the campus phone system offered similar opportunities. Through casual experimentation and due diligence, students learned how to perform humorous tricks. Drawing inspiration from the more traditional pursuit of tunnel hacking, students quickly dubbed this new activity "phone hacking."

The combined emphasis on creative play and restriction-free exploration would serve as the basis for the future mutations of the hacking term. The first self-described computer hackers of the 1960s MIT campus originated from a late 1950s student group called the Tech Model Railroad Club. A tight clique within the club was the Signals and Power (S&P) Committee – the group behind the railroad club's electrical circuitry system. The system was a sophisticated assortment of relays and switches similar to the kind that controlled the local campus phone system. To control it, a member of the group simply dialed in commands via a connected phone and watched the trains do his bidding.

The nascent electrical engineers responsible for building and maintaining this system saw their activity as similar in spirit to phone hacking. Adopting the hacking term, they began refining it even further. From the S&P hacker point of view, using one less relay to operate a particular stretch of track meant having one more relay for future play. Hacking subtly shifted from a synonym for idle play to a synonym for idle play that improved the overall performance or efficiency of the club's railroad system at the same time. Soon S&P committee members proudly referred to the entire activity of improving and reshaping the track's underlying circuitry as "hacking" and to the people who did it as "hackers."

Given their affinity for sophisticated electronics – not to mention the traditional MIT-student disregard for closed doors and "No Trespassing" signs – it didn't take long before the hackers caught wind of a new machine on campus. Dubbed the TX-0, the machine was one of the first commercially marketed computers. By the end of the 1950s, the entire S&P clique had migrated en masse over to the TX-0 control room, bringing the spirit of creative play with them. The wide-open realm of computer programming would encourage yet another mutation in etymology. "To hack" no longer meant soldering unusual looking circuits, but cobbling together software programs with little regard to "official" methods or software-writing procedures. It also meant improving the efficiency and speed of already-existing programs that tended to hog up machine resources. True to the word's roots, it also meant writing programs that served no other purpose than to amuse or entertain.

A classic example of this expanded hacking definition is the game Spacewar, the first computer-based video game. Developed by MIT hackers in the early 1960s, Spacewar had all the traditional hacking definitions: it was goofy and random, serving little useful purpose other than providing a nightly distraction for the dozen or so hackers who delighted in playing it. From a software perspective, however, it was a monumental testament to innovation of programming skill. It was also completely free. Because hackers had built it for fun, they saw no reason to guard their creation, sharing it extensively with other programmers. By the end of the 1960s, Spacewar had become a diversion for programmers around the world, if they had the (then rather rare) graphical displays.

This notion of collective innovation and communal software ownership distanced the act of computer hacking in the 1960s from the tunnel hacking and phone hacking of the 1950s. The latter pursuits tended to be solo or small-group activities. Tunnel and phone hackers relied heavily on campus lore, but the off-limits nature of their activity discouraged the open circulation of new discoveries. Computer hackers, on the other hand, did their work amid a scientific field biased toward collaboration and the rewarding of innovation. Hackers and "official" computer scientists weren't always the best of allies, but in the rapid evolution of the field, the two species of computer programmer evolved a cooperative – some might say symbiotic – relationship. Hackers had little respect for bureaucrats' rules. They regarded computer security systems that obstructed access to the machine as just another bug, to be worked around or fixed if possible. Thus, breaking security (but not for malicious purposes) was a recognized aspect of hacking in 1970, useful for practical jokes (the victim might say, "I think someone's hacking me") as well as for gaining access to the computer. But it was not central to the idea of hacking. Where there was a security obstacle, hackers were proud to display their wits in surmounting it; however, given the choice, as at the MIT AI Lab, they chose to have no obstacle and do other kinds of hacking. Where there is no security, nobody needs to break it.

It is a testament to the original computer hackers' prodigious skill that later programmers, including Richard M. Stallman, aspired to wear the same hacker mantle. By the mid to late 1970s, the term "hacker" had acquired elite connotations. In a general sense, a computer hacker was any person who wrote software code for the sake of writing software code. In the particular sense, however, it was a testament to programming skill. Like the term "artist," the meaning carried tribal overtones. To describe a fellow programmer as a hacker was a sign of respect. To describe oneself as a hacker was a sign of immense personal confidence. Either way, the original looseness of the computer-hacker appellation diminished as computers became more common.

As the definition tightened, "computer" hacking acquired additional semantic overtones. The hackers at the MIT AI Lab shared many other characteristics, including love of Chinese food, disgust for tobacco smoke, and avoidance of alcohol, tobacco and other addictive drugs. These characteristics became part of some people's understanding of what it meant to be a hacker, and the community exerted an influence on newcomers even though it did not demand conformity. However, these cultural associations disappeared with the AI Lab hacker community. Today, most hackers resemble the surrounding society on these points.

As the hackers at elite institutions such as MIT, Stanford, and Carnegie Mellon conversed about hacks they admired, they also considered the ethics of their activity, and began to speak openly of a "hacker ethic": the yet-unwritten rules that governed a hacker's day-to-day behavior. In the 1984 book *Hackers*, author Steven Levy, after much research and consultation, codified the hacker ethic as five core hacker tenets.

In the 1980s, computer use expanded greatly, and so did security breaking. Mostly it was done by insiders with criminal intent, who were generally not hackers at all. However, occasionally the police and administrators, who defined disobedience as evil, traced a computer "intrusion" back to a hacker whose idea of ethics was "Don't hurt people." Journalists published articles in which "hacking" meant breaking security, and usually endorsed the administrators' view of the matter. Although books like *Hackers* did much to document the original spirit of exploration that gave rise to the hacking culture, for most newspaper reporters and readers the term "computer hacker" became a synonym for "electronic burglar."

By the late 1980s, many U.S. teenagers had access to computers. Some were alienated from society; inspired by journalists' distorted picture of "hacking," they expressed their resentment by breaking computer security much as other alienated teens might have done it by breaking windows. They began to call themselves "hackers," but they never learned the MIT hackers' principle against malicious behavior. As younger programmers began employing their computer skills to harmful ends – creating and disseminating computer viruses, breaking into computer systems for mischief, deliberately causing computers to crash – the term "hacker" acquired a punk, nihilistic edge which attracted more people with similar attitudes.

Hackers have railed against this perceived misusage of their self-designator for nearly two decades. Stallman, not one to take things lying down, coined the term "cracking" for "security breaking" so that people could more easily avoid calling it "hacking." But the distinction between hacking and cracking is often misunderstood. These two descriptive terms are not meant to be exclusive. It's not that "Hacking is here, and cracking is there, and never the twain shall meet." Hacking and cracking are different attributes of activities, just as "young" and "tall" are different attributes of persons.

Most hacking does not involve security, so it is not cracking. Most cracking is done for profit or malice and not in a playful spirit, so it is not hacking. Once in a while a single act may qualify as cracking and as hacking, but that is not the usual case. The hacker spirit includes irreverence for rules, but most hacks do not break rules. Cracking is by definition disobedience, but it is not necessarily malicious or harmful. The computer security field distinguishes between "black hat" and "white hat" crackers – i.e., crackers who turn toward destructive, malicious ends versus those who probe security in order to fix it.

The hacker's central principle not to be malicious remains the primary cultural link between the notion of hacking in the early 21st century and hacking in the 1950s. It is important to note that, as the idea of computer hacking has evolved over the last four decades, the original notion of hacking – i.e., performing pranks or exploring underground tunnels – remains intact. In the fall of 2000, the MIT Museum paid tribute to the Institute's age-old hacking tradition with a dedicated exhibit, the Hall of Hacks. The exhibit includes a number of photographs dating back to the 1920s, including one involving a mock police cruiser. In 1993, students paid homage to the original MIT notion of hacking by placing the same police cruiser, lights flashing, atop the Institute's main dome. The cruiser's vanity license plate read IHTFP, a popular MIT acronym with many meanings. The most noteworthy version, itself dating back to the pressure-filled world of MIT student life in the 1950s, is "I hate this fucking place." In 1990, however, the Museum used the acronym as a basis for a journal on the history of hacks. Titled *The Journal of the Institute for Hacks, Tomfoolery, and Pranks*, it offers an adept summary of the hacking.

"In the culture of hacking, an elegant, simple creation is as highly valued as it is in pure science," writes *Boston Globe* reporter Randolph Ryan in a 1993 article attached to the police car exhibit. "A Hack differs from the ordinary college prank in that the event usually requires careful planning, engineering and finesse, and has an underlying wit and inventiveness," Ryan writes. "The unwritten rule holds that a hack should be good-natured, non-destructive and safe. In fact, hackers sometimes assist in dismantling their own handiwork."

The urge to confine the culture of computer hacking within the same ethical boundaries is well-meaning but impossible. Although most software hacks aspire to the same spirit of elegance and simplicity, the software medium offers less chance for reversibility. Dismantling a police cruiser is easy compared with dismantling an idea, especially an idea whose time has come.

Once a vague item of obscure student jargon, the word "hacker" has become a linguistic billiard ball, subject to political spin and ethical nuances. Perhaps this is why so many hackers and journalists enjoy using it. We cannot predict how people will use the word in the future. We can, however, decide how we will use it ourselves. Using the term "cracking" rather than "hacking," when you mean "security breaking," shows respect for Stallman and all the hackers mentioned in this book, and helps preserve something which all computer users have benefited from: the hacker spirit.

Appendix B – GNU Free Documentation License

Version 1.3, 3 November 2008
Copyright © 2000, 2001, 2002, 2007, 2008 Free Software Foundation, Inc.

http://fsf.org/

Everyone is permitted to copy and distribute verbatim copies of this license document, but changing it is not allowed.

Preamble

The purpose of this License is to make a manual, textbook, or other functional and useful document "free" in the sense of freedom: to assure everyone the effective freedom to copy and redistribute it, with or without modifying it, either commercially or noncommercially. Secondarily, this License preserves for the author and publisher a way to get credit for their work, while not being considered responsible for modifications made by others.

This License is a kind of "copyleft", which means that derivative works of the document must themselves be free in the same sense. It complements the GNU General Public License, which is a copyleft license designed for free software.

We have designed this License in order to use it for manuals for free software, because free software needs free documentation: a free program should come with manuals providing the same freedoms that

217

the software does. But this License is not limited to software manuals; it can be used for any textual work, regardless of subject matter or whether it is published as a printed book. We recommend this License principally for works whose purpose is instruction or reference.

1. APPLICABILITY AND DEFINITIONS

This License applies to any manual or other work, in any medium, that contains a notice placed by the copyright holder saying it can be distributed under the terms of this License. Such a notice grants a world-wide, royalty-free license, unlimited in duration, to use that work under the conditions stated herein. The "**Document**", below, refers to any such manual or work. Any member of the public is a licensee, and is addressed as "**you**". You accept the license if you copy, modify or distribute the work in a way requiring permission under copyright law.

A "**Modified Version**" of the Document means any work containing the Document or a portion of it, either copied verbatim, or with modifications and/or translated into another language.

A "**Secondary Section**" is a named appendix or a front-matter section of the Document that deals exclusively with the relationship of the publishers or authors of the Document to the Document's overall subject (or to related matters) and contains nothing that could fall directly within that overall subject. (Thus, if the Document is in part a textbook of mathematics, a Secondary Section may not explain any mathematics.) The relationship could be a matter of historical connection with the subject or with related matters, or of legal, commercial, philosophical, ethical or political position regarding them.

The "**Invariant Sections**" are certain Secondary Sections whose titles are designated, as being those of Invariant Sections, in the notice that says that the Document is released under this License. If a section does not fit the above definition of Secondary then it is not allowed to be designated as Invariant. The Document may contain zero Invariant Sections. If the Document does not identify any Invariant Sections then there are none.

The "**Cover Texts**" are certain short passages of text that are listed, as Front-Cover Texts or Back-Cover Texts, in the notice that says that the Document is released under this License. A Front-Cover Text may be at most 5 words, and a Back-Cover Text may be at most 25 words.

A "**Transparent**" copy of the Document means a machine-readable copy, represented in a format whose specification is available to the general public, that is suitable for revising the document straightforwardly with generic text editors or (for images composed of pixels) generic paint programs or (for drawings) some widely available drawing editor, and that is suitable for input to text formatters or for automatic translation to a variety of formats suitable for input to text formatters. A copy made in an otherwise Transparent file format whose markup, or absence of markup, has been arranged to thwart or discourage subsequent modification by readers is not Transparent. An image format is not Transparent if used for any substantial amount of text. A copy that is not "Transparent" is called "**Opaque**".

Examples of suitable formats for Transparent copies include plain ASCII without markup, Texinfo input format, LaTeX input format, SGML or XML using a publicly available DTD, and standard-conforming simple HTML, PostScript or PDF designed for human modification. Examples of transparent image formats include PNG, XCF and JPG. Opaque formats include proprietary formats that can be read and edited only by proprietary word processors, SGML or XML for which the DTD and/or processing tools are not generally available, and the machine-generated HTML, PostScript or PDF produced by some word processors for output purposes only.

The "**Title Page**" means, for a printed book, the title page itself, plus such following pages as are needed to hold, legibly, the material this License requires to appear in the title page. For works in formats which do not have any title page as such, "Title Page" means the text near the most prominent appearance of the work's title, preceding the beginning of the body of the text.

The "**publisher**" means any person or entity that distributes copies of the Document to the public.

A section "**Entitled XYZ**" means a named subunit of the Document whose title either is precisely XYZ or contains XYZ in parentheses following text that translates XYZ in another language. (Here XYZ stands for a specific section name mentioned below, such as "**Acknowledgements**", "**Dedications**", "**Endorsements**", or "**History**".)

To "**Preserve the Title**" of such a section when you modify the Document means that it remains a section "Entitled XYZ" according to this definition.

The Document may include Warranty Disclaimers next to the notice which states that this License applies to the Document. These Warranty Disclaimers are considered to be included by reference in this License, but only as regards disclaiming warranties: any other implication that these Warranty Disclaimers may have is void and has no effect on the meaning of this License.

2. VERBATIM COPYING

You may copy and distribute the Document in any medium, either commercially or noncommercially, provided that this License, the copyright notices, and the license notice saying this License applies to the Document are reproduced in all copies, and that you add no other conditions whatsoever to those of this License. You may not use technical measures to obstruct or control the reading or further copying of the copies you make or distribute. However, you may accept compensation in exchange for copies. If you distribute a large enough number of copies you must also follow the conditions in section 3.

You may also lend copies, under the same conditions stated above, and you may publicly display copies.

3. COPYING IN QUANTITY

If you publish printed copies (or copies in media that commonly have printed covers) of the Document, numbering more than 100, and the Document's license notice requires Cover Texts, you must enclose the copies in covers that carry, clearly and legibly, all these Cover Texts: Front-Cover Texts on the front cover, and Back-Cover Texts on the back cover. Both covers must also clearly and legibly identify you as the publisher of these copies. The front cover must present the full title with all words of the title equally prominent and visible. You may add other material on the covers in addition. Copying with changes limited to the covers, as long as they preserve the title of the Document and satisfy these conditions, can be treated as verbatim copying in other respects.

If the required texts for either cover are too voluminous to fit legibly, you should put the first ones listed (as many as fit reasonably) on the actual cover, and continue the rest onto adjacent pages.

If you publish or distribute Opaque copies of the Document numbering more than 100, you must either include a machine-readable Transparent copy along with each Opaque copy, or state in or with each Opaque copy a computer-network location from which the general network-using public has access to download using public-standard network protocols a complete Transparent copy of the Document, free of added material. If you use the latter option, you must take reasonably prudent steps, when you begin distribution of Opaque copies in quantity, to ensure that this Transparent copy will remain thus accessible at the stated location until at least one year after the last time you distribute an Opaque copy (directly or through your agents or retailers) of that edition to the public.

It is requested, but not required, that you contact the authors of the Document well before redistributing any large number of copies, to give them a chance to provide you with an updated version of the Document.

4. MODIFICATIONS

You may copy and distribute a Modified Version of the Document under the conditions of sections 2 and 3 above, provided that you release the Modified Version under precisely this License, with the Modified Version filling the role of the Document, thus licensing distribution and modification of the Modified Version to whoever possesses a copy of it. In addition, you must do these things in the Modified Version:

A. Use in the Title Page (and on the covers, if any) a title distinct from that of the Document, and from those of previous versions (which should, if there were any, be listed in the History section of the Document). You may use the same title as a previous version if the original publisher of that version gives permission.

B. List on the Title Page, as authors, one or more persons or entities responsible for authorship of the modifications in the Modified Version, together with at least five of the principal authors of the Document (all of its principal authors, if it has fewer than five), unless they release you from this requirement.

C. State on the Title page the name of the publisher of the Modified Version, as the publisher.

D. Preserve all the copyright notices of the Document.

E. Add an appropriate copyright notice for your modifications adjacent to the other copyright notices.

F. Include, immediately after the copyright notices, a license notice giving the public permission to use the Modified Version under the terms of this License, in the form shown in the Addendum below.

G. Preserve in that license notice the full lists of Invariant Sections and required Cover Texts given in the Document's license notice.

H. Include an unaltered copy of this License.

I. Preserve the section Entitled "History", Preserve its Title, and add to it an item stating at least the title, year, new authors, and publisher of the Modified Version as given on the Title Page. If there is no section Entitled "History" in the Document, create one stating the title, year, authors, and publisher of the Document as given on its Title Page, then add an item describing the Modified Version as stated in the previous sentence.

J. Preserve the network location, if any, given in the Document for public access to a Transparent copy of the Document, and likewise the network locations given in the Document for previous versions it was based on. These may be placed in the "History" section. You may omit a network location for a work that was published at least four years before the Document itself, or if the original publisher of the version it refers to gives permission.

K. For any section Entitled "Acknowledgements" or "Dedications", Preserve the Title of the section, and preserve in the section all the substance and tone of each of the contributor acknowledgements and/or dedications given therein.

L. Preserve all the Invariant Sections of the Document, unaltered in their text and in their titles. Section numbers or the equivalent are not considered part of the section titles.

M. Delete any section Entitled "Endorsements". Such a section may not be included in the Modified Version.

N. Do not retitle any existing section to be Entitled "Endorsements" or to conflict in title with any Invariant Section.

O. Preserve any Warranty Disclaimers.

If the Modified Version includes new front-matter sections or appendices that qualify as Secondary Sections and contain no material copied from the Document, you may at your option designate some or all of these sections as invariant. To do this, add their titles to the list of Invariant Sections in the Modified Version's license notice. These titles must be distinct from any other section titles.

You may add a section Entitled "Endorsements", provided it contains nothing but endorsements of your Modified Version by various parties—for example, statements of peer review or that the text has been approved by an organization as the authoritative definition of a standard.

You may add a passage of up to five words as a Front-Cover Text, and a passage of up to 25 words as a Back-Cover Text, to the end of the list of Cover Texts in the Modified Version. Only one passage of Front-Cover Text and one of Back-Cover Text may be added by (or through arrangements made by) any one entity. If the Document already includes a cover text for the same cover, previously added by you or by arrangement made by the same entity you are acting on behalf of, you may not add another; but you may replace the old one, on explicit permission from the previous publisher that added the old one.

The author(s) and publisher(s) of the Document do not by this License give permission to use their names for publicity for or to assert or imply endorsement of any Modified Version.

5. COMBINING DOCUMENTS

You may combine the Document with other documents released under this License, under the terms defined in section 4 above for modified versions, provided that you include in the combination all of the Invariant Sections of all of the original documents, unmodified, and list them all as Invariant Sections of your combined work in its license notice, and that you preserve all their Warranty Disclaimers.

The combined work need only contain one copy of this License, and multiple identical Invariant Sections may be replaced with a single copy. If there are multiple Invariant Sections with the same name but different contents, make the title of each such section unique by adding at the end of it, in parentheses, the name of the original author or publisher of that section if known, or else a unique number. Make the same adjustment to the section titles in the list of Invariant Sections in the license notice of the combined work.

In the combination, you must combine any sections Entitled "History" in the various original documents, forming one section Entitled "History"; likewise combine any sections Entitled "Acknowledgements", and any sections Entitled "Dedications". You must delete all sections Entitled "Endorsements".

6. COLLECTIONS OF DOCUMENTS

You may make a collection consisting of the Document and other documents released under this License, and replace the individual copies of this License in the various documents with a single copy that is included in the collection, provided that you follow the rules of this License for verbatim copying of each of the documents in all other respects.

You may extract a single document from such a collection, and distribute it individually under this License, provided you insert a copy of this License into the extracted document, and follow this License in all other respects regarding verbatim copying of that document.

7. AGGREGATION WITH INDEPENDENT WORKS

A compilation of the Document or its derivatives with other separate and independent documents or works, in or on a volume of a storage or distribution medium, is called an "aggregate" if the copyright resulting from the compilation is not used to limit the legal rights of the compilation's users beyond what the individual works permit. When the Document is included in an aggregate, this License does not apply to the other works in the aggregate which are not themselves derivative works of the Document.

If the Cover Text requirement of section 3 is applicable to these copies of the Document, then if the Document is less than one half of the entire aggregate, the Document's Cover Texts may be placed on covers that bracket the Document within the aggregate, or the electronic equivalent of covers if the Document is in electronic form. Otherwise they must appear on printed covers that bracket the whole aggregate.

8. TRANSLATION

Translation is considered a kind of modification, so you may distribute translations of the Document under the terms of section 4. Replacing Invariant Sections with translations requires special permission from their copyright holders, but you may include translations of some or all Invariant Sections in addition to the original versions of these Invariant Sections. You may include a translation of this License, and all the license notices in the Document, and any Warranty Disclaimers, provided that you also include the original English version of this License and the original versions of those notices and disclaimers. In case of a disagreement between the translation and the original version of this License or a notice or disclaimer, the original version will prevail.

If a section in the Document is Entitled "Acknowledgements", "Dedications", or "History", the requirement (section 4) to Preserve its Title (section 1) will typically require changing the actual title.

9. TERMINATION

You may not copy, modify, sublicense, or distribute the Document except as expressly provided under this License. Any attempt otherwise to copy, modify, sublicense, or distribute it is void, and will automatically terminate your rights under this License.

However, if you cease all violation of this License, then your license from a particular copyright holder is reinstated (a) provisionally, unless and until the copyright holder explicitly and finally terminates your license, and (b) permanently, if the copyright holder fails to notify you of the violation by some reasonable means prior to 60 days after the cessation.

Moreover, your license from a particular copyright holder is reinstated permanently if the copyright holder notifies you of the violation by some reasonable means, this is the first time you have received notice of violation of this License (for any work) from that copyright holder, and you cure the violation prior to 30 days after your receipt of the notice.

Termination of your rights under this section does not terminate the licenses of parties who have received copies or rights from you under this License. If your rights have been terminated and not permanently reinstated, receipt of a copy of some or all of the same material does not give you any rights to use it.

10. FUTURE REVISIONS OF THIS LICENSE

The Free Software Foundation may publish new, revised versions of the GNU Free Documentation License from time to time. Such new versions will be similar in spirit to the present version, but may differ in detail to address new problems or concerns. See http://www.gnu. org/copyleft/.

Each version of the License is given a distinguishing version number. If the Document specifies that a particular numbered version of this License "or any later version" applies to it, you have the option of following the terms and conditions either of that specified version or of any later version that has been published (not as a draft) by the Free Software Foundation. If the Document does not specify a version number of this License, you may choose any version ever published (not as a draft) by the Free Software Foundation. If the Document specifies that a proxy can decide which future versions of this License can be used, that proxy's public statement of acceptance of a version permanently authorizes you to choose that version for the Document.

11. RELICENSING

"Massive Multiauthor Collaboration Site" (or "MMC Site") means any World Wide Web server that publishes copyrightable works and also provides prominent facilities for anybody to edit those works. A public wiki that anybody can edit is an example of such a server. A "Massive Multiauthor Collaboration" (or "MMC") contained in the site means any set of copyrightable works thus published on the MMC site.

"CC-BY-SA" means the Creative Commons Attribution-Share Alike 3.0 license published by Creative Commons Corporation, a not-for-profit corporation with a principal place of business in San Francisco, California, as well as future copyleft versions of that license published by that same organization.

"Incorporate" means to publish or republish a Document, in whole or in part, as part of another Document.

An MMC is "eligible for relicensing" if it is licensed under this License, and if all works that were first published under this License somewhere other than this MMC, and subsequently incorporated in whole or in part into the MMC, (1) had no cover texts or invariant sections, and (2) were thus incorporated prior to November 1, 2008.

The operator of an MMC Site may republish an MMC contained in the site under CC-BY-SA on the same site at any time before August 1, 2009, provided the MMC is eligible for relicensing.

ADDENDUM: How to use this License for your documents

To use this License in a document you have written, include a copy of the License in the document and put the following copyright and license notices just after the title page:

Copyright © YEAR YOUR NAME. Permission is granted to copy, distribute and/or modify this document under the

terms of the GNU Free Documentation License, Version
1.3 or any later version published by the Free Software
Foundation; with no Invariant Sections, no Front-Cover
Texts, and no Back-Cover Texts. A copy of the license is
included in the section entitled "GNU Free Documentation
License".

If you have Invariant Sections, Front-Cover Texts and Back-Cover
Texts, replace the "with ... Texts." line with this:

with the Invariant Sections being LIST THEIR TITLES,
with the Front-Cover Texts being LIST, and with the Back-
Cover Texts being LIST.

If you have Invariant Sections without Cover Texts, or some other
combination of the three, merge those two alternatives to suit the
situation.

If your document contains nontrivial examples of program code,
we recommend releasing these examples in parallel under your choice
of free software license, such as the GNU General Public License, to
permit their use in free software.

Colophon

The front and back covers of this book were designed and produced by Rob Myers using Inkscape, the free software vector graphics program. Jeanne Rasata also contributed to the cover design.

The typesetting was done by John Sullivan at the Free Software Foundation using LaTeX, GNU Emacs, Evince, and the GNU Image Manipulation Program (GIMP). The primary font is 10-point Computer Modern.

Digital versions of the book, including the LaTeX source code, are available at http://www.fsf.org/faif. Improvements are welcome, and can be sent to sales@gnu.org.